Joe Rapoport

Joe Rapoport

The Life of a Jewish Radical

Kenneth Kann

Temple University Press  *Philadelphia*

Temple University Press, Philadelphia 19122
© 1981 by Temple University. All rights reserved
Published 1981
Printed in the United States of America

Library of Congress Cataloging in Publication Data

Kann, Kenneth.
  Joe Rapoport, the life of a Jewish radical.

  Includes index.
  1. Rapoport, Joe. 2. Jews in the United States—
Biography. 3. Radicalism—Jews. 4. United States—
Emigration and immigration—Biography. I. Title.
E184.J5R334 973'.04924 [B] 80-19448
ISBN 0-87722-208-8

For My Family,

For My Colleagues in Struggle,

And Especially For Sheba My Life Companion

For My Mother And Father

Contents

Introduction

This autobiography spans the past half century of American radicalism from the movement to build industrial trade unionism to the movement against nuclear pollution. It is the story of a Jewish radical who first came to political consciousness defending his Ukrainian Jewish village during the Russian Revolution, and who remained preoccupied with the fate of his people in the Soviet Union, Europe, the Middle East, and the United States. His conversion to socialism in New York in 1923 had "a double edge—the participation in the class struggle against exploitation of man by man and the strong feeling for solving the Jewish problem by humanizing society."

I first met Joe Rapoport in 1974 at an American Civil Liberties Union (ACLU) picnic in Sonoma County, forty miles to the north of San Francisco. I was working on a study of a community of immigrant Jewish chicken ranchers who, over generations, had become Americanized. I was tape recording the life stories of the immigrants and their children and their grandchildren. This oral history project was at once a busman's holiday from the academic confines of my Ph.D. dissertation, an inquiry into my cultural roots, and an attempt to understand my own generation's rebellion in the 1960's. I came to the ACLU picnic looking for contacts, and I found one.

I already had heard of Joe Rapoport as someone I should interview, even though he did not settle in Sonoma County until 1949. When Joe was pointed out to me at the picnic, I noticed first that he was short and solid. He had the same substantial appearance that I associated with the Jewish men of his generation, but he was distinguished by bushy white eyebrows and dancing blue eyes. He was engaged in a conversation, which led into another, and I had to hover about for an hour before I could catch him alone. Upon meeting, he shook hands with the grip of a man who had done a lifetime of manual labor and organizing.

At his home a few days later, our first interview opened a door into Joe's rich life experience and my own cultural history. Joe offered a thumbnail sketch of his life from his 1900 birth into a Ukrainian *shtetl*, Jewish village, up through the ACLU picnic. I wanted to hear more and he was willing to speak on tape. Over the next few months we covered his life in five long sessions. It only suggested the depth and complexity and color with which he could reconstruct his experience. I proposed we collaborate on his autobiography.

First, I was interested in Joe's ability to set his life against great forces and events of the century. Later I became fascinated by his inability to separate his personal experience from the sweep of world history. Joe's recollection of his Ukrainian *shtetl* youth became the story of Ukrainian Jewish life under Tsarism, in war and revolution, and then under the Soviet system. Joe's tale of romance with Sheba, his wife of over half a century, became an exploration of Old World continuities in the New World. His story of becoming a hand knitter burgeoned into the saga of left-wing attempts to build industrial trade unionism and socialism in America. His preoccupation with Jewish religion and Yiddish culture, with the "insult" of anti-Semitism, became the epic of Jewish destiny in the twentieth-century world.

Joe presented a stark contrast to my own generation, which was just then becoming preoccupied with personal life after the collapse of the social movement of the 1960's. Joe never lost sight of himself as an actor on the stage of history. At an early meeting I learned he was an amateur archivist who had a rich collection of strike leaflets, organizational records, position papers, newspaper articles, union membership books, and general historical memorabilia that dated back to the 1920's. It was a record of the movements, organizations, and events in which he had participated. He was ready for his historian.

Joe's historical sensibility is characteristic of a generation that stepped out of traditional East European Jewish life and into the modern world. That long transformation, which culminated with the Russian Revolution, not only marked the end of the strangling constrictions of the Tsarist system upon Jews but also ended Jewish ghetto provincialism, Jewish religious orthodoxy, and Jewish passivity before the onslaught of anti-Semitic attack. Joe and his generation broke once and for all from the world of *their* fathers. They embraced new Jewish lives as Soviet citizens, as pioneers in Palestine, and as immigrants in America. With all the horrors of World War I and the Russian Revolution, Joe and his generation also found adventure, mobility, and opportunity. They found themselves making history.

I discovered Joe to be an accomplished autodidact. His formal education ended at thirteen; his hunger for learning was kindled at seventeen, in the fires of the Russian Revolution. He began to feed that hunger through the radical Jewish movement in New York. Joe was neither a scholar nor a theorist. Nonetheless his conversation, his telling of his life story, was studded with references to Biblical history and Biblical parables, Ukrainian and Jewish folk cultures, Russian literature and Russian history, classical and modern Yiddish literature, the writings of Marx and Lenin and Stalin, the 1920's economics lectures of Scott Nearing, the historical novels of Howard Fast, and the political world view of the radical American Yiddish newspaper *Freiheit*.

The appetite grows with the eating, as the Yiddish saying goes, and Joe fed from the boiling cauldron of East European Jewish political and cultural life in New York. That political culture grew from the 1880's and flourished through the 1930's; it still glows among its aging carriers. That political culture, that world, was poised between flight from the constrictions of the Old World and flight into the disarray of the New World. It was fueled by a centuries-long heritage of piety, of faith in the power of the written word, of persecution and Messianic expectation, of sacrifice, survival, and belief in Jewish destiny. In secular form in America this culture assumed the character of a hunger for modern learning, a fervent social idealism, and a preoccupation with modern political ideologies. It was the political culture of a transitional generation. Joe's youthful conversion to socialism was an assertion of rebellion shaped by tradition. He still looks to the teachings of the Prophets as a yardstick of social justice.

Joe spoke with great intensity about the labor movement, the Jewish radical movement, and all his attempts to effect social change. It was the kind of lived politics that my own generation experienced in the 1960's. During that decade we associated our lives with American politics, and we believed we could influence those politics through our social movement. But the consistency of Joe's political idealism and political participation for over half a century stood in dramatic contrast to the ephemeral character of the 1960's rebellion. I was drawn to Joe, as I had been drawn to the study of his Jewish community, in search of an historical anchor. In Joe and his radical Jewish movement I saw continuity and consistency of politics, culture, and comrades.

Their corner of American radicalism was shaped by the communal life of the *shtetl* and the ghetto in the Old World. Their radicalism was born in burning resentment against anti-Semitic persecution and petty capitalistic exploitation, in revolt against religion and tradition, in fervent idealism to create a just new world. Their ties were cemented through working together in shops, living together in Jewish neighborhoods, fighting to build a trade union movement, and sharing a vibrant Yiddish culture.

They fed the stream of an older American Left that maintained itself around the ideals of the Russian Revolution, the organizational durability and ideological coherence of the U.S. Communist Party, the broader movement of progressives and socialists, the pressing need to organize mass production workers into industrial trade unions, and the persistent demands for equality by ethnic minorities. But even after the virtual collapse of the Old Left in the mid-1950's, Joe and his radical Jewish comrades persisted in a coherent movement dedicated to basic social change. They have been the long distance runners of the American Left in the twentieth century.

Joe's idealism and organizational work has been tempered not only by decades of experience but also by decades of unanticipated change. I met Joe at a time when he was becoming more reflective about this. He was willing, even eager, to reevaluate past politics in the light of subsequent historical developments. His attempt to maintain principle in the face of historical contradiction is at the center of this story.

Joe's distinct experience, as a trade union organizer and a community activist, placed him in a strategic position to do that kind of rethinking. Joe spoke from the dual perspective of someone who was familiar with left-wing organizations and ideologies, but who remained with the rank and file, with the grass roots. The unique value of Joe's perspective grew out of his lifelong attempts to translate ideas into action with all the joys and frustrations of the struggle, with all the contradictions of theory and practice, and with all the demands to formulate new understandings out of past events.

As a labor historian I was most interested in Joe's evaluation of the long struggle to establish industrial trade unionism in mass production industries. The labor movement was Joe's first and most enduring radical commitment. At an early meeting he showed me his favorite picture, a carefully posed shot of the central committee for the 1923 knitgoods workers strike. Joe's closest friend, Sam Steinhart, also in the picture, drew him into the union and working class militancy through that strike. Joe's thin unlined face in the picture showed him among the youngest on the strike committee; but he was dressed in coat and tie like any self-respecting hand knitter, and he looked every bit as solemn as his comrades. Describing that strike to me fifty years later, Joe alternated between an animated recollection of clashes with manufacturers' goons and a searching appraisal of union strategies. He still was living with that strike.

Joe was living most intensely with his years as a trade union organizer in the 1930's. Left-wing activists like Joe Rapoport played a central role in building industrial trade unions during that decade. Yet the Left was ousted from the labor movement by the 1950's. Joe became a California chicken rancher because he was eased out of the knitgoods trade by mechanization and by the union he helped to build from scratch. One of Joe's fundamental concerns in this book is to explain that historical development. To this day, Joe criticizes the mainstream labor movement and maintains his belief in the working class as the primary agency of social change.

Joe has undertaken the related task of reconsidering his youthful belief in the promise of the Russian Revolution and Soviet socialism. Joe's faith in socialism has been inextricably bound up with the example of the Bolshevik Revolution, the Soviet policies of economic and social equality, the Soviet struggle for industrialization, the Soviet promise of nationality rights to ethnic minorities, and the heroic Soviet resistance to fascist aggression. With the passing of the decades, Joe had to weigh these promises and accomplishments against the lack of Soviet democracy, the periods of Stalinist terror, and especially the resurgence of anti-Semitism in the Soviet Union after World War II. Joe saw these developments first hand during three visits to the Soviet Union—in 1934, in 1963, and in 1977. To this day he calls himself "a friend of the Soviet Union," but a friend who has been "deeply disturbed" by what he saw on his last two visits.

Joe has grappled with developments in the Middle East along with his reevaluation of the Soviet Union. These problems touched upon his formative years in the Ukraine, his fundamental ideological beliefs, his loss of family in the Holocaust, and his encounters with American Jewry and the American Left. Between the wars the American Jewish radical movement, like the Soviet Union, opposed Zionism as a nationalist movement that served the interests of the bourgeoisie and Western imperialism. That position changed after the Holocaust, when Israel was born with support from the Soviet Union. Along with the majority of American Jewish radicals, Joe joyously reversed his position and supported the new Jewish state. But he also had to reckon with implacable Arab opposition to Israel, a dilemma that was compounded during the Cold War when Israel aligned with American capitalism while the Soviet Union became the main support for Israel's enemies. Joe made several journeys to Israel too where he observed the problems for himself. Today he insists upon support for the existence of Israel, but he demands the right to criticize Israeli government policies with which he disgrees.

Joe also explored the problem of continuity for the radical Jewish movement in America. That movement in its struggle to build industrial trade unionism and in its opposition to fascism operated at the center of American radicalism and American social change through World War II. During the Cold War, however, American Jewish radicals came under ferocious attack from the majority of the American Jewish community. Like the general American Left, the Jewish radicals also became separated from the mainstream American labor movement. In reaction to Stalinism, the Jewish radicals began to pursue a course apart from the U.S. Communist Party. Increasingly isolated and with a narrowing base of Jewish workers, the Jewish radical movement was left mainly with its radical Yiddish culture. As the Jewish radicals embraced that culture to maintain coherence and vision, they deepened their separation from the main currents of American life.

Joe takes his movement to task for cultural and political insularity, for not sufficiently pursuing coalition and continuity. Another of Joe's pictures, my favorite, illustrates his efforts in this direction. It shows Joe, with white hair and Western string tie, standing beside a young Native American. The picture is a document of Joe's participation in a local struggle for a Native American cultural center. It testifies to his remarkable ability to step across the gulfs of time and culture, to find solidarity with other people who have experienced persecution and who insist upon justice.

Joe has sought to apply the organizational experience of the Jewish radical movement to liberal organizations and radical movements of the post-World War II period. He is still preoccupied with the problem of how to build a radical social movement that can improve American life today and effect fundamental social change over time.

When Joe accepted my proposal to collaborate on his autobiography, he doubted that it would become a book, but he was convinced that he had a significant story to tell. Over a period of several years, beginning in 1976, we conducted seventy five tape-recorded interviews. We began with his Ukrainian childhood and continued chronologically up to the present. The interviews usually consisted of my opening up a topic and Joe talking almost nonstop. The best material came when I did not interrupt the story that he wanted to tell. Within half an hour he would be deeply engrossed in his tale, spilling it out with much animation and little reflection sometimes for several hours.

I would follow up with my own questions in a second interview on a topic. With subjects that I considered important but he did not—the actual work of the hand knitter and workshop relations, as distinct from trade union struggle—I had to question him closely to elicit information. On some topics that he was not eager to discuss, like the inner life of the left-wing movement and FBI harassment of Jewish radicals in Sonoma County, I pressed questions against strong resistance. When I approached Joe with New Left criticism that the Old Left of the 1930's played into corporate liberal reform instead of building a socialist movement, and when I advanced Hannah Arendt's charges of Jewish complicity in the Holocaust, we had uncomfortable disputes.

We usually worked around the kitchen table in Joe's and Sheba's Petaluma home. Joe had retired from chicken ranching and moved into town a few years earlier, at the age of seventy-three, only because he no longer could earn any income in an industry dominated by integrated poultry corporations. He enjoyed working with his hands around the house, but it was no substitute for working a knitting machine or a chicken ranch. The displacement of the family farmer and the displacement of the hand craftsman, two central experiences in Joe's life, were recurrent topics in our discussions.

Joe was retired, but he was not readily available for our meetings. He was active with just about every liberal, progressive, and radical organization in the county. Over the years, as I met his political allies and some opponents, I came to appreciate the respect that he commanded for patient, reasoned community work. He was not a compelling public speaker. But operating behind the scenes, discussing goals and shaping strategies, organizing people and events, he was effective.

He made regular efforts to organize me too. He initiated political discussions, invited me to meetings, and solicited my contributions. From the beginning he passed on books for me to read — Philip Foner's *The Fur and Leather Workers Union*, his friend Jacques Levy's *Cesar Chavez*, and Arie Eliav's reflections on the Jewish-Arab conflict in *Land of the Hart*. Later he started me off with subscriptions to the Jewish radical press — to *Jewish Currents* and to the weekly English supplement of the *Morning Freiheit*. Once you began taking those journals, I learned, you were a lifetime subscriber.

"Talking politics," Joe once said, "is for me like a musician playing music. It is my field of work." Politics, indeed, seemed to fill every corner of his life. Joe's and Sheba's home is filled with mementoes from travels in Europe, the Soviet Union, Israel, and South America. There is an abundance of books on history, literature, and politics, in Yiddish and Russian and English. I always preferred to explore the piles of contemporary newspapers, journals, and political circulars in various parts of the house.

In Joe's study, above his desk, is a picture of Martin Luther King and several "Freedom Award" plaques given to Joe by the local NAACP. Across the room on a dresser, along side a samovar, sits a cap given to Joe by his boyhood friend Mayer, whom Joe revisited in the Soviet Union in 1934, and who disappeared in the Stalinist terror of 1937-38. Back across the room, on the wall along side Martin Luther King, are several pictures of Vladimir Ilyich Lenin, the historical figure Joe most admires.

Both Joe and Sheba thrive on political discussion of which we had many over a delicious meal following an afternoon's work. They have no children, but they have many young friends, political activists in Sonoma County as well as the offspring of comrades from New York and Sonoma County. They seized upon my friends, too, for discussions of contemporary politics. They delight in the lively exchange of fresh views.

Joe's vitality was most apparent at the meals we shared. Despite doctor's orders to go lightly on salt, Joe took his food "sharp." He also liked it in generous quantities. When he cut bread and cheese, it was in large slabs. When he poured wine, he filled the glass to the brim. He downed the wine in one long drink, as if it was a shot of vodka, and on special occasions, Joe took out a bottle of good brandy and we toasted our enterprise.

A year after we began taping Joe's life story, I began reworking the transcribed interviews into narrative chapters in Joe's voice. I gave Joe each completed chapter and we went over it together. We have done that several times for each chapter in the book. I was repeatedly astonished at the precision with which he read the material and suggested changes of organization, interpretation, and prose. It gave me some appreciation for his craftsmanship as a hand knitter and a chicken rancher, and for his craftsmanship as a political activist who liked to organize "in-depth."

During the years of collaboration we had a number of disagreements over the selection and interpretation of material for the book. We disagreed most sharply over the history of the Jewish people and the history of the American Left. Those arguments testified to our common belief in the significance of the words we were setting to paper. In the end I added my own notes, which offer some explanations and some other perspectives on the problems that Joe raises in the text; Joe disagrees with the interpretations suggested in some of these notes.

Our most enduring disagreement was over prose. At the begin-

ning of the project I wanted to tell the story in Joe's rich
Yiddishized English. Joe urged me to write it in more conventional
English, but for several years I was captivated by the eloquence and
clarity of his spoken words. With each of my rewritings, however,
the prose became more removed from the original interviews. In
the end, I decided that Joe's Yiddish dialect, on paper, might be
treated with condescension and might not be clear to a contemporary reader. So I have written the story in a more conventional
English, but it is shaped and flavored by Joe's own language.

We were surprised and delighted when our manuscript was
accepted for publication. I would like to express our appreciation
to Temple University Press, especially to our editor Michael Ames,
for the imagination to take on this unusual project and for
countless valuable suggestions on all aspects of the book. It is a
pleasure to work with people who take pride in the books they
publish.

This book grew out of my investigation into the history of the
Petaluma Jewish community. The two projects developed together
over the past four years and became inextricably connected in my
own mind. Both projects required substantial amounts of time and
money for interviews, transcriptions, and writing. I am deeply
indebted to the California Historical Society and to the National
Endowment for the Humanities for sponsoring the Petaluma
community study and thereby affording me the opportunity to
work on Joe's life story. Grants from the Louis M. Rabinowitz
Foundation and from the Memorial Foundation for Jewish Culture,
awarded specifically for this project, were extremely helpful. All
these institutions have my admiration and gratitude for encouraging this kind of unconventional historical inquiry.

Several of Joe's old friends among the knitgoods workers, Sam
Steinhart and Louis Cooper, provided critical assistance with the
chapters on the labor movement, as did my friend Marge Frantz.
Morris U. Schappes gave us a boost through his consistent interest
in the project and then with publication of a selection in *Jewish
Currents*. Irene Paull allowed us to reprint her poem, "To Joe,
Beloved Comrade," which also appeared in *Jewish Currents*.
Rose Glickman assisted with all material pertaining to Russia and
as a general critic. Eli Katz helped as a Yiddishist and as a general
critic. Zelda Bronstein and Henry Mayer, collaborators in my study

of the Petaluma Jewish community, taught me how to place the spoken word on paper. Sheba Rapoport gave steadfast encouragement to this project from the start and was indispensable for its completion. The responsibility for all the material in the book rests with Joe and myself.

Joe Rapoport

1. Stanislavchik

The *shtetl* that I left never left me through all the years I lived in the United States. Before my eyes I can still see how it looked from atop the rolling hills. The *shtetl* was set on the hillside of a valley. It was surrounded by a peasant village, and the peasants in turn were surrounded by the fields they worked. It was a checkerboard of fields. Each peasant had his own little patch of ground with the different color of his crop—the white buckwheat, the deep green flax, the golden yellow wheat. Those little patches contrasted with the huge fields of the *pomeshchik*, the landlord.

On a clear day you could see a conglomeration of roofs in Stanislavchik. Most of the houses were covered with a red clay tile similar to the Mexican roof we see in the American Southwest. The roofs of the poorer peasants were covered by thatched straw. The better built homes had tin roofs. Towering above everything were the steeples of the two churches; they stood over the *shtetl* like watchtowers.

That part of the Ukraine was thick with woods and bushes and flowers. If you looked down on Stanislavchik in the spring, you saw a garden of flowering acacia trees surrounding the town. When you walked down from the hills, you would be haunted by a hum of beetles from the trees. They were called May beetles—they came and disappeared in the month of May.

The peasants had room for fruit trees, vegetable gardens, and flowers around their huts. But when you came closer to the center of the town, into the *shtetl*, you saw little greenery near the Jewish homes. That was because there was a limited space for the *shtetl*. We were about a hundred families—a tenth of the surrounding peasantry—crowded together along a few dirt roads. My people, my family, lived in what you could call a ghetto. There were no walls to keep us in, but there were laws which limited where we could live and what we could do.[1]

Jews were limited by the law of the land, by the Tsar's rule, to live within the boundaries of the *shtetl*. We could go to live in certain cities, but we could not have a home in a peasant village, nor could we stay in the home of a peasant overnight. Our relationship with the peasantry was based on exchange of goods. We sold them city products like hardware, kerosene, matches, needles, and ornamental goods. Our craftsmen made and sold sandals, clothes, metal implements. One Jewish family processed their sheep's wool for spinning, another had a press to squeeze oils from their grains and vegetables, another chopped their straw for cattle fodder. In exchange, the peasants sold us grain, fruit, eggs, butter, wood, and other things they grew.

The *pomeshchik*, the landlord, dominated the economy of the area. He owned the land of the *shtetl* and the peasant village for which everyone paid yearly taxes. His lands, the best land, sprawled in all directions. Most of his agricultural production was sugar beets. Where the peasant families worked by primitive hand methods, the lands of the *pomeshchik* were worked scientifically, under the direction of an *agronom*, an agronomist. The *pomeshchik* also owned a sugar mill, a distillery, a linen-processing plant, and other agricultural industries. The peasant women and the poorer peasant men worked in the fields and factories of the *pomeshchik* for a few *kopeks*. All of this was under the direction of a manager. The *pomeshchik* had an estate in our area, but I did not see him once in all the years I lived there. He must have been part of high society in Moscow or Saint Petersburg or Monte Carlo.

There were a few large Jewish merchants who contracted to buy wheat or wood from the *pomeshchik*, or who contracted to buy grains and fruits from the richer peasants. Many of the Jewish people were peddlers who traveled through the nearby peasant villages selling their wares. Much of the exchange was done at small Jewish stores in the marketplace at the center of the *shtetl*. The competition was great and the storekeepers would fight for a peasant customer who was out shopping for a pair of shoes. The peasant would go from one store to another, to be sure he was not cheated. After he found a pair that fit, after he bargained over the price, the peasant would put those shoes on a stick, throw it over his shoulder, and proudly leave as barefooted as he came.

Once a week there would be a *yarid*, a fair, in the marketplace of the *shtetl*. All through the year people would bring different products to sell at that fair. There was a big open area for people to park their buggies and display their goods. Whether you came to sell a chicken or to buy tar for wagonwheels, the bargaining was sharp. It was the accepted way to do business. That *yarid* was a noisy convention of man and animal. It was one of the delights of my childhood.

My father was not exactly a merchant, nor did he have a specific trade. He relied on a number of things to make a living. In Yiddish we called it: *Asakh melokhes un veynik brokhes*. It means "many trades but few blessings" and is equivalent to the American expression "a jack of all trades, a master of none."

My father's main source of income came from a sheep farm he rented from the landlord of a nearby estate. This was unique work for a Jew, because under the Tsar's system Jews could not own land or live on it. But a landlord rented him a farm with a herd of specially bred, high quality Persian sheep. My father bred the sheep, prepared the lambskins for sale, sheared wool for sale, and used the sheep's milk to produce a special sheep's cheese known as *brindza*.

My father's income was never too steady. The sheep farm was a half year business. If nature was kind and the market was good, he could make a living from it in the spring and summer. During the winter, he supplemented our income by preparing the sheepskins for use in hats and jackets. He did all kinds of trading for income in the winter and fall. He never was content to sit in a store and wait for customers.[2]

During the good seasons my father was splurging. One time he bought some beaver pelts from a peasant. He gave them to a tailor to use for a collar on a new coat. Did he look prosperous! My mother scolded him for extravagance: "There are more important things. We need clothes so the boys will look presentable in *shul*, in synagogue, at the holidays. We need dowries for the girls. We have to rebuild this old house." But I think she liked the idea of my father dressing well.

My father did rebuild the house in another prosperous year, but it was not his original plan. One of his best friends was a master furniture maker. One evening they were sipping tea at the samovar, or more likely they had a couple of vodkas, when my father said, "I want you to make for my living room an exact copy of the *orn-koydesh*, the holy cabinet you made for the Torah—the Penta-teuch—in the *shul*." It was a large cabinet with a magnificent hand-carved design of eagles and lions and flowers.

The day came when our friend delivered the cabinet, exactly like the one in *shul*. But when they tried to stand it up in the living room, the ceiling was too low. By this time the whole neighbor-hood was in that room. When people saw the thing being delivered, they came from all over the street to watch, to advise, to help carry it in. Now everyone offered suggestions: cut down the cabinet, dig a hole in the floor, break into the ceiling.

That living room was in the old part of the house, the section where my mother grew up. The house was divided into two parts by my grandfather, with the family of my uncle living in the other part. My uncle had modernized his side of the house, and my father decided now was the time for us to build a new, taller structure.

He talked with the neighbors about how to do it. Everyone was involved in such an important decision. Then he got a couple of house builders to put up a new structure, like an envelope over an envelope. When it was finished they tore down the inside walls and ceiling. Finally came the moment when the cabinet, which was lying covered on the floor like a dead man, was stood up in that new room. And so it remained until the day I left for America.

I always loved to go to the sheep farm with my father in the summers. I was with the shepherds in the fields from when I was a little boy. Like tradition has it, those shepherds carried a flute, which was called *supilka*. It was made from a reed that was hollowed out like a bamboo stick and then cut to size with holes. I would listen to the folk melodies they were playing in the fields.

The shepherds also told stories while they were grazing the sheep. They told of past heroes who led the people in revolt, of a peasant who distinguished himself as a woodcarver, of a villager who returned from war decorated with a medal given by the Tsar himself. At night the shepherds would sit around a fire outside, roll their cigarettes, and tell yarns about witches and sorcerers. They kept me entranced with those stories, even though I would have nightmares later.

I was five years old when my parents arranged for me to go to a *kheyder*, a Jewish elementary school, for children from poorer

families. Our teacher, the *melamed*, was a poor person who could
not go much beyond the ABC's himself. The *kheyder* was in a room
of his house with just a wooden table and a few wooden benches.
All the learning was done through repetition with the threat of
severe punishment. I felt too bored, too confined, in that small
room with dirty windows and not enough air and the *melamed*
hanging over us. I was forever thinking about hunting for berries in
the woods or swimming in the river that cut through the valley or
sliding down a hill with the wooden sled my father made.

I had one experience in the *shtetl* that looks to the stories of
Tom Sawyer and Huckleberry Finn. It was at a time when our
family was expecting a visitor from the city, a man of commercial
enterprises. My older sister Ethel gave the house a special cleaning
and prepared a great meal. She put on her best dress and displayed
her finest handwork. That evening my older brother Khayim and I
got into a wonderful fight with some other kids. Windows were
broken, stones hit other people, and the whole neighborhood
started to scream at us.

When we ran to the house, Ethel yelled that father would give us
a beating when he returned from the farm . . . that she would beat
us if we came in. That was a threat, so we ran away and hid in the
deep grass of the valley. Late that night Ethel begged a neighbor to
find us and bring us home. He assured us that we would not be
punished because Ethel would not want to disturb the guest. But
when we got inside, my sister came with a whip and gave us the
works!

During that sleepless night, crying from the whipping and
burning with revenge, Khayim and I decided to run away from our
bitter life in Stanislavchik. My oldest brother Moyshe already was in
the United States. He wanted us all to come, one by one, starting
with Khayim after his *bar mitzvah*. We decided to surprise Moyshe
and come to America now!

The next morning we pretended we were going to school, but
then we went through the back alleys as if we were going to the
river where we swam. But we continued past the river for eight
miles along a country path, instead of the road where we might be
seen, to the big railroad station at Zhmerinka. Khayim already
knew that you could get a ship to America from Odessa and you
could get to Odessa by train from Zhmerinka.

At the railroad station we learned which track carried the train to Odessa the next morning. We planned to hide under the benches to avoid the fare. Everything was going according to plan until the *balegole*, the wagonman who shuttled people between Stanislavchik and Zhmerinka, was looking to meet a passenger at the railroad station and noticed us. He said, "What are you doing here? Your mother is crying. Someone said you went to the river. They are looking for your bodies there. Everyone thinks Ethel drove you to kill yourselves. Come home!" And as soon as he said "come home," we ran away.

The next morning Ethel and the *balegole* came looking for us at the station. They finally caught Khayim late in the afternoon and they expected I would follow. But they were wrong! I stayed another night in that huge railroad station among thousands of people going in all directions. It was not until the next morning, after they treated Khayim to his favorite foods, that he would help them catch me with the promise of good food and no punishment. And so it was.

When I was older, I continued my education at a *talmud toyre*. That school not only was for the study of the Hebrew language and the Jewish holy books, but also for the teaching of Russian, mathematics, and sciences. It was in a more modern building with several teachers. Still I was not a good student. I sat in school and watched the words fly by. But that school was the beginning of higher education for my brother Khayim. From there he went to a preparatory high school in the nearby town of Bar. And from there he could have gone into a Russian high school and perhaps to the university.

Education in the Russian schools could open doors to the wider world. There was a quota of 10 percent Jewish students, so few could go. There you could learn to be a doctor, a lawyer, an engineer. In the *shtetl* we associated the uniforms of those high school students with the Tsar's government. It stimulated a certain interest, a certain envy, a certain desire among young people to break out of the walls of the *shtetl*.

It was not just through the Russian schools that young people left the *shtetl*. A youngster might go to the city to learn to be a jewelrymaker. A young blacksmith might go to become a gold-smith. Others went to start businesses. There were many more opportunities in the city. They would come back for a visit well dressed with an air of worldliness. They were more encouragement for young people to leave Stanislavchik.

My own desire to break out of the walls of the *shtetl* began from sharing a room with my grandfather. I cannot go farther back in my own family than my mother's father. All through childhood I remember him as an old man. His name was Khaskel. There were others by the same name in the *shtetl*, but people would refer to him with great respect as "Alter Khaskel ... the Old Khaskel." Some people considered him a *tsadik*, a holy man.

He was a holy terror. When he was well enough to walk around, he would stop children and check their four *tsitsis*. Those were tassels attached to a prayer shawl you wore under your shirt. Each *tsitse* had so many knots and if, God forbid, one became loose, that was not kosher anymore. It lost its power to God and opened the road for the devil to reach you.

My grandfather would stop the kids on the road and examine every one of their tassels and knots. He always had some cookies in his pocket. If everything was all right, you would get a cookie and everyone would be happy. If not, and if you were not fast enough, you would get a whack with my grandfather's walking stick. He scared the life out of us.

My grandfather was a pious man. As long as I can remember, two days a week he was fasting and praying with all the honesty of his soul. For several years he was bed-ridden—just skin and bones— but nobody dared stop him from fasting. And as long as I can remember, he kept a little sack of soil from Israel under his pillow. A peddler sold it to him. My grandfather believed that little earth gave him the holiness of the Holy Land, that it would be to his good standing when he faced the Creator.

Friday was considered a holy day for a pious man to die. Then he would come to the heavens just before the *shabes*, the Sabbath, just as the people in the *shtetlekh* throughout the world were sitting down for the *shabes* meal. So when you died on a Friday afternoon, you arrived to share the holiest of the holy feasts.

One Friday in the early afternoon my grandfather said to my mother, "My daughter, call together the family." And she did. She called together her brothers, their wives, and their children. My grandfather's children and their children, we packed to an overflow that little room where he lay. He asked for his *talis*, his prayer shawl, and he blessed all present. Then he closed his eyes and died. Thus, let us believe he found a seat of honor at the holy of the holy feasts in heaven.

That was a small incident in my life, but it stays with me. Throughout my boyhood I shared a room with my grandfather, and he tyrannized me. He forever was scaring me with stories of the *dybbuk*, the devil. We were forever doing things to ward off evil spirits from our room. He made me do honor to my right foot when I put on my pants by using my right foot first. The same thing with putting on my boots and washing my hands. There was a morning prayer, a noontime prayer, an evening prayer that he made sure I did every day or he would punish me. When he died, I felt liberated from this imposed worship. I not only stopped following it, but I hated it.

A year after he died I prepared for my *bar mitzvah*. That was when the congregation would declare me an independent Jew, a man. Then the good deeds and the sins would be my own. But I was annoyed by the demands of my father to do the preparatory rituals, especially with the *tfiln*, the containers of holy prayers which you tied to the forehead and the upper part of the left arm. Then you had to wrap the leather thongs seven and a half times down your arm, and when it came to the hand you went so many times around the middle finger. Then came prayers and the kissing of the thing.

That was the pinnacle of my resentment. If I didn't do this morning ritual, I wouldn't get my breakfast. Not to kill the time entirely, I would hide other reading materials inside the prayer book. That's when I started reading serials of Sherlock Holmes and stories of Jack London and tales of Garibaldi. Wonderful fantastic stuff! It wasn't honest, but I hated that daily ritual.

I resented doing the preparations for my *bar mitzvah*. I went through the motions at the ceremony, but I had not even learned the elementary prayers by heart. My father gave me a good tongue lashing after. He told me, "You didn't know the prayers. You put me to shame before the entire *shtetl*. I do not believe you will say *kaddish* [prayer to commemorate the dead] when I die."

All of this haunted me from when my grandfather was living. The actual disbelief in God came later, when the Bolsheviks took over and taught atheism. I was ready for them! And up to the present day I remain nonreligious. I believe anyone has a right to exercise his religion, but at the same time I insist that someone else cannot condemn me for not sharing his religious beliefs.[3]

My father would go to *shul*, but he was not pious. My mother was a pious person, a true believer like her father. She never inspired religion in me, but I always respected her devotion. She was a wonderful person ... very human. She carried a great load with six children, all the household work, and helping my father with the income. She worked hard because she wanted life to be good for the children. But no matter how hard she worked, she said her prayers. Even though the prayers were not required of women, she knew them all by heart. I can remember her standing by the oven, baking *khale*, egg bread, and saying her prayers.

On the long winter nights my mother and sisters would pluck goosefeathers in the evenings. Sometimes neighbors would join them. The snow outside would be halfway up the house, while inside we sat around the *hrube*, which was an oven made from fieldstones built between two rooms. They would be plucking those goose feathers to make mattresses and pillows for dowries. While they did their handwork, they sang songs ... folksongs ... social singing, almost like prayers.

I remember, even before I understood what Jerusalem really was, my mother plucking goose feathers and singing about Eretz Yisroel, the Land of Israel. There was one song about a bird: "Great God in heaven, when I die a great bird will take me to Jerusalem." This yearning for Zion was woven into her consciousness, into the consciousness of all the people in the *shtetl*, long before we had any contact with the modern Zionist movement. Everything in our daily life was connected with the prayer, *Le-shanah ha-ba'ah biyerusalayim*, "Next year in Jerusalem." This wish to return to the Holy Land was repeated several times in prayer every day. It was a yearning through the centuries for freedom from persecution. Modern Zionism built on this religious fervor. In our home, in almost all the homes of the *shtetl*, there was a portrait of Dr. Herzl, the founder of modern Zionism, hanging on the wall.

The Torah and especially the Talmud, the interpretation of the laws in the Torah, were forever under discussion in the *shtetl*. What was the meaning of a certain passage, a certain word? Why was a dot placed on the left side of a certain letter? Why was one letter a little wider than another? You could talk for days and weeks on the interpretation of a trifle. In the wintertime, when there was not much work to be done outside, the men would gather round the *hrube* after prayers in *shul*. There they would drink a *shnaps*, a whiskey, and discuss the holy books of Jewish learning.

Great honor was given to the most learned men, to the rabbi and the religious leadership in the community. The rabbi was the final authority in these discussions. He was responsible to maintain the traditions of the Jewish people. He would be the one to interpret the Jewish laws for everyday living or in the case of a dispute between Jew and Jew. We had no government court for Jews in Stanislavchik, so the rabbi carried the authority to solve a Jewish problem.

Honor also went to the rich, to those who could buy the best seats near the Torah at the western wall of the *shul*, who could buy the honor of reading the best chunks of Torah at services. But there was resentment too. Sometimes someone would get insulted because he would be called on to read third when someone else paid more to read first. In the middle of the service voices would be raised, and before you knew it, there would be a fight. If it was *shabes*, so much the better, because then the brass candlesticks would be handy to knock the hell out of each other. Bang! Right there in the *shul*! I got trampled in one of those fights when I was a little boy. My mother's brothers, who were very learned, had a little *shul* in one of their homes, so they would not suffer the indignity of being shoved aside by the rich at the big *shul*.

There was much superstition in the religion of the *shtetl*. In the Jewish cemetery there was a special room for final rites before they would earth the body. There always was a pail full of water and a clean towel in that room. It was for the souls of the dead, who would come to say their prayers at midnight. They had to wash up, because you had to be clean to pray. Once I spent a night in that cemetery on a dare from friends. I was terrified that my grandfather would rise out of his grave to punish me for not saying my prayers.

The fact that witches and dead people were supposed to be roaming around at night used to scare the wits out of me. My grandfather forever warned me about the devil at the river, the devil at the cemetery, and especially *domovoi*, the house devil. "If you have to go up to the attic after dark," he said, "get what you want and walk backwards to the door. Retreat with your face to *domovoi*. Then it can't get power over you. If you see it, call out the name of God, *Shadai*, and you will be saved." Even when I was maturing into manhood, I had an uneasy feeling about going up into that attic at night.

The Jewish people picked up many of the peasant superstitions. To protect against demons stealing milk from our cow, my father would spread poppyseeds across the threshold of the cow shed. If my mother got scared at night, she would say a prayer against the Evil Eye; but she would call it *gut oyg*, the Good Eye, because she didn't even want to mention Evil Eye. To get rid of a curse from the Evil Eye, my aunt Rivka once called in a peasant woman who could appeal to spirits. She melted wax and made all kinds of sayings. When a bubble appeared in the wax, she had extracted the evil spirit that was making my aunt sick.[4]

Our lives in the *shtetl* were guided by religious beliefs, by the rhythms of the Jewish ceremonies, especially the *shabes*. The coming of the *shabes* was called the coming of a *kale*, a bride. My mother would prepare all day—cleaning the house, polishing the silver candleholders, cooking the food—for the Friday dinner. That was the best meal of the week, but my favorite was on Saturday afternoon. Because there could be no cooking on Saturday, on the Sabbath, my mother placed that food in the *hrube* on Friday afternoon and cooked it slow and crispy overnight. We called it *tsholnt*.

My father would return from the farm on Friday afternoon for the *shabes*. Just before dark my mother would light the holiday candles. We wore our best clothes and we went through a beautiful ceremony at dinner. We'd sing special songs which were very melodic, very happy. And after the meal there would be a gathering of all the aunts and uncles and children in the family. There would be more singing. There would be reading of Sholom Aleichem. It was a family holiday, a celebration every Friday night.

When I was old enough, sometimes I would go to the sheep farm for a couple of days so my father could be home for *shabes*. It was a great change from the *shtetl*. The empty fields were lonely in the early spring, before the shepherds were there. The winds were strong and the rains were heavy in March and April. At night I would hear weird noises from the wind blowing against the hollow straw in the thatched roof. I attributed the noise to the dead in a nearby peasant cemetery. The sound of a train passing by a few miles away would be a friendly voice for me.

The sheep farm was scary at night. But during the day I had the freedom of the fields, the rolling hills, the wide open stretches of land. I would ride a horse bareback across the fields. I enjoyed the feeling of power and freedom when I gave the horse all the speed it wanted, galloping off in no special direction. That was something I couldn't get in the *shtetl*.

There also was unpleasantness at the farm, especially an incident I never forgot. One day when I was at the farm with my father, a policeman came round. He questioned the legal right of my father to stay on that farm and he hinted it would be ok if my father would give him cheese and lambskins. My father agreed. The following day I had to drive a wagon twenty *versts*, about twelve miles, to the precinct town to deliver that bribe. It burned my hands and it burned my feet and it burned my temper. I never forgot the shame that my father had to bribe his way to live even partly on that isolated farm.

That shame haunted me as it haunted the Jewish people. There were many instances when, in order to make progress outside the prescribed areas of Jewish life, we had to buy, bribe, and steal our way. There was an oppression of the Jewish people, a hatred of the Jewish people, under the Tsar's system. And sometimes there was outright attack—pogroms—that were instigated by supporters of the Tsar. Those pogrommakers were organized throughout Russia in groups known as *Chernosotentsy*, the Black Hundreds. They would sidetrack the dissatisfaction against the Tsar and turn the peasants against the Jewish people instead.

The Ukraine, for all its beauty, was not just the romanticism of fields and gardens. The peasant population suffered terribly under the Tsarist system. They paid high taxes to feed the landlords, the church, and the Tsar's bureaucracy. That whole system was corrupt, and they had to pay bribery on top of taxes. The richer peasants, those with fifteen acres and a horse for plowing, lived comfortably. But the peasants with an acre or less lived in one

room huts which they shared with the piglet and the chickens.
They were forever hungry, forever dissatisfied, forever a danger of
revolt.

At times of great suffering and dissatisfaction the Tsar would
deflect the danger of revolt by turning the people against the Jews.
It was easy to do because we were strangers in our homeland—a
separate people with a separate language, a separate culture, a
separate god. The Tsar's church would preach religious prejudice,
accusing the Jewish people as anti-Christian, as God-killers, as
people who used Christian blood for Passover rites.

There also was the belief that the Jew lived off the peasant ...
that the Jew was shrewd and cheated the peasant. The Tsarist
system was arranged so the peasant made the bread while the
Jewish people were barred from the land and forced to be
middlemen. The peasant knew how to bargain, but the Jewish
people had centuries of experience at it. That was the only way we
could live under the Tsarist system, and it bred constant antagonism. Even if there were no shady manipulations—and sometimes
there were—the peasant suspected he was being taken by the Jew.
And since the Jewish people could not own land, we had to keep
our accumulation in goods and it was more visible.

So it was easy for the Tsar's officials to stir up the peasants by
declaring the Jews had all the money. When the Tsar gave the
green light to the Black Hundreds, the pogrommakers, the peasants could rob, rape, and kill the Jewish people without risk of
punishment.

In the cities, where the actual contact between peasant and Jew
was further removed, where the peasant just saw the glitter of gold
in store windows, the hatred was greater. Since the personal
contact was not there, as in the small towns, the big city pogroms
were terrifying. The great pogrom in Kishinev at the beginning of
the century always was in our memory.[5]

There was a great danger of a pogrom in my own *shtetl* after the
1904 war with Japan. That war, that defeat at the hands of the
Japanese on the Siberian tundras, brought great suffering to the
Russian population. It set off a huge revolt, the 1905 Revolution,
and the Tsar was forced to make democratic concessions. But
once again the Tsar turned the peasantry against the Jewish people
to divert the dissatisfaction.[6]

The pogrom was prevented in Stanislavchik because the Jewish people organized a self-defense committee. When the peasants gathered in the marketplace to prepare for the onslaught against the *shtetl*, one of the self-defense leaders rode in on horseback with a torch. This was the blacksmith, a person who had close contact with the peasants. The rabbi and the wealthy merchant had the most prestige within the *shtetl*, but the peasants respected the blacksmith as someone who worked with his hands. He warned them: "You are preparing to rob our houses and assault our women. We have people with burning torches ready to fire your straw roofs. We shall do to you what you do to us. Go home. Let us live in peace. We need you. You need us."

There was another reason for no pogrom that day. Poverty forced many peasants to find industrial work in the cities. One of the Stanislavchik peasants, Mitka Dobrovolskii, left to work on the railroad in Zhmerinka and became a socialist leader. He spoke in our marketplace that day. He pointed out that the enemy was not the Jewish people but the system which led to such conditions. He spoke for socialism, for a basic change to improve the lives of all the people, Ukrainian and Jewish. I was only six years old at the time, but as I grew up I heard stories of how Mitka Dobrovolskii saved the *shtetl* from a pogrom in 1906.

Incidents like that fed the dreams of many young Jewish people that socialism would be the salvation to our problems. Already in 1905 there was across the street from us a young bagelmaker, Sasha, who was preaching the overthrow of the Tsar and the introduction of socialism. I knew him well because I always was over there eating the egg bagels that crumbled. One day after the revolution the Tsar's police came for him. He fled through the back door from those clumsy peasant police, and he never returned to Stanislavchik. Again I was too young to understand what happened, but the stories were passed down to me about Sasha the bagelmaker and the promise that socialism would make a better life for the Jewish people and the Ukrainian people.

The Jewish population usually had friendly relations with the peasants. My father knew peasants in nearby villages who would let him stay overnight if it was necessary. In Stanislavchik there were a few peasant families who would let us pick fruit from their trees. I had a few peasant children as friends. But there always was that separation. I felt strange going into a peasant hut. I felt uneasy going through the peasant village alone—a peasant kid might throw a stone or a dog might attack. In peaceful periods the friction between the two peoples was more sharply expressed by the children. There were forever gang fights between the Ukrainian kids and the Jewish kids down by the river where we swam and skated.

It was not just coming from the Christians. We too were taught religious antagonism. When my father would pass a church or a cross in a field, he would spit three times. Automatically! When Jewish people referred to the city Belaia Tserkov, which means "white church," we would call it *schvartze time*, which means "black unholiness." Where our worship places were holy, theirs were *tref*, unclean. Where their holy day was Sunday, ours was Saturday. Where they took off their caps in church, we put on the *yarmlke*, the skullcap, in *shul*. And so it went. We did the opposite and denounced what they did with the vehemence of religious fervor.

I believe the reason for this attitude, besides the persecution we suffered at the hands of Christians, was to maintain our own religion and traditions. Over the centuries in the Diaspora, the Jewish people struggled to maintain their identity as a people, so the children in coming generations should not fall prey to the Christian church. When a Jewish child would marry a gentile, the parents would mourn as if someone had died. The best way to prevent that was to ridicule Christianity. The Jewish people sought to maintain their separation even though it cost a lot of grief through history.

And so it was. The *shtetl*—my *shtetl*—was a small self-contained world. We were about five hundred people living on top of each other. We knew what the other was cooking each night. We knew when families were fighting and when neighbors were feuding. We lived on the street, in the public. The children met in *kheyder*, in *shul*, and at the *mikva*, the public bathhouse. When we went shopping we knew the shopkeepers and their *yikhus*, their background and status. We knew when someone was sick, when a doctor came, when there was an operation. We knew each other from childhood to the grave. It was like a big family.

Of course, there never was much love between the rich and the poor. The blacksmith was appreciated for his usefulness, but honor was given to the rich merchant. He could sit at the front of the *shul* with the learned men. He could pay people to haul water for him. He could marry off a son to the beautiful daughter of a poor family. The rich would give charity. They would invite the poor into their homes for a holiday meal. But the one who gives and the one who receives have different attitudes. It was not class struggle like you found in the cities, but there was that division in the *shtetl*.[7]

The closeness of the *shtetl* was reflected in the nicknames of people. Derogatory names! Someone named Yankl was called Yankl Parekh. *Parekh* means "head covered with scabs," which referred to a head rash he had as a child; but it also means "ugliness" in behavior, and this Yankl was a person who did not keep his word to friends. The best tailor in the *shtetl* was called Avrom Got, Abraham the god, because he acted like a dictator when it came to deciding the color and style of a suit for a customer. One of the blacksmith's sons, a heavily built person, was called Yisroel Ox. A woman often was referred to by her husband's nickname, and so was a son.

My father was called Yisroel Boydik. The translation of *boydik* means "inspector," but there was a sarcasm attached to it with my father. Once he brought in a lamb from the farm on Friday afternoon to be processed for the *shabes* meal. It had to be slaughtered by the *shoykhet*, according to the law of Israel. The *shoykhet* was the ritual slaughterer, a person who had the respect of the community. After he cut the lamb's throat, my father pulled off the skin for the examination, the *boydik*, to see that there was no contamination. The *shoykhet* was attending to something else and my father was in a hurry, so my father did the inspection himself and loaded the lamb onto his wagon. My father knew as much as the *shoykhet* about sheep, but he didn't have the legal stamp for slaughtering and inspecting.

Then comes the *shoykhet* and says, "Yisroel, where you taking the lamb? It wasn't inspected yet."

My father said, "You can go home. *I* am the inspector!"

From then on my father was known in the *shtetl* as Yisroel Boydik! And to this day the children and grandchildren of my brothers, when they greet me they say, "Hello, Yosl Boydik!"

So we lived closely and there were feuds, but at times of joy the

doors were opened to everyone. The wedding of my sister Ethel
was such an occasion. It was a big celebration with all the relatives
and the whole neighborhood. They were married in a traditional
ceremony in the best room of our house, a special fancy room that
was opened only for special rejoicing. There followed dancing and
eating and drinking. Months ahead we got deposits from the
musicians, to be sure they came. My uncle, who paid them for each
song, marked the wall each time. And the food! The caterer was
the best in the area; the taste of *flodn* and strudel dipped in honey
stayed with me for months. I was only ten, but I never forgot that
party. It continued for three days and three nights, almost without
stop. It was a festivity for the whole *shtetl*.

The spirit of the holidays also brought us together. *Simkhas
Torah* was my favorite holiday when I was young. It celebrates the
finishing of the reading of the Torah. It is read in *shul* a chapter a
week, with as many chapters as there are weeks in the year. This is
how the average person in the *shtetl* knew the Torah so well.
When you finished the last chapter, you began over again, year
after year. And naturally, the day of finishing the Torah was like
New Year's Eve. There were whiskeys in *shul*, there were parties,
there was singing and dancing in the streets. One of the Yiddish
poets described how the people were mixing:

Hand on shoulder, the beard in the sky;
Let there flame a dance.

Such was the life of the *shtetl*. The Jewish people with all their
variety and divisions lived their lives and did their work—the
merchants who traded with the peasants, the craftsmen who
produced for the peasants, the *shoykhet* who processed the
livestock, the rabbi who had to make a living too. There was the
gossip, the arguments over Torah in *shul*, the bargaining at the
marketplace. The life of the *shtetl* was flowing along certain
patterns. We were living like an island which was not completely
isolated, but nevertheless like an island within a sea of humanity.
This was until World War I and the Russian Revolution, which
brought frightening disturbances, terrible destruction, and a new
form of life.

2. War and Revolution

*J*first saw the Cossacks when I was thirteen years old. After my *bar mitzvah* I went to work as a printer's apprentice in Bar, a nearby provincial city where by father was born. That year marked the third century of rule by the House of Romanov, the Tsars of Russia. Throughout the land there was celebration, the establishment of monuments, and especially military demonstrations. It was in Bar that I saw the Cossacks on parade, a sea of soldiers on the march. I was fascinated by the beauty of those tall mountain people. They wore red and black uniforms sewn to shape. They carried hand-designed daggers, long sabres, and cavalry rifles. Every horse seemed like a fiery beast ready to take off into space, but they were marching by the hundreds in perfect precision. I was awed by the power of that demonstration. Little did I know that it was part of the Tsar's preparation for the First World War. And little did the Tsar know that he was digging his own grave.

The actual declaration of war in August 1914 hit the Jewish people, as it hit the entire Russian people, like a lightning bolt out of a clear sky. A few people may have seen it coming in the newspapers, but we did not read newspapers in Stanislavchik. Our main source of information about the world was from the merchant who returned from a trip to the big city. What did we know about international affairs?

We started to learn when the war broke out. All young men of age were drafted immediately. Many resented going, especially among the Jews. Why should the sons of a people who were insulted and degraded by the Tsar willingly give their lives to defend that system?

It was no wonder that some Jewish boys from Stanislavchik maimed themselves to avoid being drafted. They did it under the pressure of parents. My aunt Rivka took my cousin Itsik to another *shtetl*, where there was a man who specialized in such things. Even my aunt Rivka, who had a very strong character, was sick to see what was done to Itsik.

She said, "Two men pinned him down on the floor. The 'specialist' was poking his finger into the internal parts of the belly to create a hernia. He was tearing Itsik's guts with nothing to deaden the pain! The cries are still ringing in my ears!"

I was several years younger than Itsik and not expected to be taken into the army. But she turned to me and said, "I am happy I have prevented him from going into the army and possibly never seeing him again. But I beg you, never let be done to you what I did for Itsik."

Very few, however, avoided the army. There was a tight control over the population by the Tsar's military machine. I heard the cries of relatives and neighbors for their sons who were taken.[1]

Everything went smoothly the first winter of the war. The Tsar had a large army ready to march and a huge reserve to draw upon. Russia was a giant country with almost endless human resources. The peasants used to say, "*Shapkami zabrosim*, with our caps we will route them." There was confidence that Russia would be victorious in a short time.

In the early spring of 1915, when my father began preliminary work on the sheep farm, the shepherds had been drafted into the army. I was learning the printing trade in Bar. It was an exciting place, a city with ten thousand Jews. There were cobblestone streets, cement sidewalks, schools, businesses, even a movie theater. On a hill there was a beautiful park where I gathered with young people to sing and play and forge friendships. I wanted to remain there, but I had to return and help my father on the sheep farm.

In Stanislavchik we followed the war closely. The men would discuss the military strategy in *shul*. After the official prayers, they would gather round the stove to map out movements of armies and argue about strategies. They would go on and on, from one thing to another, but inevitably they would look to the Jewish books of learning to interpret the war.

At that time I read *War and Peace* more than once. It helped us younger boys understand the war. We saw how Napoleon's invasion had been unsuccessful against the defensive Russian strategy. In this war, however, Russia began with an offensive strategy. The overconfidence and bumbling of Russian generals is described in Alexander Solzhenitsyn's *August 1914*. Solzhenitsyn's writings on Russia after the revolution are questionable—he is anti-Soviet and antisocialist—but his *August 1914* gives a good description of the rot and corruption of the Tsarist armies at the beginning of the war. Numbers alone could not do the trick. Russian Army after Russian Army was cut down by the Germans. First we heard rumors of it in Stanislavchik. Then the evidence started to come back with news about lost lives and with returning soldiers who were maimed.

Working on the sheep farm gave me intimate contact with the peasants of neaby villages. Instead of spinning the yarns of the past, they told stories of how the army took their young men, then their livestock and feed, leaving the plow stuck there in the ground. It was like a locust descending upon the body of Russia. The hurt was cutting deep.

Our lives were interwoven. As the peasants produced less, it affected the Jewish people. Any livelihood based on exchange was hurt. The merchant could not get manufactured goods, the blacksmith could not get iron, the tailor could not get cloth. Prices soared and we had to start trading valuables for food. The supply ran short on both sides. As the months passed, the *shtetl* began to go hungry.

With the battlefield slaughter and the hunger came epidemics. Soon there were almost daily funerals in Stanislavchik. Several of my friends died from typhus. I caught it and was bed-ridden for months. I didn't know what hit me. I attribute my survival to my sister Sorke, who looked after me through it all.

The *shtetl* was never the same again. The children who left, the economic hardships, the deaths . . . our way of life was disturbed forever. We continued to celebrate the holidays, but without the gaiety of the past. A woman could light the candles on *shabes*, but it was not the same without candlesticks. Candlesticks were essential to the celebration—they brought the spirit of *shabes* into the home. But finally we had to exchange our candlesticks for bread. And then came the day when we didn't have candles.

More and more we were living close to the results of the war. I still remember the railroad station at Zhmerinka, in the winter, with trainloads of soldiers' bodies packed one on top of the other.

Those bodies were frozen through and through. When they fell, they sounded like glass. The bodies had been returned for burial in the Ukraine, but they remained at the railroad station. When the spring sun started to thaw those frozen corpses, the stink and disease were released.

It reached a point where the people would not take it any longer. In the army there was grumbling; in the factories there was dissatisfaction; among the peasantry there was resentment. Intelligent leaders started to talk about the futility of feeding the Tsar's system with the lifeblood of the people. In Stanislavchik we heard reports of discontent across Russia. Strangers passed through with leaflets asking how long we would tolerate the slaughter, the starvation, the epidemics. People like Mitka Dobrovolskii returned to Stanislavchik and worked underground. Hundreds and thousands of leaders across Russia pointed out that the people had to get rid of the Tsar.

Even liberal minded landlords started to see the futility of the war. Thinking people of the middle class—industrialists and bankers and merchants—saw the disaster that befell Russia. They too concluded that the Tsar had to go. It was in March of 1917 that the agitation culminated in the overthrow of the Tsar. The leader of the movement was a lawyer by the name of Alexander Kerenskii. We heard by proclamation that the Tsar was under arrest and that Russia was on the way to becoming a republic.

There is an old folk saying: "*Ven a vorm krikht arayn in khreyn denkt er as s'iz gornisht ziser oyf der velt*, when the worm creeps into the horseradish, he thinks there is nothing sweeter in the world." Despite all the pain and oppression under the Tsarist system, there still were segments of the population reluctant to make such a radical change. This was true among the Jews as well as the peasants.

After the prayers in *shul* there were heated discussions about the new development. Some remembered when Alexander II, the Tsar-Liberator who emancipated the peasants, was assassinated. His son Alexander III instituted a bloody repression of everything liberal. Then, as in every period of restlessness, the Jews became scapegoats and there was a wave of pogroms.[2] Now people questioned whether the Tsar could be removed so easily, and if he was removed who would replace him?

The Jewish people feared any disturbance in which the *shtetl* would be ravaged. But the majority of people in the *shtetl* greeted the new government with hope. Most of the Jewish population was elated by the establishment of a liberal democratic form of government. The majority of the Jewish people were poor and had the feeling of good riddance to the Tsar.[3]

With the removal of the Tsar there were hopes for immediate peace. Kerenskii made the mistake of his life when he called upon the people to continue the war till a victorious conclusion. At the same time, Kerenskii established a republic and allowed free expression of opinion against the war he perpetuated. All kinds of political parties suddenly came to life with programs of peace and democracy. Some brought forth slogans from the 1905 Revolution. Within a few months the people started to see that there was no basic change. The political parties appealed to the people to get rid of Kerenskii.

Things were happening too fast for us to understand in Stanislav-chik, but we tried. Public meetings began to occur in the market-place. A peasant would come to buy a pound of salt or to sell a rooster, and he would ask, "Did the war stop yet?" The peasants thought the Jewish people had more knowledge of what was happening. The stores were practically empty, so the storekeepers would walk into the street for a discussion. A few people would start talking, soon there would be ten, and before you knew it there were a hundred. There was expression of opinion, there was argument, and the people became acquainted with the various approaches to new developments.

One of the most influential speakers was Mitka Dobrovolskii. I grew up with the story of how he saved the *shtetl* from a pogrom in 1906. Now he spoke in the marketplace when he came to visit his family in Stanislavchik. I would drop everything when I heard that he was speaking. I did not know his political affiliation, but I liked what he stood for. He would tell us, "The day is past when a landlord can sell three hundred souls—three hundred serfs—for a hunting dog." He wanted to push the revolution much further, and he did just that. (Later we heard he perished fighting with a partisan detachment. In New York I wrote an article on him as a Stanislavchik hero.)

I remember one meeting in the marketplace where there was a

Jewish speaker, a provincial lawyer from Bar. He got up on a wagon and talked about freedom of conscience and freedom of speech. He spoke perfect Russian. I was proud to see him up there. A Jewish person speaking to a gathering of peasants and Jews was a revolutionary development in our area. It showed a growing fraternization of all the people.

A peasant mounted the wagon after that learned Jewish man. He was one of the poorer peasants, but he had a gift of thought and speech. He said, "We need more than the nice phrases of the previous speaker if we are to live better. We must end the war. We must have more land. Kerenskii is serving the rich and the powerful. We got rid of the Tsar; we must get rid of Kerenskii. We must get rid of the landlords and the church too! We'll be our own landlords! We'll have real freedom!"

This peasant showed how leaders came forth from the people. He received the greatest applause. That lawyer with his brilliant tongue and university expressions certainly was put in place!

In a short period of time in the days of Kerenskii, the boundaries started to break down for the Jewish people. Suddenly, a Jew could pick himself up and travel anywhere, even to Moscow! The Zionist movement came to life with the message that Jews should go to Palestine. The Jewish Bund preached that Jews should join the fight for socialism. Almost overnight there was a hunger for Jewish culture. Now you opened a Jewish book, you read Jewish poetry, you learned a Jewish folksong and it sounded good. Suddenly the *shul* in Stanislavchik was being used for a lot of cultural and political meetings.[4]

There was a double process all across Russia. On one side was democratic expression and appeal to the will of the people. On the other side was pressure against further change and for continuation of the war till victory. In the confusion of that double pull, the Bolshevik Party came forth with the clearest antiwar position. It was during this period that Lenin, Trotsky, and other Bolshevik leaders returned from exile. They built a coalition of revolutionary groups around a minimal program: "peace, bread, land." Details, it seems, they left for later.

The Bolshevik program started to vibrate in the big cities, in the industrial centers. Their slogans inflamed the imagination of millions in the countryside. Their message reached the soldiers on the battlefields, who were bitterly disappointed by the continuation of the war. Even though Kerenskii weakened the machinery of the Tsar, he could not get a firm grip on the soldiers. When the Bolsheviks issued a call to establish soviets, councils of workers and peasants and soldiers, the soldiers on the battlefields held meetings, elected delegates, and sent them back to confer in the cities.[5]

A neighbor, the son of a Jewish tailor who had been inducted into the Tsar's army, returned to Stanislavchik with a red armband on his army uniform. It meant that he had been elected as an army representative to the soviet. He walked with pride. This boy who had been nothing in the life of the *shtetl* returned a leader, a military leader, a military representative to the soviet. Only yesterday no Jew could even be an army officer.

The beginning of the Bolshevik Revolution came without disturbance in our area. In October of 1917 we simply heard a declaration that the Bolsheviks had assumed power in Petrograd, Moscow, and other cities. At first the people of our area remained neutral. But as the revolutionary struggle develped, as opposition to the revolution developed, there was a new round of discussions about where people stood and what was ahead.

When the Bolsheviks took power, they had the problem of holding the battlelines against the Germans until a peace could be negotiated. At that same time, there developed a bloody civil war in the interior, not only between the Bolsheviks and the military machine of the old system but also with the nationalist movements fighting for their own independence.

The Ukrainians had nationalist aspirations from long ago. They too were an oppressed people whose language and culture were discouraged by the Tsar. During the Kerenskii period, and especially after the Bolsheviks took over, the Ukrainian nationalist movement came to life. It was not only teachers starting to glorify Ukrainian culture, but it was a Ukrainian nationalist independence movement. They built armies before our eyes with soldiers who returned from the Tsar's army. Under the leadership of their own ruling classes, the Ukrainian people began to establish their own government.

At first it was peaceful when a Ukrainian Nationalist Army took over our area. But then the Bolshevik Armies came with promises

of land for the peasants and Ukrainian national autonomy in a
federation of Russian peoples. When the Bolsheviks came, there
was fighting with the Ukrainian nationalists. The situation was
never static. An area could be under the Bolshevik system one day,
Ukrainian nationalists another day, and the Tsarists yet another day.
There were foreign occupations too—the Germans, the Poles, the
Romanians.

In my own memory, this is the hardest period I have lived
through. Whenever there was an upheaval in Russia, the Jewish
people paid the biggest price, and this was no exception. The
changes in armies brought disaster. In the beginning, the people of
my *shtetl* were sympathetic to the national aspirations of the
Ukrainian people. Some Jewish artisans were more sympathetic to
the Bolsheviks, but the richer Jewish people opposed the Bolshevik attack on private property. The Jewish people, even in
Stanislavchik, were not one solid group. But when we did not take
guns in hand to join the Ukrainian Nationalist Armies, the entire
Jewish people were declared enemies and Bolshevik collaborators.[6]

This harkened back to the tragic experience of the Jewish
people with Bogdan Chmielnitskii, who led the Ukrainian people
against Polish domination in the seventeenth century. When the
Jewish people did not join with Chmielnitskii, and when some
Jewish merchants collaborated with the Poles, it was interpreted
that the Jewish people opposed the Ukrainian independence
struggle. The result was a massive slaughter. To this day we
remember with a shudder "*in Khmelnitskis tsaytn*, the days of
Chmielnitskii."[7] (Yet, up to the present under the Soviet system,
Bogdan Chmielnitskii is considered a national liberator in the
Ukraine without a word of criticism against his slaughter of the
Jewish people. You can still see a statue of him in Kiev.)

There was a similar experience in the revolution. When the
Jewish people did not join against the Bolsheviks, the Ukrainian
nationalists tried to raise the ire of the peasantry against us. There
was a long history of anti-Semitism and pogroms in the Ukraine and
in the Ukrainian nationalist movement, but this was something
new. This was an organized onslaught by Ukrainian nationalist
military forces joined by parts of the general Ukrainian populaton.

The advance detachments of the Ukrainian Armies usually

started the pogroms. They came in ahead of the armies and they found the *shtetl* helpless. Small bands of robbers, who traveled near the Ukrainian Armies, also used the chaos to violate the *shtetl*. Once it started, peasants from the village would join in.

The Jewish people were an easy target since we were concentrated together in the *shtetl*. Over the years we could accumulate only goods and money, not land. Even in the homes of the poor, they could find something valuable to steal and some woman to violate. There was ravaging, there were degradations, there was murder.

We soon developed a sense of impending danger. With the approach of a Ukrainian Nationalist Army, we hid our valuables. The young people would hide in a basement, in the fields and woods, or with friends among the peasants. The robbers invaded like locusts and took what they could. When it was over, we came out from underground as if a new world opened before us. Coming out of hiding, still alive, still able to stretch full length and reach for the sky, was a renewal of life. You must go through such an experience to understand.

If the Jewish people had some sympathy for the Bolsheviks during this period, it was because we felt our lives were safer with them. This was in spite of losing property through the Bolshevik program of confiscation and nationalization. With the Bolsheviks there was greater respect for our dignity, greater security for our lives. And when you live, you hope!

It has been said that the Bolsheviks also committed atrocities against the Jewish people during the revolution. We had such an experience in Stanislavchik. An advance detachment of a Bolshevik Army came in and made a pogrom as good as the Ukrainian nationalists. In fact, it began at my house. In the old part of the building there was a walled-up room, a hiding place, that had not been discovered through all the pogroms. Even the neighbors began to hide their remaining valuables in that room. I was not there at the time, but I knew exactly what happened when I came home later. I saw the handwork from Sorke's dowry scattered in the street.

This pogrom was especially disturbing because it was done by a Bolshevik detachment. We had started to believe that although the Bolsheviks would not honor private property, they opposed rob-

bing and killing civilians. This attack gave us a feeling of hopeless-
ness that we would be exposed to pogroms from the Red Army
too.

But in a short time, when the larger units of the Bolshevik Army
came into Stanislavchik, we learned that detachment had been part
of a defeated Ukrainian Army. They had promised to fight under
Communist leadership, but they still carried the poison of
Ukrainian anti-Semitism. Those soldiers were dispersed into other
units and the Bolshevik officers of the detachment were tried for
failing their responsibility. They were found guilty and shot before
our eyes.[8]

The period of change from one power to another always was the
most dangerous time. Since our area was a strategic point, near the
huge railroad junction at Zhmerinka, there were frequent battles
and changes of power. The armies would fight all around Zhmerinka, shooting at everything but the railroad station in the middle.
One time there were cannonballs flying over our heads from
armies on both sides of Stanislavchik.

There were periods of tranquillity when an army held power for
weeks and even months. After they arrested any active sympathizers of their opponents, they would institute their own policies,
confiscate what property they wanted, and introduce their own
money, which was just a legal way of robbing the people.

The money came in all sizes. First the Tsar's *ruble* was replaced
by Kerenskii money. It was on 2″ × 2″ squares because of the
paper shortage, but it was printed by the ton. The Ukrainian
nationalists, to show they were stronger, had big pieces of paper
with large denominations ... beautifully printed and completely
worthless. The Bolsheviks had their money too. Our area reverted
to barter—I once saw a peasant waiting in line to pay for a theater
ticket with a piglet—but we had to give an occupying army what
they wanted for their money.

Despite the insecurity over property, these longer occupations
did not carry that pogrom character of murder, rape, and insult.
You couldn't really call these periods "normal," but you could
adapt. My mother used to say, "Defend us, dear God, from what we
get used to."

It was just a matter of time before the Bolsheviks confiscated the
sheep farm my father rented from a landlord. That prized flock of

Persian sheep was simply distributed among the peasantry to be bastardized. My father knew how to live by exchange of goods, like buying some salt in Zhmerinka to trade with a peasant who had an extra sack of grain. We still had some valuables for barter, and we had produce from our tiny vegetable garden.

Despite all the hardships, life did not stop for me. From the early days of the revolutionary period, Jewish culture blossomed in Stanislavchik. Instead of going to pray at *shul*, the young people began discussing Jewish literature, Russian literature, and even Ukrainian literature. The vast churning of people during the war and revolution brought a new teacher of Yiddish into Stanislavchik. Although he was not much to look at, he was able to marry one of our most beautiful girls because of his education and worldliness. He brought a lot of knowledge into the *shtetl*. He set up groups for the study of Yiddish literature. He organized a Yiddish dramatic group that staged several shows. There were a couple of young people who began to write their own poetry. We had regular cultural evenings for the recitation of literature and the singing of folk songs. That is when I experienced my first real urge for learning.

The older folks ridiculed us. They asked what more is there to learn than the talking of Yiddish and the study of the Torah in Hebrew. But one evening, after a tongue lashing from my father for wasting my time at Yiddish cultural meetings, I discovered something else. When I happened to walk out of the hall during a performance, I found my father listening outside. He said, "I just wanted to know how you spend your time." Education was on![9]

During this time Zionists came through Stanislavchik preaching that the Jewish people should leave Russia and establish a homeland in Palestine. One Labor Zionist came to recruit me at home. He said that the Jewish people, like every other people, needed their own nation and their own working class fighting for socialism. He argued that the security and dignity of the Jewish people required it.

This was something new to me. It was a political Zionism, not the belief of my grandfather—the belief of the Jewish people through the centuries—that the Messiah will come to take the Jewish people to Zion. I was more sympathetic to the ideas of this Zionist, but after my grandfather I was annoyed by any ideas of returning to Zion. With two brothers and a sister in New York, America was more attractive. I did not join this group, but he did recruit some friends who later went to Palestine and pioneered in the establishment of Israel.

One period of tranquillity came when the German Army occupied large parts of the Ukraine. They were correct in their dealings with the population. They didn't steal; they didn't confiscate; they didn't carry out pogroms. Since Yiddish was close to the German language, some of the Jewish merchants acted as middlemen for them. The Jewish workers and the Jewish young people who had returned from the war were not in sympathy with this counter-revolutionary occupation force. But the broad section of the Jewish population, while they played no role in the German occupation, appreciated that no one bothered them. (Twenty-five years later, when the Soviet government warned the Ukrainian Jews to flee the invading Nazi armies, many remembered the Germans as civilized conquerors. That mistake cost many Jewish lives, including part of my own family.)

During those periods of calm, Stanislavchik was less isolated from nearby villages and towns. It was dangerous to travel, but you would take a chance. You were prepared for danger. But one of those times something hit my family, something we lived through for twenty-four hours, which reflects those tragic days for the Jewish people.

My sister Sorke had a chance to visit her fiancé in a nearby *shtetl*. The *balegole*, the wagonman, was traveling there with an empty wagon. He offered Sorke a ride and she accepted with pleasure. They went, but they did not return that evening as planned. The following day a peasant came into Stanislavchik with a report that the *balegole* was found murdered in a wheat field. The body was there. The wagon was there with its cargo. The horses were there. Nothing else.

This report was devastating to my family. We were convinced that Sorke was murdered or taken off with the murderers. The sorrow of my parents is indescribable. She was the youngest girl, the closest to my mother. There was a special warmth, a special devotion between them. The grief that hit my mother, that hit all of us, broke my heart. I still can't talk about it calmly.

The lucky conclusion was that the parents of Sorke's fiancé had insisted she remain with them overnight. When the *balegole* was leaving, they said it was too late for her to travel safely. She stayed with them that night and returned later the next day, a few hours after the report. The joy of reunion I don't have to describe.

The murder of that *balegole* without any robbery was a warning to the *shtetl*. It meant the Jewish people could be killed without any material benefit to the murderers. At the time the word "genocide" was not known to me, but I saw an indication that the Jewish people were in line for complete destruction.[10]

My personal reaction to these attacks—in addition to loss of nearest and dearest—what was eating my gut, was the insult! It was the insult that anybody might violate my sister, rob us, or shoot us. It was the insult of being afraid! This, to a great degree, influenced me at the age of eighteen to take the gun into hand.

There was another influence on myself and the other young people. That was the Kishinev pogrom, a bloody massacre in the capital of Bessarabia in 1903. It aroused the great Jewish writer Chaim Nachman Bialik to write his monumental poem *"Shkhite Shtot*, City of Slaughter."* We interpreted that poem as a warning: don't be murdered without resistance. Although I later learned there had been Jewish resistance in the working-class quarters of Kishinev, at this time I took it as a message to mobilize. Take arms! Fight the pogrommakers!

With this in mind we organized a group for self-defense of the *shtetl*. To me this was a restoration of dignity and self-respect. If we are to die, let us do it fighting!

We organized the self-defense group at a meeting in the *shul*. We met in secret because our parents would be opposed. They believed that a Jew with a gun would be a provocation for punishment . . . that if one Ukrainian was killed in a skirmish there would be an attack upon the entire *shtetl*. We saw that our parents were depending upon prayer to God. We felt that prayer was not the most effective weapon against the pogrommakers.[11]

There were about a dozen of us sixteen to nineteen years old. We had free picking of guns and ammunition left by retreating armies. We did not organize to fight the marching armies, but to drive out the advance detachments and the bandits that made pogroms. Our defense group was quite effective against small groups that could not exact vengeance upon the *shtetl*.

We always kept a lookout in the center of town, the market-place, especially at night. Whenever we expected Ukrainian Nationalist Armies to occupy the area, we would be ready for the advance detachments. When seven or eight riders would come into town and start to break into a home, we would drive them off with gunfire. They deserved to be shot.

There were times when the Ukrainian Army was as dangerous to us as the advance detachments. When they broke through the rearguard of the Red Army and entered Stanislavchik looking for Bolsheviks, they came with guns blazing. With the excuse that people might be hiding Bolsheviks, they would raid homes, steal, shoot anyone on sight. Those raids were pogroms.

Once when that happened, I ran to hide in the deep grass of the valley with my friends Nokhem and Mayer. A Ukrainian soldier came by and took aim at our rabbi, who also was hiding out there. The three of us fired and cut down that murderer. We rescued the rabbi and ran for our lives. We knew where to hide. We knew every bush, every tree, every twist and turn of the area. It was home ground.

Nokhem, Mayer, and myself drew together within the self-defense group. We had been close friends as boys growing up in Stanislavchik, and as we matured during the war and revolution we became even thicker than under normal circumstances. We each had sisters: all our talk about defending our families meant our sisters, because girls were most endangered by attacks. Nokhem's younger sister, Rose, was quite attractive. We used to spend time together walking and talking. If I had remained in Stanislavchik, she was the girl I wanted to continue my life with. After I went to the United States, my nearest friend Mayer married her.

Nokhem, Mayer, and myself were together constantly. We saved each other's lives on several occasions. Once Ukrainian nationalist soldiers arrested Nokhem and demanded to know where I was hiding. He knew, but he would not tell. They beat him to a pulp with the steel cleaning rods of their rifles. After the soldiers got tired of beating him, he made his way to our hiding place and collapsed. It was a demonstration of devotion which is cemented only during such a period of danger.

I had a taste of that steel rod on my own back. Once I was arrested by the Ukrainian nationalists when I was in Zhmerinka buying kerosene to exchange with the peasants for food. The soldiers were rounding up all the young men in the streets. When I gave them my name, expecting to be released, they singled me out with a few others and took me back to their barracks. They kept me overnight for questioning.

There is no heroism when you face severe punishment or death. I was scared. In the morning they questioned if I participated in the struggle against Ukrainian independence. They were searching for some connection with the Red Army. But it was not just questioning—it was a beating with fists and rods. Finally they went off for food: "Leave the Jew on the floor. He'll not run."

When I heard the outside door slam, I slowly made my way to the inside door, then the outside door, then the bushes and over the barracks fence. Half running and half crawling, I made my way home across the fields. To my parents, who heard I was taken by the soldiers, I was just returned from the dead.

The Ukrainian nationalists may have singled me out because someone in the village gave them my name. There were a couple of young Ukrainian nationalists, sons of the landlord's manager, who were stool pigeons reporting people they held grudges against. They were vicious anti-Semites who liked to beat up Jewish young people. Our self-defense group fought them anytime, on any level.

During one fight I ran home for my rifle. It was on a Saturday afternoon. After the *shabes* meal, we would go for a stroll along the road leading out to Zhmerinka. Boys and girls would walk together, sing songs, brag about adventures. On one side of the road was the landlord's estate and on the other were homes of the richest Jewish merchants. Further out you reached a well with water that bubbled out of the earth. When the sun shone through the trees surrounding the well, the water had all the colors of the rainbow. That water was crystal clear, ice cold, with a special sweet taste. It was a public area where we would sit, talk, play games. It was a part of our lives.

On this particular Saturday afternoon those two Ukrainian fellows, tall and strong and handsome, came marching through that area with canes. They singled out a couple, insulted the girl, and started to beat up the boy with their canes. Mayer, Nokhem, and myself came over and a fight broke out. I thought they had a pocket gun and I was afraid the peasants would come to give them more help ... so I went a-runnin' to get my gun. But my mother got a hold of me first: "You want to fight? Fight! But no guns! I want you back." To my mother I listened.

(During a period of occupation by the Red Army, those two anti-Semites were arrested and taken away. They never returned. Rumor had it that they were shot as counterrevolutionaries.)

At the beginning my father objected to our self-defense group, but there was nothing he could do to stop my participation. Arguing did no good and soon the parents realized that our protection allowed people to sleep at night. Everything will fight for its life and we were no exception.

Our self-defense group did lay low when a Ukrainian Army itself would be taking over our area. They would be looking for young people who sympathized with the Bolsheviks or who fought in self-defense groups. One time when there was great danger, we were forced to leave Stanislavchik. We followed the Red Army to Vinnitsa, which was a large city forty miles from Stanislavchik.

In Vinnitsa we heard about a Red Army detachment that was being organized to fight a bandit group that was threatening a nearby *shtetl*. The Bolsheviks considered pogrommakers to be enemies of the people. Although we were fleeing danger, we volunteered for another danger. We didn't want to join the Red Army, but we did want to save that *shtetl*. So Nokhem, Mayer, my cousin Itsik, and myself joined up.

That new Red Army detachment was entirely Jewish. Some were members of Jewish self-defense groups from other *shtetlekh* who came to Vinnitsa for the same reasons we did. There also was a group of Jewish city ruffians with city dress and city ways who laughed at those of us from the backwoods of a *shtetl*. It was my first contact with this type of city Jew.

At the railroad station in Vinnitsa, where our detachment was to board a train, a Ukrainian bandit leader—a pogrommaker—was being held. As we stood there on the station platform, we heard a yell: "The bandit is escaping!" We saw him running across the tracks toward the wheat fields. Five of us leveled our guns, fired, and shot him. Automatically! This was the kind of reaction you would have to a pogrommaker in times of restlessness. It was "either-or"...either you were ready to respond or you never would be ready.

We took the train to the area where that *shtetl* was under attack. After a night's fight in the woods, we broke up the bandit group, which was composed of local peasants, and we rescued the *shtetl*. On the train back to Vinnitsa, however, I heard stories that some of those Jewish city ruffians committed wrongs upon the Ukrainian peasants where we had fought. There were rumors of robbery and rape. They bragged: "We gave the bastards a taste of their own." I did not personally see anything, but such things happen in the process of war and retaliation. When we returned to Vinnitsa, the leader of our detachment was arrested. I met up with that guy twenty years later in New York, and he would not say a word about the entire incident.

In Vinnitsa we found the Red Army preparing to retreat before the same Ukrainian Army that was taking over Stanislavchik. The volunteers in our punitive detachment were ordered to be distributed among the regular Red Army units. My cousin Itsik decided to retreat with the Red Army. Nokhem, Mayer, and myself snuck away and returned into Vinnitsa. We landed at an inn, where we hid until the advancing Ukrainian Army established control over the city.

At that inn I was amazed to run into an old neighbor from Stanislavchik—Sasha the bagelmaker, the young socialist who ran away from the Tsar's police in 1906. I was not conscious enough to inquire about his political beliefs and there was not time to exchange much information. But he was glad to find me in a self-defense group in Stanislavchik.

I saw another familiar face at that inn. There was a family from another *shtetl* who also came to Vinnitsa for a better chance to survive the invasion. I recognized one of their teenage daughters as a kid who had visited her aunt in Stanislavchik years ago. Any stranger walking in the *shtetl* was noticed. But now she was a beautiful young lady and I noticed her all the more. I tried to start a conversation about recognizing her, but I did not get anywhere. This, however, was not the last time I met up with her.

It took three days of disturbance before the Ukrainian Army established order in Vinnitsa. During that entire period the three of us were hiding in the attic of that inn, living on a few cucumbers. Then we crossed the forty miles of fields and forests back to Stanislavchik.

When I returned home, my aunt Rivka demanded to know what happened to her son Itsik. No matter how much I explained, she cried, "You saved yourself and let him go down! Where are his bones? Where is his grave?" Then she sat down on the floor of our house, in the Jewish tradition of men sitting on the ground for seven days of mourning for a dead person. She said, "You are responsible for Itsik's death. I will sit seven days of *shive* in your house!"

Itsik returned a few months later. He had retreated with the Red Army to Kiev, and there he stayed with a family until it was safe to go home. After the joy of reunion, Itsik started to brag about his adventures with the daughter of that family. He showed us a picture of a beautiful girl. "She was very human, very friendly," he said, "She was good to me."

We were envious until one day my aunt Rivka walks in, very disturbed, screaming, "Oy, what a disaster! What a tragedy! You should see her!"

"What are you talking about?"

"You don't know? Itsik didn't tell you? That 'beauty' came here to marry him. Look at me," she said. She was old, with a face like a prune. "I am a beauty compared to her! I had to hide him and pay her a ransom to go away!"

I was not politically alert during the revolution, but my respect for the Bolsheviks was growing. I temporarily joined with that Red Army detachment because of the Bolshevik oposition to anti-Semitism and pogroms. Even the richer Jews in Stanislavchik began to appreciate the Bolsheviks after the ravaging of the Ukrainian nationalists. Those were the days when Lenin gave real leadership. He understood how to win people over to a just cause. It became clear that it was just a matter of time before the Red Army would prevail in the Ukraine. The peasants were turning more and more to the Bolsheviks.

The Ukrainian nationalists made a great mistake by opposing distribution of the landlords' lands and goods to the peasants. They made a great mistake by tolerating mistreatment of the peasant population. This was reflected in a local uprising of the villages near Stanislavchik against a Ukrainian Nationalist Army. There already were deep grievances against the Ukrainian nationalists. Whenever they took over our area they would promise the peasants a glorious Ukrainian national culture and then they would demand every head of livestock, every last piece of bread. The peasants did not take too kindly to that.

Once a Ukrainian nationalist detachment began robbing a nearby peasant village and mistreating the women. When a peasant found a soldier raping his wife, he picked up the soldier's rifle and killed him. The gunfire brought the rest of the soldiers and they arrested the peasant. Someone sounded the alarm, the church bell, and the peasants from all the nearby villges came running from the fields. They took that detachment as prisoners.

With the Ukrainian Army a few miles away in Zhmerinka, there was a danger of reprisal. The peasants called together the entire population of the villages for a meeting in the marketplace in Stanislavchik. The wise men of the villages warned the men to arm themselves and to brace for an army attack.

The Jewish people immediately understood that our lives were in danger. To join the fighting villagers would expose us to retaliation by the Ukrainian Army. Not to join might mean retaliation from the peasants. What to do? When the peasants gathered in the marketplace, the Jewish people met at the *shul*.

The older people advised the younger people to flee. The younger people insisted that we must live together with the peasants, even if it meant falling together. Most of us went to join the peasants in the marketplace. We found a crowd armed with pitchforks, scythes, threshing sticks, and a few rifles. We entered with our weapons and we were accepted.

A stranger was addressing the crowd. He said, "I come from the Ukrainian Army at Zhmerinka. It is retreating before an advancing Bolshevik Army and there will be no attack upon you. I suggest that you hide in the thicket of woods along the road outside the village. I will give you a signal if the Ukrainian Army plans to attack. If they retreat, I will give you another signal and you can march into Zhmerinka."

Someone yelled out, "It doesn't smell good. Why should we trust you?"

He identified himself as a Bolshevik assigned to the Ukrainian Army to do just what he was doing. He gave all kinds of logical explanations why he was with the people. He convinced us to advance to that thicket.

At the time for the signal, there was a cannon shelling of the thicket. It was a total betrayal! That speaker in the marketplace was a provocateur of great skill who succeeded in misleading us. Several were killed and wounded by that bombardment. We all started running back to Stanislavchik.

There was a quick meeting of peasants and Jews in the marketplace. Everyone felt the danger. With the record of the Ukrainian nationalists, we knew the young people would be shot on sight. It was decided that all the young people should leave the area.

The next morning I joined a group of Jewish youngsters fleeing into the unknown. We didn't dare travel by road for fear of meeting a Ukrainian Army detachment. The September rain made for hard walking across the soaked fields. Finally, after hours of walking, we came to a village. We were exhausted and hungry and soaking wet. We were scared for ourselves and for those we left behind. The peasants of this village knew through their grapevine what happened. They gave us their best food; they washed our clothes; they gave us the most honored spot to sleep—on top of the oven. It was the only time I saw such a warm reception of a Jewish group in a Ukrainian village.

The next day we marched on to a *shtetl* that was miles and miles farther from Stanislavchik. The Jewish population housed and cleaned and fed us. Their young people accepted us like returning relatives. In fact, when I returned to the Soviet Union in 1934, I found that one of the boys in our retreat married a girl he met in that *shtetl*.

After two weeks the Ukrainian Army was forced to retreat, and we returned to our families. The Ukrainian Army had come into Stanislavchik the day we fled, but they were mild with the population. They accepted the explanation that the young people fled, and there was no punishment. They did not want to cause another revolt. It seems they felt the breath of the advancing Red Army. When that Red Army took power in our area, it was greeted as a liberator.

The Red Army was our only real contact with the Bolsheviks during the civil war. As it drove out the armies of the Tsar and the Ukrainian nationalists, it began to institute the Bolshevik program. There started a slow change of life and beliefs.

There was confusion at the beginning of the transformation, before clear guidance and new leadership came forth. First, we had to get rid of the petty functionaries of the Tsar's bureaucracy. They were a cancerous growth on the body of the people. They were removed from leadership. Those who were zealots, who were oppressors of the people, were called to account with beatings and even shootings.

There was great confusion over the question of land in the beginning. When the landlords or their managers disappeared, it was just a matter of time before the peasants took over the property. At first the division was chaotic. No peasant had use for the big house of the landlord, but animals, machinery, even parts of machinery were grabbed. The peasants were hungry for wood and suddenly you would see them driving out of the landlord's forest with as much as they could carry in a wagon. The richer peasants, who were more audacious, began to claim large chunks of the landlord's estate.

The Bolsheviks slowly began to institute orderly confiscations instead of robbery. Then the livestock and machinery and land could be used collectively and efficiently later. Under the Bolshevik occupation the big house of the landlord was turned into a people's center for information and redistribution. That's where you went to get more land or to get your ration of salt. That's where my family went, under the supreme guidance of my aunt Rivka, to get a larger plot of land for a vegetable garden.

There was an outcry of protest by the Jewish people when the Bolsheviks began their program. We did not have the implements or the experience to take a piece of land and make a living. Most Jews remained in the *shtetl*, but we were impoverished by the confiscation of our goods for the Red Army, for the workers in the city, and for redistribution. Homes and personal possessions were not taken, but that accumulation of goods had been the basis of our livelihood. Now there was not even freedom for the Jewish people to exchange goods in the marketplace. We had to depend upon the Bolshevik government for food it appropriated from the peasants. At first there was very little.

The redistribution was done under Bolshevik guidance through our own committees of poverty. Those committees were selected publicly in the marketplace. Poor people were chosen on the basis of honesty and good relations with their neighbors. If there was no objection from the crowd—and sometimes there was—the person was elected. It was not a well organized method of selecting leadership, but it perfectly suited the needs of the times.

I served on one of those committees for distribution of goods in the *shtetl*. It was done very well. The change was crude at first, and sometimes it was too severe. But at the same time there was the humanism of equal shares of food for all. The committees knew who needed what.

There always was resentment from the wealthy Jews. They continued to curse the Bolsheviks, even after the Red Army stopped the pogroms of the Ukrainian nationalists. Those who had carried the power of leadership, who had the prestige of the seat near the western wall of the *shul*, who were looking at Jewish life from the top down, they never made peace with the Bolsheviks.

There also was resentment from the religious people. Bolshevik education—or propaganda, if you wish—linked the Russian church, and to a lesser degree the Jewish *shul*, with the old Tsarist system. The Bolsheviks denounced religion as the opium of the people. It was a blow to the life of the older Jewish people, but for the first time I felt that no one could pick on me for not going to *shul*. I felt liberated!

The majority of the Jewish people had good reason to support the Bolsheviks. We lived a life of oppression, of pogroms, of fear under the Tsarist regime. It could not be compensated for by the accumulation of gold in the hands of the rich. The wealthy merchant had a lot to lose, but the majority of the Jewish people was poor. They had everything to gain with the promise of redistribution of wealth. And the Jewish intelligentsia, who under-stood more deeply the transformation of Russia, welcomed the new society as a promise for Jewish culture, for education, for freedom. There was great Jewish support for the Bolsheviks.[12]

As time passed I came to admire two giant figures among the Bolsheviks. I learned that under the leadership of Lenin the struggle for peace and the struggle for reorganization of Russian life was taking place. I learned that under Trotsky's leadership the Red Army was resisting the forces of the Tsar. For a split second, in fact, there was in my own mind a question over whether to join the *Krasnaia Gvardiia*, the Red Guard, as the Red Army was then called.

There was a Jewish doctor who came to Stanislavchik from the city to serve the health needs of our area. He took a liking to me and he once told me, "Things are settling down. You need an education, a career. I advise you to enter a Bolshevik military school. I can arrange it for you."

I consulted with Nokhem and Mayer. We concluded that I should not rush, that I should not join yet. We consulted again when I had a sudden chance to leave Stanislavchik with a family that was going to America. My friends feared that I would join the Red Army. They regarded America as a great opportunity for me and my family. I finally did cast my vote for leaving.

By the time of my departure in 1919, I was beginning to learn about the new Soviet society. First, things had to be taken apart before rebuilding. I was there long enough to see the abolition of landlordism and banking, the redistribution of land and goods, the transformation of the police into a grievance militia, and the emergence of local leadership responsible to the people. I did not stay long enough to see the accomplishments after the civil war, to see the pieces put back together. I learned that story from a distance.

My own future was different, but before I left Russia I had seen human lives mowed down to maintain privilege. I was not class conscious, but I had an understanding of the division between rich and poor, oppressor and oppressed. Even before I came to the United States, my sympathy was with humanism, with the struggle for justice and equality.

3. Emigration

*E*veryone in Stanislavchik had friends and relatives in America. From their letters we heard about the easy money, the prosperous way of life, the chance for education and further advance. They reported there was no discrimination, no pogroms against the Jewish people. America was a legend to us.

We heard the stories ourselves from the people who came back to visit Stanislavchik, who came to bring the rest of their family to America. They looked like they were coming from outer space! They wore heavy shoes with wide noses instead of points; they explained that Americans needed big comfortable shoes. They wore fine suits with a different cut of cloth. Across the vest would be a gold chain. Every few minutes they would take a big gold watch out of the vest pocket and look at it in a manner that drew everyone's attention. They would stand around in the marketplace and tell stories about the good life in America.

Not all the reports were so favorable. One fellow came back from New York to resume his old life driving a wagon in Stanislavchik. He found the work too hard and the living too different there. He demonstrated what America was like to us children: "I will show you a special American apple. Taste it." We almost broke our teeth when we bit; it was hard on the outside! But when it was opened, it had a sweet and juicy wine colored pulp around litle seeds. A pomegranate! "*Azelkhe epl vaksn in Amerike,*" he told us. "Such apples are growing in America."

My brother Moyshe was the first to go to America from my family. He had help from a distant cousin, a coppersmith, who was established in New York. Moyshe worked for that cousin a year, and then he started his own business. Soon came pictures of Moyshe in fine American clothes standing in front of his store. Every few months he would send us five dollars, which was a lot of money. Then he started to bring over the family. First it was my oldest sister Shlima and her family. Then went the middle brother Khayim who already had tried once to run off to America with me. Before another could go, the war broke out. We were completely cut off from America.

Around 1919, in the third year of the revolution, we heard that *landsmanshaftn*, organizations of countrymen in the United States, were sending "delegates" to smuggle people out of the Ukraine. This was hard to believe when a civil war was raging in Russia and there still was war with the neighboring countries. But one day a rumor started to circulate that a family with American relatives was reached by such a delegate and was preparing to leave Stanislavchik. When I inquired, they confirmed that they planned to leave for the Romanian border in a few days. They said there would be room for me to come along.

My friends Nokhem and Mayer encouraged me to go, but there still was the question of my family's opinion. My mother had died from cancer a few months before, and a good part of my interest to remain died with her. I was reluctant to leave my father and sisters, but they insisted I go, not only for me but for themselves. Ethel sewed a five *ruble* gold piece into the lining of my jacket and said, "This is for an emergency. You must reach Moyshe with news of our situation. He will bring the rest of the family to America."[1]

On a December morning in 1919, with the sky still dark and the roads frozen, I set out across the valley with my father to meet the other travelers. As life brings tragedy, so that morning had to be rainy . . . actually, a fine drizzle. My father was wearing an old cotton coat. His good coat with the beaverskin collar was robbed a time back. The cotton was loose in the lining of this coat, and chunks were accumulating in the corners. Those clods of cotton, as they became soaked that morning, were pulling down my father, He was bent under the weight of that wet jacket and under the weight of losing his last son.

We crossed the fields and climbed the hillside of the valley. As we walked, it became lighter. From the elevation I could see the stretches of the *pomeshchik's* lands and the checkerboard fields of the peasants and the roofs of Stanislavchik. By the colors of the roofs I could tell what belonged to whom. It was a painful moment. I was leaving my home town, the town where my mother and grandfather were raised, where I tasted the joys of youth and turbulence of war and revolution.

We arrived early at the crossroads. Soon came the wagon with that family. The moment of parting with my father was very difficult ... very emotional. It is hard to see a person cry. It is harder to see a man cry. My father was an old man, but he was someone who had kept me under his rule, someone whom I had looked up to for strength and support. Suddenly I saw him lost ... scared ... hurt. He cried, "I will not see you again."

I can still see that picture, sixty years later. It followed me all the way through and never let me forget. Now I am old, but nevertheless I still feel the pangs of life and living ... I still feel the pain of my departure from Stanislavchik.

The group of travelers included the family, the delegate, and a boy from another *shtetl*. It was a two-day journey to the Dniester River, the border with Romanian occupied Bessarabia. Since Romania was at war with Russia, it was dangerous near the border. We traveled by night and hid by day. I learned we were heading for Dzegifka, a *shtetl* along the river where we would meet up with another group. Then the delegates would arrange a border crossing by bribing the guards on both sides. American dollars could work miracles, even during war.

On the way to Dzegifka I befriended the other young fellow. His name was Srulik Stein. He told me an amazing story. During the civil war, he had been forced to join the Ukrainian Nationalist Army. He knew the Ukrainian language so well that he was never recognized as a Jew in an army of anti-Semitic murderers. Within time he became a self appointed watchdog in that Ukrainian Army. Whenever he learned about a plan to commit a pogrom, he would find a way to warn the Jewish population.

Srulik and I decided to part from the group when we reached Dzegifka. Crossing the border was extremely dangerous. To do it with a couple of wagons full of children and possessions was even more dangerous. Srulik and myself, being of military age, could be accused of desertion if we were stopped on the Ukrainian side. On the Romanian side we could be accused as Russian spies. We had to move with flexibility and cross in complete silence.

Srulik was a very cautious, even fearful fellow. In the Ukrainian

Army he had to be forever alert, even in his sleep, lest he talk out in Yiddish. During our travels he always worried. What will happen if we come to Dzegifka and have no place to stay? What will happen if we cannot find help to cross the Dniester? What will happen if we capsize on the river? He kept worrying about such questions and finally I began to call him *"vos vet zayn,* what will happen?"

We parted from the group when we came to Dzegifka. No recriminations; I met up with that family in a friendly manner for many years in the United States. We left them at an inn, where we did not want to stay because that was the kind of place a border patrol might raid. We walked from door to door, asking Jewish families if we could stay until we crossed the border.

We did find a place—nice home, parents, and, lucky us, two pretty daughters. The *balebos,* the man of the house, not only gave us a room, but he wanted us to share bread with the family. We could not accept the offer because we could not pay for their hospitality. We were proud young men—we preferred to stretch our pennies on stale bread and a herring. But when Friday came around, the family insisted their celebration of *shabes* would be disturbed if we did not attend the meal.

Within a few days we became close to that family. They were concerned about our plans to cross the border—they warned us of the dangers. Meanwhile, the girls brought us together for evenings of cultural activities with other young people, and soon Srulik and Gitl, the older girl of the family, became attracted.

The mother pleaded with Srulik: "Gitl is already engaged. It would be a dishonor if she would go back on her word." To this I added, "I fully agree. Now you must get rid of us." The *balebos* went out and secured our transportation across the Dniester in a hurry! He made arrangements for a *kontrabandist,* a smuggler, to take us.

Our parting with the family was very touching. That *balebos* was a religious man with a long gray beard and a patriarchal appearance. He asked us to bend our heads. He put the palms of his hands on them and he made a farewell prayer. Neither of us was religious, but we both were deeply moved.

At the designated time, at night again, we made our way to an old shack along the Dniester. We waited there for two long days with just a little grain to chew on and all our fears to think about. Finally, the smuggler appeared and took us across the river. There was much apprehension—we thought we were spotted by a border patrol—but there was no trouble. He brought us to the town of Soroco, on the other side of the Dniester, where we were warmly greeted by a son from that family in Dzegifka. He fed us, he gave us Bessarabian clothes, and he arranged for us to leave immediately with a peasant who was traveling away from the border. That peasant took us miles away to another *shtetl*.

Crossing into Bessarabia from the Ukraine was like stepping into Mexico from the United States. It was a different state, a different form of life, a different language, a different look to the villages. But it was not so different for Jewish people. We did not know a soul in the *shtetl* where we arrived, but we knew we would find help at the *shul*.

There we found a group of men finishing the evening prayers. We explained that we were traveling from the Ukraine to America, that we just crossed over the border and we were looking to rest for a while. The rabbi found us a place to stay with a Jewish landlord—in Bessarabia Jews could own land. He was surprised to discover that I, a Ukrainian Jew, knew all about sheep farming.

Again we were independent; we earned our own keep. We worked on that farm for several weeks. The landlord paid us in Romanian money and we started to eat better—a little cheese, fresh bread, some candy to sweeten our tea. During that time we became accustomed to Bessarabia, so we no longer feared that every passer-by would arrest us as spies. And so we started to talk about where to go next.

We landed in that *shtetl*, in Bessarabia, like parachutists in a desert. We had no idea of how to reach America. The people from that *shtetl* advised us: "You must go to Kishinev, the capital of Bessarabia. It is a large city with Jewish organizatons. They will help you contact family in America. In Kishinev you won't be lost anymore."

Again, without our asking, they helped us along the way. They secured for us Romanian documents of identification as refugees. They gave us written testimonials which guaranteed our good behavior. They made sure we had enough Romanian money for the next part of our journey. And they arranged for a peasant to take us on a wagon to Kishinev.

It was less than a day's ride to Kishinev. There we again faced the problem of where to go, whom to contact. But now we were in a city, a Bessarabian city under Romanian occupation, which was more dangerous than a *shtetl*. This time we stopped someone in the street who looked like a Jew. When he responded to our Yiddish, we told him our story and asked how to advance further to America. He directed us to a *shul* which was the office for the Joint Distribution Committee. That was a Jewish agency helping with immigration.[2]

We went there and sure enough we found Jewish people from all over Eastern Europe waiting in lines for assistance with their travels. The refugees were mostly young people going in two directions. One stream was headed for the United States and neighboring countries such as Canada, Mexico, Cuba, Brazil, and Argentina. These people were aiming to join relatives already there. The other stream was going to Palestine. After years of pogroms and devastation and humiliations, these young people believed that a Jewish homeland was the answer to the Jewish problem. They were *chalutzim*, pioneers, going to build a new Jewish life in Palestine. They received a lot of help from Zionist organizations.[3]

The Joint Distribution Committee began the process of contacting our families in the United States. Arrangements were made for us to stay with a poor Jewish family. Like on the earlier part of the trip, we avoided sponging off those who helped us. We bought our own food and ate sparingly. That is when I used my five *ruble* gold piece. We needed a few cents for a shave, a newspaper, a piece of candy. We knew that the Joint Distribution Committee would not let us starve if we ran out completely, but we never did have to accept their offer of free meals. We received help from other young people who already were getting money from relatives in America. Then Srulik got some money from a delegate who knew his brother, and we were able to help out those who were poorer than us.

At the headquarters of the Joint Distribution Committee, I met up with my cousin Gitl and a group of young people I knew from Bar, where I had been a printer for a year. Gitl was going to New York and her husband Avrom; the others were en route to Palestine. I spent time with them while I waited to hear from

Moyshe in New York. It was a period of deprivation and uncertainty for all. We did not know exactly where we were going next
or how we would get there. Yet we had a joy of freedom from fear
... freedom from the dangers of the civil war in Russia. Now we
were on the other side of the fence, headed in a new direction.[4]

As long as we were together, it was more than eating and
sleeping, waiting and hoping. The joy of youth, the strength of life
in the young, allowed us to forget all the hardships when we were
together. We exchanged experiences and plans. We sang, we read
poetry, we played cards. There was the contact of boy and girl. We
had some glorious times together. Kishinev was a real city with big
buildings, wide streets, large parks, museums, all kinds of places to
explore. It was a Jewish city—a large Jewish population, Jewish
stores, Jewish culture. We were youngsters from backwoods
shtetlekh turned loose in a wonderland.

Among that group of young people from Bar, I met Shaiva. We
had met before, first when she was eight years old and visited an
aunt in Stanislavchik. Then I met her again during the revolutionary days, when we were hiding from the Ukrainian Army at the
same hotel in Vinnitsa. She was fifteen and attractive enough to
catch my eye, but in that disturbing period our attention was
centered on survival. Now we met again in Kishinev. Her parents
sent her with that group of *chalutzim*, thinking that it would be
safer for her to go to Palestine than to remain through the savagery
of the civil war.

In Kishinev she met up with a delegate, a person originally from
her *shtetl* who had come from the United States to pick up his
family. Tsindel urged Shaiva not to go to Palestine. He said, "If your
parents only knew about the hard life in Palestine ... about the
Arab resistance to Jewish settlement! You have a rich aunt in the
United States. She will be happy to bring you there." He took away
her boots—it was wintertime—and he finally convinced her to go
to America.

Through Tsindel Shaiva met another American delegate, Pinkofsky, who came to pick up his own family in the Ukraine. To help
cover his expenses, he took money to bring other people back to
the United States. Pinkofsky had been a dentist in the American
Army during the war. He still wore his captain's uniform and
walked around Kishinev like an American general. While his group

was waiting in Kishinev for him to find the people he was paid for, they lived the good life that American dollars could provide. He told Shaiva that he was ready to return to the United States, except for one family from Stanislavchik.

"What is the name?"

"Rapoport."

My brother Moyshe had arranged with Pinkofsky to take his wife's mother and anyone from our family back to America. Pinkofsky had reached Reuchel and now she was in Kishinev. When Pinkofsky mentioned the name Rapoport, Shaiva told him where to find me.

I left Kishinev with Pinkofsky and his group. We went to the capital of Romania, Bucharest, which was a center of refugee emigration. This was a larger city, a national capital. As part of Pinkofsky's group I lived in comfort that I never experienced before. I had good food, new clothes, and clean accommodations. Whenever I would come into my hotel room, even in midday, the first thing I did was flick on the light. I was fascinated by the quickness of electricity at my command.

By this time Moyshe had sent me some money with a note: "Buy what you want. Do what you couldn't do in Stanislavchik." The first thing I did, with some other young people in our group, was to ride a *droshky*, a hired carriage, on the fine streets of Bucharest. The wheels ran on rubber and the streets were smoothly paved; we rode like a canoe on water. I imagined that even the *pome-shchik* in Stanislavchik did not ride with such comfort. We rode through the streets to the royal palace, which was open for visiting. There I saw a swan lake. I still can taste the exhilaration of that day.

But it was not a time for me to sightsee in Bucharest. I had to get out as quickly as possible. Pinkofsky had bought false passports for his group, so we could travel with ease as Romanian citizens. He had my age on the passport as nineteen, and it would not be long before my passport age would make me eligible to be drafted into the Romanian Army. Our group was large and there were repeated delays to our departure. I began to feel the breath of the Romanian Army at my neck!

From New York Moyshe also urged me to leave Romania quickly, with his mother-in-law Reuchel. His urgency was based on rumors that the United States would soon limit the flow of immigration from Eastern Europe.[5]

However, in Bucharest you could not just go in and get an American visa. There were thousands of people in line. Tens of thousands of people! There was an artificial increase of numbers because Romanian citizens would stand in line, get numbers for visa applications, and then sell the numbers when the day approached. I could wait months to apply for a visa, or I could pay hundreds of dollars for a number. I tried to buy a number.

Pinkofsky had over one thousand dollars that my brother gave him to bring back our family. But he was buying numbers to get visas for his own family first. I knew that if I was drafted into the Romanian Army, Pinkofsky would just return the one thousand dollars to my brother later, in order to use it now to bring over his family first.

I went to the line to buy a number myself. There were all kinds of sharp looking fellows with big city clothes who claimed to have numbers for sale. And in the middle of it all I noticed a guy with the appearance of a rabbi, according to his beard and clothing. He was speculating in visa numbers! That rabbi was a petty swindler! After I made his acquaintance he explained, "I do not make enough money from my rabbinical work. This helps out a little bit. So ... we are only sinning mortals. I do the best I can. I have two numbers for sale."

I went to Pinkofsky with the story. He said, "Give me the address."

I said, "No, I must do it myself."

He gave me the money and I returned with two numbers. I gave him one and kept the other to get my own visa. He tried to rough me up, but he did not get my number. Finally, after things settled down, he helped me get the visa and arranged for me to leave with his family, whom he was personally taking as far as Liverpool and the ship to America. I did not like leaving without Reuchel, but I was driven by the immediate danger of recruitment into the Romanian Army. There was no doubt she would be attended to, and she did arrive in the United States a few months after me.

(Even though Pinkofsky did bring all those people to the United States, he had to pay for his manipulations. He used other people's money to send his own family first, and when he ran out of money, he demanded more from those whose relatives had not yet come. Some people were so angry that they took him to court, and Pinkofsky landed in jail for a brief time.)

I left Bucharest by train with Pinkofsky and his family. Almost the entire train was reserved for refugees who were traveling to Antwerp in Flanders, Belgium. I had a wonderful time in that port town with other Jewish young people who were heading for America. We were from different areas, we spoke different Yiddish dialects, but who cares about borders? We explored the docks and watched ships come out of nowhere on the horizon. We rode an electric carousel with fancy horses and fishes and birds you sat on. Some people—not me—went to a *shul* to meet Belgian Jews, but they did not speak Yiddish. It was a pleasure just to eat a banana, which had a certain sweetness I never tasted in the Ukraine. We

Joe, top seated row second from left, with other members of the Pinkofsky group at a railroad station while traveling from Bucharest to Antwerp in 1921.

enjoyed ourselves. We had money and we had certainty. It was no more a question of what fate brings next.

Our trip across the English Channel was terrible. We were not used to such turbulent water. We were sick ... but happy! We felt that America was just on the other side of the pond, calling to us, and we were coming.

Pinkofsky's group traveled second class. First class, of course, was luxury par excellence. But our second class hotel in London was good ... clean ... big rooms ... excellent facilities. In the hotel restaurant I was amazed to be given two forks. Why, the richest Jew in Stanislavchik would not be served two forks, unless it was for *fleyshik*, meat, and for *milkhik*, dairy. There were all kinds of knives and spoons, there were linen table cloths and ironed napkins. And the way we were served ... all those fellows standing around ... they scared me.

I couldn't understand all the luxury, but I knew this was the way Moyshe wanted me to travel. And so it was on the liner *Aquitania*, which we boarded at Liverpool. I thought that all of Stanislavchik could fit on one floor of that ship. It was a huge floating palace with comforts beyond my imagination. It had fine restaurants, grand ballrooms ... a swimming pool! I spent most of my time in the lower part of the boat ... I felt more comfortable with the poor people in third class ... and they were living very well too. I thought only the Tsar had such luxury as the *Aquitania*. But the Tsar was dead by that time.

The entire trip was only five days. It was nothing like I had heard about immigrants spending weeks sick on a ship crossing the Atlantic. Nor did I have any problems getting off the boat, since Moyshe had insisted I go second class. Those who went third class had to go through an elaborate check at Ellis Island. Customs was just a matter of routine for second class passengers.

I arrived in New York in June 1921, a year and a half after I left Stanislavchik. Stepping down from the *Aquitania*, from the gang-plank to the street, was going from serenity to a madhouse. Everything around me was rushing and running and making a tumult. People, carts, and automobiles were speeding in all directions. I wanted to run after them and see where they were going and why they were in such a hurry.

My brother Moyshe, my sister Shlima, and their families were waiting for me. After warm greetings Moyshe said, "We'll go home and hear the story of all the hardships." I would have been quite satisfied to ride on an American wagon pulled by an American horse, but it was an automobile! My brother just sat down at the wheel and drove us off! The only automobile that I ever saw in Stanislavchik was when the son of the *pomeshchik* visited the estate at the beginning of the war. Now my brother Moyshe—or Morris, as he was called in America—drove that car just like the landlord's son. Except this car was larger, nicer. It was almost a miracle.

We landed at Morris's home in Jamaica, Long Island. I learned that he owned a music store and he was doing so well he was in the process of building a big new store in the Bronx. He had time to spare before the new store opened, so he took me around to see friends and relatives from Stanislavchik.

We drove around the countryside from area to area visiting *landslayt*, countrymen. Instead of the checkerboard fields of the Ukrainian peasants, I only saw farming which reminded me of the spacious holdings of the *pomeshchik*. I wondered if they were all landlords in America! In all these travels from town to town, I did not see any peasants. Everyone looked well dressed, well off. Who took care of the fields? Who did the work? I did not ask too many questions because I did not want to seem too backward.

I met *landslayt* who left in the years before the revolution. They were hungry for news of Stanislavchik. I spoke in Yiddish, but soon I would be surrounded by people speaking quickly in English. I admired how well they had learned the language. It took some time before I realized that the English I heard was far from perfect.

I was very impressed by my brother's way of living: the automobile, the fine clothes, the luxurious home. There was the washroom with all the conveniences, the kitchen where you did not have to carry wood and make a fire several times a day, and the bright light of electricity with no smell of kerosene. Our food in the Ukraine, even in the best days before the war, was simple. I had never tasted anything so delicious as a chocolate malted. I compared it to manna—the food of the Bible, of the Exodus, that was supposed to have the taste of all good things.

To me, Morris's new store in the Bronx was a palace. It was decorated with ornate fixtures, hand-crafted cabinets, and luscious

1. Sophie Rappaport
2. Henrieta
3. Joe
4. Irene
5. Herman Rappaport

6. Fannie Rappaport
7. David Rappaport
8. Morris Rappaport
9. Shlima
10. Shlima's husband Isaac

11. Dorothy
12. Saul Rappaport
13. Lily

Joe with his family in New York, 1921. Left to right, in top row are Morris's wife Sophie, Shlima's daughter Henrietta, Joe, Shlima's daughter Irene, Herman, and Herman's wife Fannie. Left to right in second row are Morris's son David, Morris, Shlima, Shlima's husband Isaac and Shlima's daughter Dorothy. Left to right, bottom row, are Morris's son Saul and Shlima's daughter Lily.

carpets. It was crowded with sheet music, victrolas, and musical instruments. Outside he had a huge sign on the wall: Rapoport Music Store. Whenever I passed that sign, I stopped to read it over and over.

Morris wanted me to work with him in the store during the day and learn English in school in the evening. He offered me a comfortable home, a little income, and a chance to learn the language and life of the American people.

After the deprivations and dangers of my life in Stanislavchik, I should have been happy to do what my brother advised. However, within a few months something started gnawing at me ... a growing dissatisfaction ... a feeling of confinement. It is true that I experienced the hardships of war, revolution, and emigration. But through all of that I had become independent. And up to the age of seventeen I had the freedom of the fields at the sheep farm, the freedom of riding horseback at full speed without destination. While I enjoyed the change from poverty to luxury, from danger to security, something was missing.

I just did not feel free. I did not like being so dependent upon Morris. I did not like working in a store. I felt that being in a store all hours, waiting for customers and waiting upon customers, was somehow degrading. I felt limited in my movement and I was hungry for more movement. I was hungry for seeing things, for meeting people, for exploring. It seems to me that I never stopped traveling from the day I left Stanislavchik.

4. America

I began to explore New York with friends from the Ukraine who had been in America for a few months. They already knew how to drop the proper coin in the subway and land where they wanted. On Sundays they took me to see Times Square, Central Park, and especially lower Manhattan, the hub of Jewish life in New York. The skyscrapers, the cars, the theaters, the crowds of pepole . . . it was strange and fascinating. I simply walked and looked and marveled.

My friends envied my life with Morris. They thought I had it easy, living in his home and working in his store. But soon I started to envy how they did things "the American way." They too had begun living with relatives. But they went out to work, started to learn a trade, earned a few dollars, and got their own room. It was a declaration of independence from their relatives.

One day I talked with Morris and explained my aspirations. I was very impressed by American construction—the skyscrapers, the bridges, the subways, and especially the roads. Most of the roads in the Ukraine were dirt. The main road through Stanislavchik became a quagmire in the rainy season, and when it dried out in the summer there were huge impassable ruts. I admired how machines were covering the roads so fast and so smoothly in America. I wanted to build American roads.

When Morris asked how I would become a road builder, a road engineer, I said I would start from the bottom. I would work on the roads during the day and I would go to school at night. He laughed: "Here you have the good life with me and you want to do the work of Italians!" He did not believe I meant what I said, but my mind was made up to leave the store, even if I had to pick up a temporary trade.

Harry Kessler, a friend from Stanislavchik, gave me the address of a shop where he started as an apprentice in the knitting trade. I went to that shop at One Hundred Twenty-first Street on the East

Side. It was a small dirty place, packed with a few people working at hand knitting machines and others working at pressing, cutting, sewing, and finishing. The boss needed a knitter to make collars and pockets to be sewn onto the bodies of the sweaters. He accepted me with no wages for the first two weeks, but with the promise to begin paying as I learned the work. That is where I started my adventure in the knitting industry.

That knitting shop was in a neighborhood commercial area, a marketplace, with little stores and pushcarts. People from the neighborhood would come in asking for sweaters of certain colors and shapes and sizes. We made it right there and then. The shop owner lived on that block and knew the customers. He worked on a knitting machine too, and he had several relatives working there. I liked the friendly atmosphere of the place. Soon he paid me fifteen dollars a week for making hundreds and thousands of pockets and collars. It was simple and monotonous work, but it seemed like I was learning fast.

After working there for several months, something disturbing happened. A holiday came around and the boss told me to stay home. When I got my wages at the end of the week, I found a day's pay deducted. I accepted the policy of deduction when I was sick, but I thought I should be paid when the boss stopped me from working.

The boss tried to explain that this was not a union shop, where a worker might get paid for a holiday. Because of my conception of justice—that such a holiday should be paid for—I thought the boss must be playing a trick on a greenhorn. All kinds of jokes were played on people who just arrived in America. Some friends already had placed before me a banana, expecting me to bite into it like an apple. But I already learned how to handle a banana in Belgium and I peeled it. I thought this pay deduction was another trick on a greenhorn, another banana.

When the other workers in the shop substantiated the boss, I insisted, "It is still not fair to deduct when you laid me off for the day." The boss, who regretted my stubborness, said he would pay for the holiday if I wanted, but I could not work there if I did not accept the rules of the shop. Little did he know, little did I know, that this was my first introduction to the struggle for trade union organization, for the elementary rights of the workers. I accepted my day's pay and I said goodby. It was my first experience losing a job because of my notion of justice.

Then came the question of what to do next. I still knew very little about how to knit a sweater or even how to find a job. My cousin Avrom Rubinstein showed me how to find ads for jobs in the *Morgn Zhurnal*, a Yiddish newspaper. I learned that in order to get an advertised job as a knitter, you had to be at the shop early in the morning. There was an unwritten law among knitters looking for work: first come, first served. When a group of knitters answered an ad, they would not even stand in line; one would tell the other who was next. I thought it was a good way for the workers to tackle the problem themselves.

Even when I arrived first, however, I was too shy to go in because I was not an experienced hand knitter and I did not support a family like other people looking for a job. I let the others in ahead of me, until I answered an ad at a shop in the Brownsville section of Brooklyn. There I found a number of workers— employees in that shop—waiting for the boss to open the door. We started talking and I told them I was inexperienced. They insisted I should not be shy. They said the boss was not strict and they would show me what I did not know. They actually shoved me in to apply for that job! I took an immediate liking to that group of workers.

The boss hired me right off. He just pointed to a knitting machine, taking it for granted that I was an experienced knitter, and he gave me a piece of cloth to copy. Then he walked off without further explanation.

I didn't know what to do next. I didn't even know how to start the damn machine! The other knitters watched. I immediately became a curiosity in that shop—a knitter who did not know how to knit!

The nearest knitter came over. "Don't worry," he said. "You see the needles set in the wall of the machine. The thread—the yarn— is pulled through the needles as they move up and down. The thread makes a loop as it goes in and out, in and out. The loop makes a round of stitches when you pull it across the width of the machine. You work the needles and produce the round simply by pushing the machine from one side to the other, there and back.

This particular piece requires 150 rounds. You finish each piece with a different thread, so you can work continuously and separate the pieces later."

I did that, I made a couple of pieces, and suddenly there was a tremendous bang! Under the machine was a comb that caught the cloth. Two five pound weights, hooked into that comb, pulled down the cloth so that you knitted an even stitch. Those two weights went crashing to the floor, the piece of cloth I was working disappeared, and the machine was empty as if I never worked on it!

What happened was the thread I was feeding into the machine had broken. A knitter always watched the moving thread for a knot that was too thick to pass through the needles. A knitter had to be sensitive enough to feel the jar of a heavy knot entering the needles if he did not see it. When you found such a knot, you stopped the machine and retied it. I let such a knot pass through the needles and the thread broke.

The other knitters watched to see what I would do next. And again one of them came over to explain what happened. There were ten knitters in that shop, and they all cooperated to teach me the trade. Instead of feeling that another worker was competition, they were friendly and helpful. Later, when I learned what it meant to be paid by the piece, when I learned how precious every second was for the day's production, I appreciated their attitude even more.

The Omaha Knitting Mills was like a family shop. It did not have the wall that existed between a large manufacturer and a worker—the one sitting in a fancy office, the other working in the shop, with managers and foremen in between. Here the boss worked on a machine and ate lunch with the workers. His brother and sister also worked there. All twenty people in the shop were *landslayt*, countrymen, who knew each other from the knitting industry in Warsaw and Lodz. The atmosphere was warm and the contact was close in that shop.

I liked working as a knitter from the very beginning. I was working on a hand machine, making cloth through my own efforts. Even though I would repeat a design for hundreds and thousands of pieces of cloth, skill was required and there was room for innovation. I even appreciated the monotony of the work. No matter what the design, you were pushing that machine from one side to the other, there and back, day after day. You developed a continuous rhythm. You were one of eight, ten, twenty knitters working their machines, back and forth, back and forth. If the shop was working smoothly, the sound was like the hum of a well tuned motor.

Those knitters in the Omaha Knitting Mills not only taught me how to knit, but they sort of adopted me. They saw that I was completely green, just out of the backwoods of a *shtetl*, so they began to teach me about America. They invited me along with them to the restaurant for lunch; they included me in things. They taught me to eat potato *latkes* and gefilte fish with sugar instead of pepper, the Polish way instead of the Ukrainian way. I was the only Ukrainian Jew in the shop, and they had a lot of laughs at my Ukrainian Yiddish accent.

I became most friendly with the Steinhart family, the largest

Joe at his knitting machine in the Omaha Knitting Mills, 1922. From left to right are the boss Zishe Singer, Jack Schiller, Joe, Sam Steinhart, and an unidentified knitter.

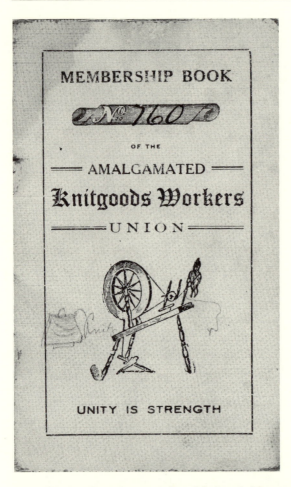

Joe's first trade union membership book. The union, the Amalgamated Knitgoods Workers Union, was a branch of the Amalgamated Textile Workers Union. Thus the spinning wheel on the front.

group of relatives working at the Omaha Knitting Mills. It was four brothers and a sister. One of them, Aaron, married Hannah, the boss's sister. Aaron's sister Jenny worked there as a mender—a person who repaired breaks in the cloth—and she married Jack Schiller, who was a knitter in the shop. I formed a strong friendship with two of the Steinhart brothers, Sam and Harry. They invited me to their homes and they introduced me to the life of the Jewish worker in New York.

Book No. 760

Joe Rapport

Initiated *Sept* 1922

❋

New York

L Shelley
Secretary

HEADQUARTERS :

76 Throop Ave
Bklyn NY

M. Ginzig, 95 Suffolk St.

The workers of the Omaha Knitting Mills never succeeded to teach me Polish Yiddish, but they did begin my education in trade unionism. There was a very weak union in the knitgoods trade at that time. The workers of my shop, especially the knitters, had trade union experience from Poland and were activists in the union here. From them I learned of plans for a general strike to organize the industry. They had to use the Russian word for strike, *zabastovka*, to explain it to me.

I found trade unionism strange in the beginning. Outside of my experience with the Red Army during the revolution, I had no contact with the radical movement. I came from the petty bourgeois population of a *shtetl* with no factory workers, no proletarians. Those workers in the Omaha Knitting Mills had to teach me what the union meant. They did not do it just through lectures and literature. They invited me to union meetings. They introduced me to other union activists. They took me along to distribute leaflets. Since I was the only knitter in the shop who was new to trade unionism, they kept encouraging me to participate, and always someone from the shop went along wth me, especially Sam Steinhart. He saw to it that I joined up with the general strike committee. It was in this 1923 strike that I began to knit out my own conception of trade unionism and the labor movement.

The strike was for growth and recognition of the union. It was an absolute necessity. The knitgoods workers labored five and six days a week, ten hours a day, for substandard wages. There was no security on the job, there was no room for complaining, and there was terrible treatment of unskilled workers, mostly teenage girls.

The union had organized a few of the small knitting shops in earlier struggles, but it was too weak to improve conditions in the trade. Most shops were unorganized, including all the larger shops, the knitgoods factories with over one hundred workers. And the manufacturers were organized in a powerful association, the National Knitted Outerwear Association. They were rich and they were ruthless opponents of trade union organization.

I first tasted that ruthlessness while I was distributing leaflets for the approaching strike. We were attacked by a group of gangsters hired by the manufacturers association. There was a fight, and the police arrested us! Something about this first clash with thugs and the police echoed my joining with the self-defense group in Stanislavchik. Without giving it much thought, I could not accept this terror against the right to hand out leaflets on the sidewalk. Indignation against the oppression of working people has grown in me since that day.

That indignation must have been apparent to the trade union activists. Despite my protests that I was green, that I did not yet speak English, they appointed me picket chairman of the strike

committee for Brownsville. I quickly realized that it was a big
responsibility to call a strike. We were calling upon people to risk
their jobs, so we had to be well prepared. We planned for the
workers to come in their shop groups to Jewish labor lyceums
across New York. The Jewish labor movement built these lyceums
for social activities, educational programs, and organizational
work. At the Brownsville Labor Lyceum we had the help of the
director, Abraham Shiplacoff, a Bundist from way back in the Old
Country. Shiplacoff saw that I was green, that none of our activists
had much organizing experience, and he helped us through that
strike.[1]

We were surprised at how many knitgoods workers showed up
at the Brownsville Labor Lyceum on the morning we issued the
strike call. There was no problem when all the workers from a
shop joined the strike. Then the shop group was responsible for
picketing their shop and keeping out scabs. But when not all the
workers struck a shop, there was trouble. Not only did we have to
fight the boss over strike demands, but we had to convince the
other workers that by scabbing they took away bread from their
friends and in the long run hurt their own families.

The manufacturers immediately began to hire scabs to replace
striking workers and gangsters to bring the scabs across our picket
lines. Most of these gangsters were "punks," as they were called,
but some were armed professionals. I learned that you could not
leave the workers of a single shop to defend themselves against
professional sluggers. You had to meet that terror with a large
body of people, with mass picket lines, mass resistance, mass
attacks on the gangsters.

I never forgot one attack from gangsters at a Sunday afternoon
strike committee meeting. In walked two stocky fellows, not very
presentable looking. They did not have the look of hand knitters
because the hand knitter was a skilled worker and well dressed.
When they walked in, there was an immediate hush from the thirty
people at the meeting. Those gangsters pulled out guns and went
toward one of the strike leaders. He retreated and they started
after him. There was a chase through three rooms, running in a
circle! I was amazed! I didn't see how they could do that among so
many people. I yelled, "Let's tackle them!" I was quieted down:

"They'll shoot and the manufacturers association will defend them." But finally the strike committee blocked the gangsters and forced them out.

The 1923 knitgoods strike was my early schooling in the struggle for workers' rights. That is when I began to learn the ABC's of trade unionism. Even though it was completely new to me, I was in the peculiar position of picket chairman in Brownsville. I had the responsibility to decide what shops should be picketed and how, to urge the workers not to be afraid, to explain what happens when a person is arrested. I had an interpreter who translated my Yiddish into English for the American, Italian, and German workers.

In that first strike I learned how the people did not have savings for a prolonged struggle, especially those with families to feed. Some of the shops that struck in force won an early settlement, but quite a few workers began returning without victory when the bosses promised no reprisals. Others were determined to fight to the finish.

The executive committee that led the 1923 knitgoods workers general strike. Joe is in the second row fifth from the left. Sam Steinhart, fourth. Originally appeared in the Forward.

At that moment came the possibility of arbitration. Some leaders from the United Hebrew Trades, the federation of Jewish trade unions in New York, had a close relationship with Governor Al Smith. He was friendly to labor and offered to nominate a mediation committee which would recommend a binding solution. Our supporters from the United Hebrew Trades urged our strike committee to accept the governor's proposal. They argued that arbitration could only help the union, and that the manufacturers association would look bad before public opinion if it refused the governor. Our strike committee did not agree.

I couldn't participate in that decision because I didn't even know the meaning of the word "arbitration." But later, as I looked back, I realized that we made a mistake. There were anarchists and extreme left wingers in our leadership who claimed we would be played dirty by the government in arbitration, but who really opposed any kind of agreement that would limit the workers. In my view, such a proposition should be accepted or rejected depending upon the strategic position of the organization rather than abstract principle. If you are too weak to gain a victory through your own force, you have nothing to lose by accepting compulsory arbitration.[2]

We did win union recognition at a number of shops, including my own. The relationship was so close at the Omaha Knitting Mills that the boss agreed before the strike to accept the general settlement. But the great majority of the manufacturers continued to resist the union even if their shop was organized during the strike. They had the full support of the manufacturers association. Some immediately broke the agreement and provoked shop strikes. Others refused to renew the contract after a year. We did not have the strength to resist the manufacturers association in shop strike after shop strike. It was just a matter of time before we lost all the shops we had organized.

Soon after the strike I moved from my brother's house in the Bronx to a room in Brownsville. Morris was still indignant because I did not remain in the store, so I did not try to explain my new radical beliefs. I could not have explained if I wanted to, because it was something I was growing into over time. Later, when I did share ideas with him and my other brother Herman, I sounded like a wild radical to them. They were both businessmen and my beliefs clashed with all their conceptions. But time proved me correct in certain matters, especially the radical movement's prediction of the disastrous collapse in 1929. My brothers attributed that prediction to my personal wisdom and I gained their respect. Ideologically we remained in different worlds, but we maintained close family relations.

I continued to work in the Omaha Knitting Mills until one of the larger unionized shops, the Lipman Brothers on One Hundred Twenty-fifth Street in Harlem, refused to renew their agreement. Harry Steinhart already had left the Omaha Knitting Mills and became chairman of that shop. He requested that I take a job there as a knitter and help him in the approaching shop strike.

Harry and I did lead that shop in a prolonged strike to renew the agreement. It was a bitter struggle. The manufacturers used relatives to scab and hired gangsters to beat up the pickets. The union was able to pay several dollars a week to each striker. Since Harry and I were single and could live on pennies, we turned over our shares to other strikers with families. But they started to see that it was futile and they began trickling off the picket line. Some went back to work in the shop, but most would not betray the union and found other jobs.

Harry and I did not give up. We wanted to discourage other unionized shops from following suit. From a political point of view, from a trade union point of view, rather than a struggle for our jobs, the two of us continued that shop strike from the fall of 1923 into the spring of 1924. That was the coldest winter of my life! We picketed from early morning to late evening, in rain or shine, in sleet, snow, and frost. We walked the picket line so long that our shoes gave out, and we didn't have enough money for new ones.

Fortunately, we both received support from our girl friends during that long strike. Harry's girl friend Sylvia Steinhart, a cousin, worked at a knitgoods shop in Brooklyn. Her boss was a leader in the manufacturers association. When he learned they were en-gaged, that Sylvia's earnings helped Harry remain on the picket line, he fired her.

I was luckier. My girl friend did not work in the industry, and she always was willing to share her meager earnings with me. She was that girl who had an aunt in Stanislavchik, whom I once met in Vinnitsa during the revolution, and whom I later met in Kishinev.

Shaiva was the one who brought me together with the delegate Pinkofsky. It was natural to maintain an acquaintance when she landed in the United States. Occasionally we would meet, go for a walk, take in a picture. At first it was nothing more than a friendly feeling ... more like a cousin relationship.

Shaiva—or Sheba, as she was called in America—was living with her aunt in a middle-class area of Paterson, New Jersey. She had it really good there after the turbulence of war and revolution. But Sheba too was bit by the bug of exploration. Her aunt kept her wings much too tied, and Sheba went off to live with another aunt in Philadelphia. She went to school, learned office work, and completely dropped her foreign accent. Later she moved to New York, to the Bronx, and we continued to spend time together. From Brownsville I would send her a postcard with a definite time and place to meet. We would go on a picnic, see a play, take a boat ride up the Hudson.

As time passed we were growing closer together. However, I lived in Brownsville, far from the Bronx, and my participation in the trade union movement kept me busy. I was meeting all kinds of new women—trade union activists, Bundists, anarchists, even vegetarians—and I hesitated to think seriously about planning our lives together. I was especially reluctant because of my low wages. I was new to the knitting trade—my wages were not high—and I started to feel deprivation from my participation in the trade union struggle. We were getting closer, but the economic problem really was a separating factor.

Then came that single shop strike against the Lipman Brothers. My economic position, instead of improving, became much worse! During that long strike Sheba made it her business that we meet more often. One day in January of 1924 we came to the conclusion that it was silly to live in two separate rooms, to pay double rent, while not seeing each other often. So we took one room for economy's sake. We started then with what we thought was practical, and not long ago we celebrated our fifty-fifth anniversary of marriage.

It was natural for young people to be drawn to someone from home in Europe. New York, that huge metropolis, the queen city of all cities fifty years ago, really was a crazy quilt of different peoples, different colors, different languages, different communities sticking together. When you arrived in New York, you were not just coming to the millions of people and all that hugeness. You landed in that patch of the quilt where you had a tradition, where you had roots, where you had branches from the past. It was like bringing the walls of the ghetto into the greatest city in the world. Nothing could be more natural than meeting other young people from home.

More than that, the life of the Jewish family was different in the United States. The American born girls were too snobby, too high fallutin', for the simple boy from the *shtetl*. It was natural to yearn for that innocence, that beauty of manner, that simplicity of past ways. It was natural to turn toward people who shared your experience. Not everyone did it, but marriage between *landslayt* was common.

Young people soon heard about each other. Someone would say, "Herman, you didn't see Fanny in Brockton?"

"No."

"Nice girl growing out there."

And the girl heard about him: "Meet your cousin Herman. A good boy. Get acquainted."

They would bring young people together. My older brother Herman did marry Fanny, a distant cousin from Stanislavchik. My brother Morris was first engaged to an American girl, who was a good attraction, but who turned out to be in a racket for the golden ring with a diamond. Morris learned something that time, and later he married Zissel, Sophie, who had lived across the road in Stanislavchik. So it was with the young people I knew from the Ukraine, and so it was with Sheba and myself.

Neither Sheba nor I was religious. We were completely free-thinkers, so we moved in together without being married. We had no need to play around with words and ceremonies. We did not take our families into our confidence. We just told them that we got engaged ... sort of. We said we did not want any special symbolism, no presents or parties. My brother Morris did not approve, so we didn't come around there very often. With Sheba's family in New Jersey there was a break. Her uncle insisted that he give me a dowry and put on a big wedding. It was like the voice of my grandfather giving me orders in America. I made a snappy reply:

"You can keep your five hundred dollars and your niece too if you insist upon those conditions!" We walked out. Period!

At that time young people in the radical movement were strongly influenced in these matters by the establishment of socialism in Russia. The new freedoms and new forms in the Soviet Union strengthened the idealism of radical minded young people here. I considered a religious wedding ceremony to be counter-revolutionary, since I accepted the slogan that religion is the opium of the people. I didn't see the need for anybody, the government included, to give us permission to come together.

Moving into that room strained relations with our families, but it drew us closer together with friends. Harry and I lost that strike at the Lipman Brothers, but we continued to work together in the union and the two couples spent a lot of time together. Sheba and I had a warm relationship with the entire Steinhart family, which continues to the present with their children and grandchildren.

Sam Steinhart became my closest friend during those years. He not only got me involved in the union, but he introduced me to Jewish cultural life in New York. Around the time of the general strike he encouraged me to join the Pitkin Avenue Jewish Cultural Club in Brownsville. Many of the members belonged to the Young Communist League, the youth movement of the Communist Party, and all were progressives ... left wingers of one kind or another. It was quite a group. Some became writers and teachers in the Yiddish language. Others grew out of the Jewish atmosphere and became lawyers, editors, and union organizers in the general American radical movement. At that time we were united by our appreciation for Yiddish culture.

In that club I met boys and girls I could talk easily with. We had evenings of singing and dancing and sharing ideas. There I was able to develop the little bit of Yiddish culture I started to pick up in Stanislavchik during the revolution. We had lecturers on all kinds of topics in the Yiddish cultural field. Yiddish writers came to read their work, including poets like Moyshe Leib-Halpern and Zishe Weinper. My education in the classical works of Yiddish literature —the stories of Mendele Mokher Sforim, Y. L. Peretz, and Sholom Aleichem; the poetry of Chaim Nachman Bialik and S.G. Frug— was greatly enriched through that club. We took pride in Yiddish

as the language of the people, a language with its own great
writers. We of the Jewish radical movement tried to enhance that
Yiddish literary tradition in the United Sates.

At the same time we took special pride in the blossoming of
Yiddish culture in the Soviet Union. In the early years of the
Russian Revolution, during Lenin's life and for a time after Stalin
assumed leadership, there was official encouragement of Jewish
culture in Russia. We heard speakers who returned from the Soviet
Union and reported on the Jewish schools, the Jewish publica-
tions, the Jewish art that was developing there. We read the new
Jewish literature that came out of the revolution. It reflected
Jewish tradition, not from a religious point of view, but rather as
the history of our people and our struggles.[3]

Everything that was fine in the Jewish secular field was expressed in our radical movement. We had schools, lecture series,
theatrical groups, literary groups, folk choruses and mandolin
orchestras. There were special summer camps where we could
take a vacation and spend time together. There were weekend
excursions for camping and hiking. There was the visiting with
friends in the evenings. All these things were a binder for trade
union and political struggles. It caught my imagination and
encouraged my participation in the movement.[4]

Brownsville, where I lived, was a center for its own Jewish life.
All kinds of Jewish people lived there, from the *alrightniks*, the
rich, to the workers in the shops. But Brownsville was mainly a
ghetto of Jewish poor people; even the businesspeople there were
at the bottom of the totem pole. The Jewish people of Brownsville
were more closely knit as a community than in the Bronx, which
was already becoming a middle-class community.

Brownsville was an easy place for Jewish immigrants to live.
There were synagogues, Jewish stores, the Jewish Labor Lyceum,
and all kinds of other places to meet. There I could eat in
restaurants where I could order food in Yiddish. On the summer
evenings young people would stroll on Pitkin Avenue to window
shop, stop and listen to a soapbox speaker, join in a debate on the
street. Lower Manhattan was the center of Jewish life in New York,
but Brownsville had its own Jewish identity.

I did not just stay in the ghetto, isolated from the rest of life in
New York. I explored the city. First I went galavanting around with

my cousin Avrom to pictures and plays and museums, until his wife Gitl arrived in America. Later Sam Steinhart introduced me to the Metropolitan Opera House, where we would wait hours for a "standing seat." It was with Sam that I saw *Swan Lake* with Anna Pavlova, who had been prima ballerina of the Bolshoi Theater in Tsarist days, and it was with Sam that I saw the great Russian tenor Fyodor Shaliapin in the opera *Boris Godunov.* The arts had been at a high level in prerevolutionary Russia, despite all the backwardness. The changing tides of history allowed me, a Jewish boy from Stanislavchik, to get a good taste of it in New York.

I tried to learn English in school while I lived in Brownsville. I wanted to be able to speak with Americans, to read the history of the land and the struggles of the people. In the back of my mind there still was a desire to become a road engineer. I hoped that if I did well enough learning the language at night school, perhaps I would continue my studies.

I felt a satisfaction attending classes a couple of evenings a week, but my education at that night school came to an unplanned early end. My teacher was a middle-aged woman of Irish descent with a strong fervor of patriotism. Years later I learned to appreciate this Irish patriotism for freedom in America, which grew out of their oppression in Ireland. But at that time I was annoyed when my teacher, before every class, made us go through a lengthy flag saluting ceremony.

Once the teacher asked us to write an essay about the school. It was an exercise in spelling and connecting words. I chose for my subject a criticism of taking up our precious time for education with that repetitious flag ceremony. It was not anti-Americanism. I was not opposed to the flag ceremony, but that it was taking so much of our time in school. I reacted as I did against my grandfather's dogmatic insistence upon religious observance.

At the next class meeting, to my surprise, the teacher singled me out by reading my essay aloud to the class. She did not discuss the grammar, but she condemned it from the patriotic point of view. Then she ordered me to salute the flag and repeat the American hymn.

I refused! I considered it a punishment for my opinion rather than a routine act of patriotism. At that point she ordered me out of the class. Afterward she brought up the issue with the school management. They considered it important enough for every teacher to ask for opinions in their classes.

When I next returned to class, I found myself placed like in a court before a jury. When I defended the right to express my opinion, the teacher said that if I didn't like America, if I didn't like American democracy, why did I come here? At that point, it seems to me, I aggravated the situation by stating, "If you have a democracy in the United States, why was Debs put in jail for his opinion against the war?"

Unwittingly, I blew up a barrel of dynamite in my face. That evening I was expelled from the school. When classes finished and the students passed into the street, some came with a soapbox and raised the question of not returning to classes until I was reinstated. I opposed that move because I knew the students were in exactly my position—they needed to learn English. Raising my right to speak was natural after my experience in the Ukraine and in the knitgoods strike, but I did not want to be the cause for stopping the education of others.

I made one other attempt at formal education, but my heart wasn't in it anymore. I deeply regreted it. As the years passed, I gave up the idea of becoming a road engineer, and I never learned to speak English correctly. Working in shops I had to talk English with people, especially in the process of organizing. My thick accent haunted me then, and it haunts me to the present.

In time I learned that understanding does not come just by living through exploitation in the shop. I discovered there is a history of labor organization, there is a rich literature you must be able to read, to digest, to explain. So if I read Marx, if I read about the American labor movement, if I read about developments in American life, it was mostly through Yiddish publications and translations. Only later could I read English, and up to the present I do not read it well enough.[5]

I did continue my education through the publications of the radical movement. I found that job at the Omaha Knitting Mills through an ad in the *Morgn Zhurnal*, and I continued to read it until the workers teased me: "That newspaper is for the boss, the man with the beard who says prayers. But you, a young man, a worker ... you should read the *Freiheit*!"

That was the newspaper of the Jewish radical movement. Reading the *Freiheit* I first learned about different trade union policies, different theories of the working class, ideas about making a total change of society. The *Freiheit* was sympathetic to the socialist movement in the world, especially in the Soviet Union. It contrasted with the *Forward*, the organ of Jewish right-wing socialism and trade union bureaucracy. The *Freiheit* gave a wonderful political education to militant Jewish youth in the 1920's. I read it religiously.[6]

At that time, I embraced the idea that socialism is the need of humanity. I believed there must be a radical change in the economy and society, in the relation of man to man. Instead of working for bosses who squeezed the people to accumulate profits and power, we wanted to take over industry and run it cooperatively for all the people. We later adopted the phrase of Abraham Lincoln—a government by the people and for the people—to express in a simple way the idea of socialism as a political system that would work for the people, that would use the genius of creation of the people.

At that time the Russian Revolution was a terrific influence upon me ... upon the radical people of the world. It was the first crack in the capitalist world, the first breakthrough of socialism. We read John Reed's *Ten Days That Shook the World*, and we saw the possibility of socialism everywhere. We glorified the accomplishments of the revolution, the Bolshevik attack on private property and exploitation, the change from Tsarist oppression in Russia. It was an example that socialism can be built.

The influence of the Russian Revolution was especially great among Jewish radicals. At that time and up to the present, I had strong feelings about solving the problem of the Jewish people. I had lived in the ghettos of the Ukraine, and I had felt the insult of anti-Semitic attack. I appreciated the Soviet encouragement of Yiddish culture, the new opportunities for Jewish people to participate in Russian life, the promise of a national homeland for the Jewish people in the Birobidzhan province in Siberia. To me the Soviet Union offered living proof that the problem of the Jewish people could be solved under socialism.[7] It gave my participation in the radical movement a double edge—the participation in class struggle against exploitation of man by man, and the strong feeling for solving the Jewish problem by humanizing society.[8]

But how to do it? What was the road to socialism? I was just learning in the 1920's through my participation in building a strong trade union movement. Although my own knitgoods union dwindled after the 1923 strike, I started to participate in other activities of the left-wing needle trades workers in New York. I went around from one thing to another, trying to understand what was happening. I was advised to join certain committees, meet certain activists, attend certain meetings. Between seasons, when I could not find work as a knitter, I would help other unions in the strike hall, join a demonstration or a picket line, raise money to support strikers. I stayed as long as I was of use, and I received a tremendous schooling in the different areas of trade union organization.

At the end of 1923, I was invited to represent the knitgoods workers at a left-wing conference of the Trade Union Educational League (TUEL). We met under the leadership of William Z. Foster, who came to the Communist Party through his struggles on the trade union front, especially the great steel strike of 1919. The TUEL was an educational organization of advanced trade unionists fighting for trade union democracy, for a living wage, and for industrial unionism. Through the TUEL, I discovered that it was not just the left-wing needle trades workers who struggled for progressive trade unionism. I met activists from the steelworkers, the miners, the shoemakers, and other industries. At that conference, I saw leadership and program on a much higher level than what I learned from my brief participation with the knitgoods workers and the left-wing needle trades workers. That conference, that organization, cemented my conception of the proper way to build trade unionism.[9]

During that period, in the mid-1920's, there was a great battle for control of the International Ladies Garment Workers Union (ILGWU). That struggle developed between the more advanced, more aggressive needle trades workers who fought for democratic industrial unionism, as against the ILGWU bureaucracy. Those ILGWU bureaucrats were right-wing socialists who were more interested in their own welfare than the good of the workers.

When the left-wing group grew in strength and began to win control of locals, the bureaucracy expelled left-wing leaders and even entire locals.

Irving Howe, in *World of Our Fathers*, twists the history of this conflict. He tells it from the standpoint of the *Forward*, from the standpoint of right-wing socialism and trade union bureaucracy. He makes all kinds of insinuations against the left-wing movement, especially Ben Gold and the left-wing fur workers, for using gangsterism. This accusation is a blood *bilbul*, a falsehood, like the accusation that the Jewish people used Christian blood for Passover.

Yes, the left wing had an apparatus of young workers who could handle themselves. But this was for defense against gangster attacks from the right-wing leadership and the manufacturers. In fact, I was in that apparatus . . . I was among the workers who defended the offices of the expelled left-wing locals from the ILGWU goons. For many years we had to defend our movement from the labor terror of the social democratic leadership of the ILGWU.

Gangsterism by the Left was not necessary because we had mass support and mass mobilizations. I remember, in particular, one mass meeting of the left-wing opposition within the ILGWU. We filled Yankee Stadium with tens of thousands of workers! Not only was it called without official leadership, but it was a demonstration against the leadership! That took a lot of hurt and a lot of understanding by the workers. It took a willingness to take a chance. That meeting, that entire fight for control of the ILGWU, was a revelation to me.[10]

Some of the advanced knitgoods workers participated in the ILGWU fight, but as individuals rather than as a trade union group. Our affiliation was with the Amalgamated Textile Workers Union because the knitter, like the textile worker, made a kind of cloth. A few years later, when the Amalgamated had dwindled, we did turn to the ILGWU for help. We went to the leadership and explained that the majority of workers in the knitgoods industry were of the garment industry type—pressers, cutters, operators, and finishers who put together the garment. The ILGWU made quite an effort to help us—with organizers, an office, printing materials—but that failed too. All our efforts to organize knitgoods workers met the stone wall of opposition from the manufacturers association.

After that, a small group of us just stuck together with the hope that one day we would be able to organize a knitgoods union. We were rank-and-file workers rather than trade union leaders. We worked in the shops and we maintained contact with the workers. In the rare cases when a single shop strike broke out, we would be there to help the workers. We did not have the strength to function openly on a broad base, but we knew the time would come for that. We were union conscious idealistic activists. We had a vision that someday we would end the injustices in the knitgoods shops. That progressive trade union outlook sustained us through the years of the open shop in the knitgoods trade.

Even without a union there was beautiful cooperation between knitters. Most of the shops in the knitgoods trade were small and relationships were strong. People who worked together in a shop for a short period of time were drawn closer together than people who lived in the same apartment house for years. You were a captive group, bound together not just by the walls of the shop, but by the need to help each other with the machines, to get leverage against the boss, to grumble if the foreman would insult a worker. Over the years, the knitters met in different shops, established reputations, got to know each other and their families. There was an underground solidarity of knitters despite differences of ideological outlook, religious belief, and nationality.

There were unwritten rules about how the knitter should behave in the shop, even without a union. A knitter was a skilled worker who earned good wages, but he became his own driver under the piecerate system. Some knitters would work on their own time—separate cloth at lunchtime—for greater production and a few more pennies each day. This disturbed most knitters ... union conscious knitters. We put a value on our earnings, on high production. We believed in doing a day's work. But we thought you should not be so tired at six o'clock that you could do nothing but rest at home in the evening. A union conscious knitter would clean up, put on a coat and tie, and go out to a meeting in the evening.

To me the knitters were an elite of union conscious craftsmen. Most were Jewish immigrants, but they were completely different from the people in my *shtetl*. They had a high Jewish cultural

education—usually self-education in history and literature and
politics. Many had been in trade unions in the industrial cities of
Poland. They were people who without any rules or regulations
would *never* cross a picket line. During periods of organization,
you would reach out first to the knitters because they understood
unionism and they would not betray you to the boss. It was these
union attitudes and these personal relationships that kept our
group of activists going, despite the failure to organize the
knitgoods workers in the 1920's.

During those years in the 1920's, I became completely devoted
to the left-wing Jewish movement—the trade union activities and
the Jewish cultural work. I started drifting apart from my old
Ukrainian friends. Srulik Stein, who traveled with me to America,
went into the delicatessen business. Business and I never clicked!
Harry Kessler, who first suggested that I try the knitting trade,
became a knitgoods manufacturer! That was a taboo to me—living
off other people's labor, off the labor of knitters like myself! My
cousin Avrom, who was a tinsmith, did have some contact with the
radical movement, but he always remained on the outside looking
in. And Harry Steinhart dropped out of the movement. He became
a fur worker, then a fur merchant, then antiradical and anti-
Communist. We drifted apart too.

With Sheba it was the opposite. She was politically detached
when we moved in together. I still spent a lot of time with the
movement, a lot of evenings taken away. Once it came to an open
discussion. We came to the conclusion that she could not change
my way of living, and I would not impose it upon her. But after that
I did invite her to more left-wing gatherings, and it was just a
matter of time before she became involved in political activities
too. It began as a sideline, but eventually she helped build her own
office workers union and later became expert at trade union
insurance programs. Although I was involved in many Jewish
cultural activities that never interested her, we could share a lot of
trade union experience.

When Sheba and I decided to get together during the Lipman
Brothers strike, we found a place through advertisements in the
Freiheit. We rented a tiny room with kitchen privileges in the
Bronx apartment of the Shatz family. Harry Shatz was a carpenter
who traveled around the garment district, tools in hand, building

worktables, cabinets, and partitions in the shops. He and Yeta and the two children occupied the largest bedroom in the apartment; Yeta's sister was in the next bedroom; and we brightened up the dreary third bedroom with our love.

There was a warm atmosphere in that apartment. The Shatzes came from our area of the Ukraine, so we could talk our Ukrainian Yiddish, share our folk expressions and folk stories. When Yeta saw that Sheba knew as much about cooking as me, which was zero, she helped Sheba learn. Harry and I organized a Jewish cultural club with other left wingers on the block. As the children were growing up, they became a part of our lives too. We had a family feeling with the Shatzes, and we still maintain friendship with them.

After living with the Shatzes for three years, we began to think about seeing more of the United States. Many young people in the radical movement were hitchhiking to California at that time. It was a natural desire for Sheba and myself. In leaving the Ukraine, we already had yielded to one call to see another part of the world. Back in Stanislavchik I had read Russian translations of Jack London and other authors who wrote about the American West. In New York we heard more about California—the warm weather, the palm trees, the way of life. Hitchhiking carried the romanticism of crossing the country close to the earth. It was the romanticism of a boy and girl going off together. It was the call of the unknown that started when we left the Ukraine.

While we were considering a trip, someone warned us about staying in hotels without being married. So one day we went off to city hall and got married. When my brother Morris happened to read the notice in the newspaper, he followed it up by throwing a surprise party with relatives and friends. There was no pressure of religious ceremony or any of that. We had a good time! And soon after our marriage, we had a reconciliation with Sheba's family in New Jersey.

In the summer of 1927, we learned that some friends were about to travel by automobile to California. They said we could join them. We had to be ready within two days, and we were! We quit our jobs, we moved out of our room, and we left half our savings, seventy-five dollars, with Morris. We "Shuffled Off to Buffalo" (that was a popular song at the time) in a four cylinder Oldsmobile.

We stayed with *landslayt* in Buffalo, Detroit, and Chicago. Even in Iowa we landed with a family from Stanislavchik who had done business with my father and who were related to Morris's wife Sophie. They accepted us as family and kept us in Waterloo for a few days.

From Iowa we drove north and west into the Dakotas. We saw fields that were larger and richer than the lands of the *pomeshchik* near Stanislavchik ... fields where wheat and corn stretched away from the road to the horizon. It was a beautiful serenity around us. We traveled slowly and pleasantly with stops to touch the earth and chew on a kernel of grain.

The four of us grew together like a family. Sheba and Ann cooked the meals on the Coleman stove with food we bought from farms we passed. Osol and I took care of the car and the sleeping gear. We traveled with one pup tent and one cot for each couple. Only when you are very young and very much in love can you do that and tolerate each other.

When we reached the Black Hills of South Dakota, it was not just going into our first mountain area, but it was going into a wilderness with no *landslayt* in reach. We marveled at the raw majestic beauty of the Black Hills—the dark evergreens, the granite peaks reaching for the sky, the magnificent views. I had never seen such tall mountains.

From there we were cutting across the prairies of Wyoming. It was long distances, long stretches between one village and the other. Most of the roads were gravel. If the gravel was low it was called a washboard road, because it was like riding on a washboard. When the road was freshly covered with gravel the ride was smooth, but the tires would not grab and travel was slow. No matter. We enjoyed looking out at the endless fields of prairie brush. We really knew we were in the West when we heard the howling of coyotes at night.

The people were friendly. As we came deeper westward, they would look at our license plate when we stopped at a gas station: "Hey! A long way from home!"

"Sure are."

"How far you going?"

"California."

"A long way to go!"

"Sure is."

After long expectation we reached Yellowstone National Park, the miracle of all miracles. The mountains, the waterfalls, the canyons, and above all the bubbling geysers . . . no, it did not make me think of Stanislavchik. I never saw anything in the Ukraine to compare with that corner of America the Beautiful.

We went all the way up to Glacier Park, Montana; the road across the park was just being built by a group of engineers. We came down through Butte, the copper center with the IWW traditions. And then on through Salt Lake City, the Great Salt Desert, across Nevada, and across the Sierras into California. After three months of travel in that little dinky, we finally saw our first palm tree.

We landed in San Francisco, and we parted with our friends. First we had to refill our empty treasury. Sheba immediately found a job as a saleswoman in a department store. I soon learned there were no knitting mills in San Francisco. But there happened to be a radical labor conference in San Francisco, and at the conference I learned that a knitter could find work in Los Angeles. Sheba remained working in San Francisco while I went to Los Angeles with some delegates from the conference.

At that time the radical movement was fighting two great injustices. One was the Mooney and Billings case; the other was the case of Sacco and Vanzetti. While we were traveling to Los Angeles we learned that Sacco and Vanzetti were executed. It was a shock to us. It was a shock to the world. There was every indication of a frame-up, a deliberate execution of two people for not going along with the philosophy of life in the United States.

From the conversation in the car, I learned that the San Francisco conference had been concerned with the factional struggle within the Communist Party. I knew about that fight between the Lovestone group and the Foster group in New York. It was a bitter conflict, ending friendships and dividing families. I never was a factionalist in the left-wing movement. My interest was closer to the struggle to build trade unionism. But the Communist Party factional struggles did affect questions of trade union program, methods, and leadership. It affected greater numbers of workers than those in the Communist Party. My sympathy was with the Foster group. I respected Foster's leadership in the steel strike of 1919 and in the TUEL. But there I was in the car, a captive of

two Lovestonite Party functionaries, people who really were
steeped in the political life of the left-wing movement. All I could
do was listen and learn more about their views and how the
factional conflict was developing in California.[11]

I was more preoccupied with finding work immediately. One of
the people in the car offered that I stay with him until I found a job.
His family accepted me like a relative, and through them I began
meeting people in the Los Angeles radical movement.

Instead of going around looking for a job, I invested my few
dollars in mailing out postcards to all the knitting mills in Los
Angeles: experienced knitter from New York wants work. Just
before I completely ran out of money, one of those knitting mills
responded. The boss started me at twenty-five dollars a week,
which was a terrific amount of money at the time, and soon he paid
me a dollar an hour for a forty hour week. Sheba came down from
San Francisco and found work in an office.

We remained in Los Angeles for a year. Our life there was filled
with new experiences. It was the period before the depression, a
period of prosperity and optimism. Yes, there was a labor movement, there was a struggle. There was and there will continue to
be a struggle between the haves and the have-nots. But our life in
Los Angeles was one of relaxation, of new people, of new interests.

Not everything was new. That Lovestonite might have later
regretted inviting me into his home, because the factional struggle
in Los Angeles was even sharper than in New York. Los Angeles
was at that time a provincial town. The labor people were drawn
closer together, and their ideological divisions were sharper. The
split was so close that if one person missed a meeting, his absence
gave the other faction a chance to adopt resolutions and mail them
right off to New York as a victory. It was a question of one vote, and
I was a new vote!

Despite the factional struggles, we still were people of the same
movement. The radical Jewish movement in Los Angeles was alive
with the same idealism and activity as New York. There were all
kinds of affairs at the Jewish Labor Center—lectures, parties, strike
benefits, Tom Mooney support meetings. Sheba and I spent
weekends on excursions from the warmth of Los Angeles into the
snow-covered mountains; we explored the beaches, visited lakes,
traveled into the desert.[12]

Sheba and Joe on a day excursion into the mountains around Los Angeles, 1928.

Even before Sheba arrived I met up with a good group of young people on a trip into the mountains from the Jewish Labor Center. We traveled together in a rented flatbed truck. As usual, when young people of the radical movement got together, song was inevitable. This was a characteristic of the Russian people, the Ukrainian people, and also the Jewish people. We sang folksongs, songs of the people ... songs that would urge on the workers ... people's songs of struggle and victory.

One voice on that truck was ringing out, beautiful and hardy, leading from one song to another. In Russian we called such a songleader *zapivalii*. I immediately took a liking to that *zapivalii*. I made my way to him over the weekend and learned his name was Yankl Rabinoff. When we became more friendly, I learned that he and his wife Dora were part of a young group living in two houses near the Jewish Labor Center. There was a flare of enjoyment of life in those houses. At the same time, they were steeped in labor struggle, in the fight against the bureaucracies of the Amalgamated Clothing Workers and the ILGWU. This was the type of carefree serious minded youngsters we picked up friendship with in Los Angeles.

We lived with another young couple, Alex and Sylvia Kraus, who also were in the radical movement. They were sympathizers of the Lovestone faction, but we thoroughly enjoyed each other's company. Three of us worked and Sylvia was the *baleboste*, the housekeeper. She was very beautiful and very vivacious. However, Alex and I had a constant struggle when she became, all of a sudden, a vegetarian! I have committed many sins in my life, but vegetarianism was not one of them. We still lived in harmony, but after supper Alex and I sometimes went for a walk that ended in a delicatessen on Brooklyn Avenue.

We lived in Boyle Heights, the Brownsville of Los Angeles. We had a beautiful little cottage with a fountain in front, with palm trees and strange fruit growing around us. The weather was forever pleasant, even when it rained. Everywhere were orange blossoms, miles and miles of orange blossoms. Los Angeles was like a huge village dipped in green. Even the poorer areas were like living on boulevards.

We had a new way of life in Los Angeles. We were not traveling in a crowded subway, we were not living in a cramped apartment, we were not suffering through the hard winter of New York. There was a fight to organize trade unions in Los Angeles, but we were not really a part of it. Although I worked in an open shop, the pay was good, the boss appreciated my work, and there was no jealousy among workers. It was not the harsh struggle for existence like in New York.

We thoroughly enjoyed our life in Los Angeles. We enjoyed it so much that one day we decided we had too much of a vacation. We had a yearning to return to New York, to the routine of our life there, a life we considered more interesting and more fruitful than what we had in Los Angeles.

The friendships that we made in Los Angeles were deep and lasting. Later the Rabinoffs came to New York and Yankl became an activist in the knitgoods industry. Within time Alex Kraus became a businessman and an opponent of the radical movement; we parted ideologically, but we maintained a warm friendship up to the present. There were all kinds of other people we met up with again over the years, especially when we later returned to live in California. That year in Los Angeles was a memorable and rewarding period in our lives.

After goodby parties, we left Los Angeles in my first car. It was a wonderful car, a second-hand Chevrolet of 1923 vintage. It was a

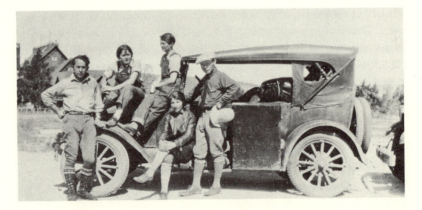

Joe and Sheba, with friends and first car, returning from Los Angeles to New York in 1928. From left to right are Joe, Ida Gaffin, Sheba, Lena Kendzer, and Abe Kendzer.

touring car with a top that came down. And it had a special
feature—a front seat that could be lowered back and slept on. We
traveled in class, in a car we could turn into a bed!

We returned to New York just before the 1929 stock market
crash and the Great Depression. Sheba went back to work in an
office and became active in the office workers union. I found a job
at a knitting mill, and I rejoined that small group of rank-and-file
knitgoods activists. We still met regularly; we still hoped that the
struggle of 1923 would not be lost. We believed that someday we
would do something about organizing the workers of the knitgoods industry.

5. Organizing the Unorganized, 1929-34

The depression hit the country like lightning from a clear sky. During the 1920's there was an air of prosperity which I associated with the popularity of the silk shirt. Skilled workers shared in this prosperity, but the overwhelming majority of working people did not. As radical economists explained, that kept down buying power and brought about an imbalance between production and consumption. The left-wing movement predicted economic trouble, but we were ignored.

The collapse hit working people hard. There was unemployment and there was a lack of means for everyday life. The ruling classes had nothing prepared for security against homelessness and hunger. Hoover advised the people to sell apples, but who could buy them? It was a time of fear and resentment.

The skilled workers in strong unions could make a fight to protect their positions, to retreat with their faces to the enemy. But because we were not organized in the knitgoods industry, we had to submit to big wage cuts, longer hours, sweatshop conditions, and long periods of unemployment. We were helpless.

Our group of union conscious knitgoods workers held together. We were two dozen class conscious activists who continued to meet after the knitgoods general strike of 1923. The manufacturers were strong enough to prevent any large strikes or labor organization, but our group continued to discuss possibilities, to talk with other workers. We kept the flame of trade unionism burning in the knitgoods trade.

There was a core of dedicated people in that group. Sarah Chernoff was a fiery rebel, a militant worker who was way ahead of her time; she was a dynamo among women in the industry. Her

husband, Harry Weinstein, was just the opposite—phlegmatic,
scholarly, and very cautious. We had another worker intellectual,
Solomon Zaslovsky, who followed economic and political developments through the *Wall Street Journal.* Like Harry he was always
pessimistic about our prospects for organizing knitgoods workers,
and like Harry he could not give up the idea. Sam Steinhart was
another important voice in the group. He could have been a fine
organizer, but there was something about him—an air of freedom,
a refusal to be completely tied down to organizational responsi-
bilities—that made him hesitate at taking leadership; instead he
would encourage me. And there were others who were constant
in their devotion, whom history should remember: Jackob Nickon,
Rose Eisman, Jack and Jenny Schiller, Nettie Markov, Isaac and
Adele Spevack, Bessie Shinehouse, I. Avner, Albert Fleischer, Fred
Scheer, Anna Savitsky, Willy Miller, Jack Yanow, and more.

Over the years we became a solid tested group of activists.
Because our trade was unorganized in the 1920's, we did not have
problems of trade union bureaucracy and the factionalism of
the Jewish trade union movement. We were rank-and-file activists,
not trade union officials. We had wide contacts in the knitgoods
shops, and we had a good reputation among the workers. We had a
solid base to begin organization when the time came.

At the beginning of the depression, our knitgoods group was
affiliated with the National Textile Workers Union, which was part
of the Trade Union Unity League (TUUL). It was a period of
militancy for the left-wing labor movement. We organized our own
radical industrial unions, separate from the main body of labor in
the AFL. That development was influenced by factional struggles in
the Soviet Union and the policies of the Profintern. But it also was
the result of growing restlessness of unorganized workers and
their desire for industrial unionism.

Our knitgoods group affiliated with a textile union because
knitters made cloth, like textile workers, but for knitted garments.
The National Textile Workers Union, the first of the separate left-
wing unions, grew out of a collection of militant textile strikes in
New England and the South in the 1920's. It began before the
TUUL and the official left-wing policy of dual unionism in 1929.
The National Textile Workers Union was a response to the super-

exploitation by the textile mills, the growing militancy of the workers, and the do-nothing policy of the AFL. It was an early symptom of what was to come in the depression.[1]

I saw the militancy of those textile workers first hand. For whatever reasons—perhaps because I showed some consistency and ability in the knitgoods workers struggles, perhaps because I was young and easy prey—William Z. Foster called me into the TUUL office and requested that I go to New Bedford, Massachusetts as a TUUL organizer. The TUUL was sending organizational help for the textile workers who emerged as leaders in the New Bedford cotton mill strike. When I protested that my English was poor and I had limited leadership experience, he said, "I'll be the one to judge your ability. You are one of the people who holds the knitgoods workers together. And if you think your English is bad, just listen to those Portuguese workers in New Bedford."

I was forever getting involved in one thing or another, and I went there for a couple of months. I found those workers up against an aggressive textile industry that was shifting to new factories and cheaper unorganized labor in the South. It was like today's multinational corporations, which move across international borders in the search for cheap labor.

The New Bedford textile workers put up a good struggle, but by the time I arrived they had been forced back to work, except for the strike leaders who lost their jobs. The defeat was felt very strongly. But a strike is never lost in principle; the workers learn from defeat and gird for the next battle. The TUUL organizers worked to keep a semblance of organization alive. We couldn't do much then, but out of that strike came some dedicated young radicals who stuck with the struggle for trade unionism in the textile industry. Those textile strikes of the 1920's are part of the historic tradition behind the fight to organize textile workers today.[2]

I admired the militancy of the National Textile Workers Union—it was years ahead of its time with those textile strikes—but our knitgoods group ran into trouble in that union. The leader, Albert Weisbord, was radical in his ideas, but when it came to the knitgoods industry, he applied a theoretical approach without the benefit of practical experience.

At the beginning of the depression, Weisbord wanted us to

approach organization of our knitgoods shops as if they were huge
textile mills. He insisted that we organize secret shop groups and
put out an underground newspaper. We explained that our shops
were too small and the time was not right . . . that such an approach
would expose the union conscious workers, who would become
noticed in the small shops of our trade. Since I was the knitgoods
workers representative on the national committee of the textile
union, Weisbord attacked me personally for not recognizing new
methods of organization and for insubordination. He even called
us before William Z. Foster and the TUUL. The national leadership
in the end agreed with us.

We just could not make any headway in the knitgoods shops. As
the depression deepened, the discontent was strong and the need
for organization was greater than ever. But there were few
outbursts of resistance. There was a fear of completely losing the
job, an uncertainty of what else was possible than to go along with
conditions as they were. There was little our group could do to
organize the knitgoods workers in the early days and years of the
depression.

During this period I helped the radical movement organize
Unemployed Councils in neighborhoods across the city. We
demanded a moratorium on the payment of rent as long as there
was unemployment and the closing of banks. Landlords were
evicting people who could not meet their payments . . . just
throwing the furniture and the families onto the streets of New
York with no place to go. We would come with a group of people
and move those families right back into their apartments. Sometimes we could reason with the landlord. Sometimes we fought
with the police. I participated in dozens of support struggles for
people who were evicted.

Those of us in the Unemployed Councils also preached that the
workingman on the job should extend solidarity to the unemployed. We did that in a number of ways, especially through large
militant demonstrations. We demanded unemployment compensa-
tion, more jobs, and a general improvement in conditions.

I paid my own penalty for joining the historic unemployment
demonstration at Union Square on March 6 of 1930. Tens of
thousands of demonstrators covered the square and overflowed
into the sidestreets that day. There were dozens of well-known

speakers. The sentiment was so strong that all kinds of people, including Sarah Chernoff, just got up on the platform and spoke their piece.

That demonstration became a bloodbath when the police attacked. They arrested the leaders and dispersed the demonstrators. Grover Whalen was the New York police commissioner; we called his police the Whalen Cossacks. They rode their horses into tightly packed crowds, beating people with clubs regardless of age or sex. The fire department also was there, using the full force of fire hoses to wash us out of the square.

Those of us who had experience with police attacks brought tools for self-defense and for cutting the fire hoses. The demonstration was broken up, but our resistance advanced the fighting spirit of the unemployed. That militant demonstration was on the front page of newspapers across the country.

And what happened to me? The following morning, when I returned to work, the boss came over to my machine. "Joe, why didn't you come to work yesterday? Were you sick?"

"No, I went to the demonstration of the unemployed. It was quite a showing ... a hundred thousand people."

"Is that right?" he said. "A hundred thousand people! You're fired! Now it's a hundred thousand and one!"[3]

The left-wing movement grew rapidly in those early years of the depression. The radical workers really carried on a fight. We saw the growing dissatisfaction, and we mobilized the people. It was not only the workers in the shops and in the city neighborhoods but also the veterans who marched on Washington and the farmers who organized to stop the banks from taking their land. The slogans, the meetings, the demonstrations of the left wing had an influence. The struggle vibrated across the country.

About that time, in 1931, our knitgoods group picked up the question of what to do. We knew the New York knitgoods workers were restless. It was not openly expressed, but we thought there was enough dissatisfaction to make another attempt at trade union organization. We thought that this time the knitgoods workers would not be cowed by the fear of losing the job.

But how to go about it? Our knitgoods group was still a local in the National Textile Workers Union, but that union never recovered from the defeated textile strikes of 1928 and 1929, especially the Gastonia strike. We needed some elementary support like a place to meet, an organization to lean on, a full time organizer, or at least someone to put out our leaflets in good English. Our group had functioned for years as a spark among knitgoods workers, but we really were starting from scratch.[4]

We decided that a garment union, not a textile union, should be our organizational base. The textile element in the knitgoods shop—the hand knitter, the mender, the winder—was starting to be replaced by new power machinery. The workers who finished the knitted garments—the pressers, cutters, operators, finishers, etc.—were similar to other needle trades workers. At one point in the 1920's, we had received some organizational help from the International Ladies Garment Workers Union (ILGWU) and we decided to approach them again. It was an established union with organizational resources and experienced leadership.

Our committee met with David Dubinsky, who was then ILGWU secretary-treasurer, and we offered to begin organizing the knitgoods shops for the ILGWU. We had a reputation as a scrappy group of radicals who were not sympathetic to the ILGWU leadership, but we never had been a dual union in conflict with them. Nonetheless, he refused to help us. He said that all their resources were going toward organization of dressmakers, cloakmakers, and the rest of the needle trades with a history of struggle.

Then we went to the Needle Trades Workers Industrial Union (NTWIU) with whom we were more sympathetic all the time. Why did we not go to the left-wing right away? We thought that our first task was to organize the unorganized and that it was more realistic to affiliate with the stronger ILGWU. We did it as an instant reaction, just because we worked in the shops and we saw the need for knitgoods workers to organize a union.[5]

We met with the national leadership of the NTWIU—Ben Gold, Rose Wortis, Joseph Boruchowitz, and the others. We knew them from our participation in left-wing trade union struggles going back to the 1920's. In fact, at one point in the fight for control of the ILGWU, I slept for several nights in the offices of the blousemakers local to help repulse any attack from the ILGWU bureaucracy. That was part of the cement that kept our movement together over the years.

Again we offered to begin organizing knitgoods workers. We

requested their support, and we offered to give up a percentage of our own wages to pay an organizer. They agreed with our evaluation that it was time to organize the knitgoods workers. They said we could affiliate with the NTWIU and they would help us. They recommened that I be appointed as organizer of the new knitgoods workers trade union.

My arguments about my lack of experience did little good. My own group agreed with the recommendation, and the majority opinion had to prevail. It became a question of taking the opportunity to do what I preached.

I decided to begin organizing the trade with my own shop, the Simon Knitting Mills, where I had the personal confidence of the workers. I began with the hand knitters, who were the most important producers in the shop and who had a background of trade union experience. I consulted with a couple of them, and they agreed to speak with a few other workers. We decided to omit from the early stages of organization any workers who were opposed or who might be scared because they supported families.

We invited each of the workers we spoke with to lunch at a cafeteria. That kind of procedure was natural because when you work in an open shop you cannot talk freely. Over lunch I explained that we were building an inside organization of the shop. I explained that our work had to be completely under-ground, to avoid firings of workers before we were ready to defend ourselves.

Each one of the workers agreed to speak to another worker in confidence. When you work together in a shop for months and years, you become acquainted one to one with other workers. That was the basis of our approach. We would not yet refer to ourselves as a group, but we would talk about the spirit of organization in the garment industry and see if they agreed that our shop could do something too. We left out those workers who showed the slightest hesitation.

When we had a third of the shop behind us, we called them to-gether at that cafeteria. We put up the demand that the boss recognize us as a shop group for discussion of terms of work. I warned them that the boss might fire us, but that organization had to start somewhere. They accepted the plan.

When I went to the boss with our demand he said, "Why pick on me? There is no union at other knitgoods shops!" Then he fired me.

After I was discharged, we called a meeting with all the workers, because if there was a strike it would involve everybody. We decided that the boss did not have to recognize us as a union, but he must agree to rehire me and to meet with a workers' committee on questions of wages, hours, and grievances. To take away the edge, we would promise not to impose union shop conditions until other shops were organized and faced the same conditions.

The following morning the small group that started the organization arrived an hour early and formed a picket line with strike signs. Immediately the boss called the police to chase us away. But the boss was shocked to discover that no worker wanted to cross that picket line. The workers knew the demands were just—not exaggerated—and that was important. Even the cops let us alone when they found out we were not stopping people by force and we were willing to negotiate.

The boss was caught in the middle of an order, in the middle of the busy season. Our approach was so simple and so just, it was easier for him to accept. He agreed to take back the workers and to recognize a shop committee.

The workers elected a shop committee with me as the shop chairman. I continued working there for another month to make sure they got used to the idea of complaining and negotiating. Then I called a shop meeting and told them the union demanded my time. The majority was opposed at first, because they felt my leadership was like an umbrella protecting them. But a couple of workers argued that if more shops could be organized, they might win union recognition within time. This reasoning was accepted.

(I arranged for a beautiful young woman, Edith Berkman, to replace me as a hand knitter in that shop. The boss protested—he didn't believe a woman would be strong enough for the work. After all, he had an investment in his machines, and they had to produce. But Edith was an experienced knitter from Poland, and she produced like everyone else when he gave her the chance. Edith had been a TUEL organizer in the famous Gastonia textile strike, and later she became a needle trades organizer. I saw her in Los Angeles a few years ago and she said, "Joe, do you remember when you arranged for me to become the first woman hand knitter in the industry?")

That successful strike at the Simon Knitting Mills was the beginning of organizing the knitgoods workers in the 1930's. Our group began using the same system in other shops. We worked through the personal contacts we developed over the years, especially with the hand knitters. In this manner, we started to organize shop after shop in Manhattan and Brooklyn.

The manufacturers resisted, especially through the National Knitted Outerwear Association. They used all the old tactics— scabs, gangsters, injunctions, and arrests. Sometimes they put up really vicious resistance. One of our most bitter early struggles took place at the H & M Knitting Mills, where Sam Steinhart worked and led a strike for recognition of the shop committee. That employer with the help of the manufacturers association hired gangsters to terrorize the strikers. In one of the attacks against our picket line, a gangster stabbed Sam. The wound was a fraction of an inch from his heart. He was laid up for weeks in the hospital. Sam returned to leadership in our struggle to organize the trade, but he had to nurse that wound for years after.

One of the shops I helped to organize during this period belonged to Harry Kessler, the *landsman* who first advised me to become a hand knitter. When Harry refused to recognize a shop committee, the majority of his workers declared a strike. Since Harry and his brother were former knitters, they started to work the machines themselves during the strike. That kind of inter-ference led to clashes, verbal and otherwise, outside the shop. Harry became very angry at me. I tried to explain that trade union organization was a process in the industry . . . that I could not make an exception for him. But for years after I organized his shop, when we ran into each other at my brother Morris's house, there was a coolness between us.

Sometimes the organization problems were as much with the workers as with the manufacturers. I had a hard time with the workers at the Jay Brothers Knitting Mills, a large sportswear shop with many skilled workers from other needle trades. They worked at knitgoods shops, during the slack seasons at their own shops. When I came to distribute leaflets at the Jay Brothers Knitting Mills, I recognized several cutters and operators who participated

in the struggles of the dressmakers and the cloakmakers in the
1920's. I did not approach them at the shop door, where we might
be seen, but I cornered them a block away. I told them what we
were doing and asked for their cooperation.

I met with a group of trade union veterans from that shop. They
refused to help out. They argued that their jobs in the knitgoods
shop were only temporary and that the shop would be too difficult
to organize. I saw that I couldn't make first base with them. I was
the novice at organizational activities in that meeting.

I went to Joseph Boruchowitz, one of the respected veteran
leaders in the NTWIU, and told him the story. He said, "Joe,
sometimes I envy that you are organizing an industry where most
of the workers have no sophisticated trade union experience.
These old timers think they know all the answers." He was not
exactly anxious to speak with them, but I insisted and he did. He
convinced them to eat lunch with the pressers and the knitters, to
talk union, to prepare the ground inside. Eventually we organized
that shop.

It was after the election of Roosevelt that trade union organization really began to develop in the knitgoods industry. When
Roosevelt openly declared himself in favor of labor organization,
he stirred up demands of working people for trade unions.
Roosevelt's steps were vague in the beginning, in the NRA period,
when he opened the way for manufacturers to establish company
unions. The left wing denounced Roosevelt as antilabor. But
workers in almost every industry began to organize trade unions
and fight for better conditions. This especially was true in the New
York needle trades. There was an outpouring of desire to organize,
like the breaking of a dam, and this was felt by our small knitgoods
workers union.[6]

The manufacturers continued to resist. At first they opposed any
suggestion of recognizing a shop committee. But we were in a
stronger position when we could tell a manufacturer that other
shops were organized, that we didn't want to put him out of
business, and that we didn't want to scare other employers with
extreme demands. Although the union's connection with the shop
committee gave the boss an uneasy feeling that there was organizational support behind his workers, it also reassured some bosses
that the shop committee would not make unreasonable demands.

As soon as our shop committees began to take root, they would demand that a representative of the union be present during negotiations with the manufacturer. At the same time, we began to popularize the idea of union recognition. We started to hold regular general meetings open to all the workers in the trade. Those public meetings attracted workers from the open shops— old contacts and new ones—who helped our work.

Our approach amazed the leadership of the NTWIU. The organizational drives in the needle trades usually *began* with a general strike for union recognition in the trade. The workers were consulted, but at general membership meetings, not as shop workers in their own shop groups. Those general strikes began with union workers setting up picket lines in front of all the shops and stopping the other workers from entering. It worked only when there was strong organization and traditions of struggle.

There also was the system of "pulling" shops. This was when the workers in a shop might want to join the strike, but they were afraid to go openly against the boss. So they would send someone down to the strike hall and he would say, "Send a committee into the shop and say 'Everybody down!' It will be an excuse that 'we are being forced' and everybody will go."

Because we were starting from scratch, because we were rank-and-file activists, we were able to adopt fresh methods that were suited to the knitgoods industry. Our approach was underground and from within. It was a method of solid organization from the bottom up, worker by worker, shop by shop. We didn't try any premature general strike with the "pulling" of shops. We organized in depth.

Even though we did not yet have union recognition, we began to function the way a union should—as a real democracy. We had general membership meetings, but the real basis of our organization was the shop committees and the committee of shop chairmen. That's where the workers could participate in real discussion. That's where solid leadership developed. Just *because* we did not have paid union officials coming to settle things with the manufacturers, the shop committees had to be strong and democratic.[7]

As we grew in size we added a few more full time organizers, including Sarah Chernoff. She was very capable, especially organ-

izing the women of the trade. There was one strike at the Zion
Knitting Mills in Brownsville where she gave leadership to seventy-
five Italian working girls. The owner of that shop, a religious
Zionist, failed to intimidate those girls with the police. Then that
religious man, for whom walking into church would be like eating
khazer, ham, actually got the local priest to help him break the
strike. But Sarah aroused the militancy of those girls. Her Yiddish
accent was as thick as mine, but she was a militant woman who
was understood no matter how she said it. Those kids stuck by her
like chicks to a mother hen. As she expressed it, "They wear the
crosses on their necks, but you can talk to them class struggle." She
organized that shop.

Our leadership was honest and idealistic with the class struggle
first in mind. Take Sol Reeve, another of our organizers—a skilled
cutter, intelligent, sharp in defense of his beliefs, a courageous
militant on the picket lines. Or take Louis Cooper, who was not a
full-time organizer; he came forth as a shop leader during the
Dorfman Brothers strike and became a consistent participant in
our union struggles. The knitgoods workers appreciated their
devotion. They knew the record of our entire group. We had been
doing organizational work every day and every week for years and
years. When we approached the workers to organize in 1932 and
1933, we were known and trusted.

We were helped by approaching the workers as part of the
Needle Trades Workers Industrial Union, which was known as an
honest and fighting union. We were able to lean on the NTWIU for
advice and support as well as reputation. We had space in the
union office, which was in the garment district near Seventh
Avenue and Twenty-eighth Street. The streets below the office
were like a labor marketplace with workers milling about all day.
That was reflected inside the building. There was a constant
circulation of workers coming to union headquarters with complaints, looking for jobs, looking for consultation with leadership,
or just sharing experiences.

Sometimes it was so noisy that it was impossible to sit in your
cubicle and talk. But it was a good thing that happened in our
union office. The people had confidence that they could come and
get help. They could come and feel at home. To go see an ILGWU
leader was like seeing a politician or a manufacturer in his office.

Workers were not the only ones who made noise in our union office. On several occasions, there were terror attacks from strong-arm committees of the right-wing unions and the manufacturers. At one bloody raid, in the middle of the day, they not only smashed furniture, but they started shooting and they accidentally killed an old man selling bagels in the office. Then the people lost their fear and headed for the gangsters. The gangsters ran down the stairs with guns drawn. They met the police who heard the shooting and came running. There was a big gun battle and several of those gangsters were killed.

I remember another incident in Ben Gold's office, which was next to mine. At first, when I heard a tumult from Ben's cubicle, I thought it was just an old time furrier who came in to raise hell. Noise in Ben Gold's office was nothing new. But when I heard it develop into a fight, I ran in and saw two men hitting Ben.

I walked over to one, lifted him from behind, and carried him into the hall. I said, "Shame on you! Coming in here and fighting with Ben! This is a union office!"

He just turned around, clobbered me with a lead pipe, and ran out. My shoulder hurt for weeks, but I did not tell anyone about my attempt to scold that gangster.

The national committee of the NTWIU was composed of delegates from the different needle trades. I represented the knitgoods workers. I got a real education from those discussions, especially from listening to Rose Wortis. She was clear minded, politically alert, and completely dedicated. Ben Gold, the leader of the NTWIU, was a powerful speaker who could explain complicated problems in a simple way. He was a real people's leader who was loved and revered by everyone. Louis Hyman, Irving Potash, Sarah Dorner, Rose Kaplan, and Charlie Nemeroff were other leaders who were well accepted by the people. That entire NTWIU leadership helped form my own conception of the correct way to build trade unionism.[8]

Our knitgoods group had great respect for the NTWIU leaders, but we also had some bitter clashes with them. In the beginning, they appreciated the steady growth of our organization. We were bringing in new shops without much pain or trouble. We were making improvements in hours and wages in our shops. We were building a base. But there came a time when the NTWIU insisted we call a general strike for union recognition and the thirty-five hour work week.

This was at the middle of 1933, when the spirit of unionism was sweeping the country. The ILGWU was making a big drive to organize the needle trades, and it decided to call a general strike. The NTWIU leadership felt the left wing had to take the strike initiative too, or we would be branded as scabs and left behind.[9]

The NTWIU asked our knitgoods department to join the general strike. We were growing slowly, but definitely, and we thought that a general knitgoods strike would be disruptive. Many of our workers had just gone through shop strikes to win recognition of their shop committees and improvement of conditions. They were not ready to strike again, and even though there were no union contracts, we had verbal agreement with manufacturers that we would not come right back with new demands. That moderation and keeping of promises made it easier to organize the open shops.

We thought a general strike would be premature for knitgoods workers. This was not just the opinion of our executive committee, but our shop chairmen and shop committees too. We thought that *we* should choose the time to fight for major demands. We did not want to go into battle just because there would be a general strike in the other needle trades.

Something else was happening in the knitgoods trade that made us even more reluctant to call a general strike. The ILGWU had started up a dual union of knitgoods workers. There was a group of Lovestonites, former Communist Party members and sympathizers, who were accepted by Dubinsky in the ILGWU. Some of those Lovestonites were clothing cutters, pressers, sewing machine operators, and specialists in other trades who worked in knitgoods shops during the slack season in the dressmaking shops and cloakmaking shops. They were members of the ILGWU, and they were ideologically opposed to the NTWIU. When they saw our organizational progress, they spelled it out to Dubinsky and the ILGWU: "If you do not organize the knitgoods workers, you will have a growing Communist control there."[10]

Dubinsky knew that we had come to him first, but he gave them the go-ahead to organize a knitgoods local of the ILGWU—Local 155. It was one of the rare instances when the ILGWU, not the left wing, organized the dual union.

The situation was further complicated by the efforts of the United Textile Workers Union to organize knitters. It started a local for mechanics who worked in the new shops that produced only knitted cloth on power knitting machines and then sold the product to garment shops for finishing. The United Textile Workers, like the ILGWU, belonged to the AFL. Even though the two unions had a jurisdictional fight in the knitgoods industry, they made a pact to work against our knitgoods local of the NTWIU.

The ILGWU dual union was our main problem. At the time when the NTWIU called upon us to join the general strike of 1933, we already felt hampered by ILGWU Local 155. It was not as easy to organize a shop when the manufacturer knew he could bargain with another union or when the ILGWU might scab on our striking workers. It was the beginning of a struggle between the two unions over who would represent the knitgoods workers.

It wasn't so bad yet. We came from the depth of the knitgoods industry. We had the confidence of many workers. We were carrying on a good fight against the open shop. Our union democracy won over the loyalty of the workers in our shops. But we were not yet well entrenched, and we did not feel ready to fight both the manufacturers and the ILGWU in a general strike.

We clashed with the NTWIU leaders on this issue. They criticized our settling shops without union recognition and contracts; they did not appreciate our democracy with real power in the shop committees; they claimed we had no confidence the workers would follow us in a general strike; they insisted we did not feel the tenor of the times. At first it was a quiet debate. When we refused to give in, they denounced us in a public meeting of the NTWIU national committee at the summer camp of the Jewish radical movement. I was right up on the platform in that camp auditorium, packed with needle trades workers, when leader after leader attacked us as weaklings and opportunists. They really did a job on us.

We were left with the choice of withdrawing from the NTWIU or submitting to the strike decision. We felt that going independent would weaken us in the long run, so we submitted. They assigned Alex Kolkin to act as manager of the knitgoods department during the general strike, and I was exiled to the bail committee. Kolkin was an able man, but he did not have roots in the knitgoods trade. It was a marriage without love.

That strike opened the gates for ILGWU Local 155. Our workers were not enthusiastic to strike, and our credibility with the manufacturers was destroyed. We clashed with the ILGWU along with the manufacturers' gangsters in our efforts to organize open shops. We had a fight just to keep our own shops intact. When *we* broke our agreements not to come right back with new demands in our organized shops, those manufacturers had a new opportunity to eliminate our union or to negotiate with the ILGWU, which they considered the lesser evil.

We had a bitter fight with ILGWU Local 155. If they could not win over our workers to their side, they tried to arrange sweetheart contracts with the manufacturers. Then, while our workers were still on the picket lines, they started to bring scab workers into our shops. Those scabs carried ILGWU Local 155 membership cards. Many of them were uneasy about crossing our picket lines, but they claimed ILGWU Local 155 had a union contract with the manufacturer.

At the shops where they sent in scabs, we mobilized large groups of workers to picket. In the process of trying to talk with the scabs in a peaceful way, we had skirmishes with them, with their ILGWU leaders, and with the manufacturers' thugs. The police joined the attacks on our picket lines. Many of us were arrested several times during the strike.

We lost some of our most important shops. Take the Levine Knitting Mills, one of the larger shops in Brooklyn, which we had organized from the inside, on the basis of recognition of a shop committee. During the strike, the cutters in that shop negotiated with the manufacturer to switch over to ILGWU Local 155. There was no shop meeting with discussion and a vote by workers. It was an underhanded raid! We were not strong enough to stop them. We had some devoted people in that shop who were forced to join Local 155 or find another job. I remember the chairlady Anna Beresin coming to me crying when they finally had to submit. It was a personal tragedy for her to return to her shop and join the ILGWU.

We had another situation with the Links and Links manufacturers in Ridgewood. Links and Links was the name for a knitting machine that made a soft stitch material for children's garments. It was a special part of the knitgoods industry with mostly German workers. Before the strike, the Links and Links manufacturers, who had their own organization, sent a lawyer to negotiate a settlement with us on the basis of thirty-seven and a half hours a week, union recognition, and some improvement in working conditions. The Links and Links knitters were willing and we of the knitgoods union were willing, but the NTWIU leadership insisted that we could not settle for thirty-seven and a half hours in some shops and then demand thirty-five hours in others.

We knew that attempting to impose the thirty-five hour work week on Ridgewood and our other shops would make the ILGWU more attractive to the manufacturers. Most of the shops in the industry worked forty-eight and forty-four hours a week, and we already had won forty hours in the shops we organized. Our job was not to squeeze the organized manufacturers, but to strengthen our position by organizing other shops until we were strong enough to fight for better industrywide conditions.

That demand for thirty-five hours was too extreme, but the NTWIU leadership imposed it upon us. Throughout the strike, when the ILGWU was settling shops on the basis of thirty-seven and a half hours, we could not back down from thirty-five hours. That lawyer from the Links and Links manufactuers had handed us a bonanza on a silver platter, and we had to refuse it. Those workers did strike, and we lost their shops to the ILGWU.

We managed to maintain our base, instead of falling apart as we feared, because we started sending our people back to work in shops where we won agreements. We tried to reach understandings with those manufacturers to allow their workers to start work a little later, so we could use them to strengthen our picket lines in the mornings and organize more shops. Some manufacturers went along with it, but soon we had to start sending back workers whose shops were filling up with scabs. Otherwise we not only would lose the shops, but we also would have unemployed workers, to whom we were morally responsible.

Those general strikes in 1933 were a great victory for the ILGWU. The NTWIU grew, but the ILGWU gained a strong control over the New York needle trades. We never learned which knitgoods local emerged strongest from the knitgoods general strike. We estimated that our numerical strength was about equal to ILGWU Local 155, with about fifteen hundred members apiece in an industry with eighteen thousand New York workers. But they had started very weak and made tremendous gains in the strike. They could not have tackled us except through that confusing situation with three striking unions and two kinds of settlements and all kinds of deals with manufacturers.[11]

We were forced into that general strike with those unrealistic demands at what should have been a time of careful, steady building for us. I wish we could have been more independent of the NTWIU. We received a great deal of assistance from them, but we were placed in a position where we had to make a mechanical translation of the methods, the timing, and the demands of the general needle trades to our own knitgoods industry. That militant general strike might have been correct for the other trades in the NTWIU, but the knitgoods workers did not have their kind of entrenched organizations and traditions of struggle. That militant strike might have been the political demand of the time—the militant policy of the Profintern in the early 1930's—but it was not the need of our workers at that moment!

The NTWIU leaders should have realized that and left us alone. They should have honored the radical movement's slogans of fighting trade union bureaucracy, of building trade union democracy. They should have accepted the opinion of the knitgoods workers about a knitgoods strike.[12]

After the strike there was a period of consolidation. We continued to reach out to the unorganized workers in the open shops, but we always had to protect ourselves from ILGWU raids. They were trying to knock us out of the field and take over our organized shops. It was a terrible situation, which helped the manufacturers hold down the tide of union organization in the knitgoods industry.

The momentum was with ILGWU Local 155. Before the 1933 general strike, they were a small group of outsiders with hardly any organized shops. Now they were an established organization with most of the larger shops and with as many members as us. They

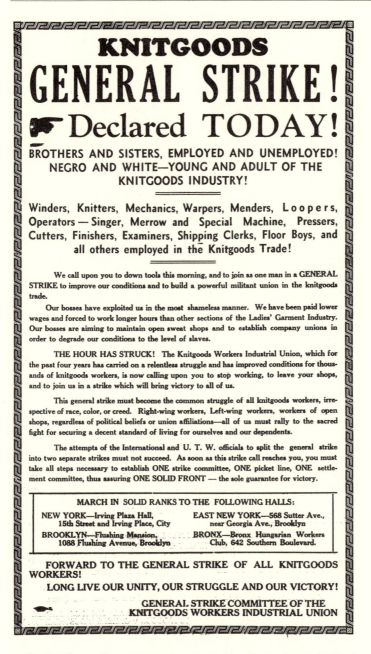

KNITGOODS
GENERAL STRIKE!
☛ Declared TODAY!

BROTHERS AND SISTERS, EMPLOYED AND UNEMPLOYED!
NEGRO AND WHITE—YOUNG AND ADULT OF THE
KNITGOODS INDUSTRY!

Winders, Knitters, Mechanics, Warpers, Menders, L o o p e r s,
Operators — Singer, Merrow and Special Machine, Pressers,
Cutters, Finishers, Examiners, Shipping Clerks, Floor Boys, and
all others employed in the Knitgoods Trade!

We call upon you to down tools this morning, and to join as one man in a GENERAL
STRIKE to improve our conditions and to build a powerful militant union in the knitgoods
trade.

Our bosses have exploited us in the most shameless manner. We have been paid lower
wages and forced to work longer hours than other sections of the Ladies' Garment Industry.
Our bosses are aiming to maintain open sweat shops and to establish company unions in
order to degrade our conditions to the level of slaves.

THE HOUR HAS STRUCK! The Knitgoods Workers Industrial Union, which for
the past four years has carried on a relentless struggle and has improved conditions for thousands of knitgoods workers, is now calling upon you to stop working, to leave your shops,
and to join us in a strike which will bring victory to all of us.

This general strike must become the common struggle of all knitgoods workers, irre-
spective of race, color, or creed. Right-wing workers, Left-wing workers, workers of open
shops, regardless of political beliefs or union affiliations—all of us must rally to the sacred
fight for securing a decent standard of living for ourselves and our dependents.

The attempts of the International and U. T. W. officials to split the general strike
into two separate strikes must not succeed. As soon as this strike call reaches you, you must
take all steps necessary to establish ONE strike committee, ONE picket line, ONE settlement committee, thus assuring ONE SOLID FRONT — the sole guarantee for victory.

MARCH IN SOLID RANKS TO THE FOLLOWING HALLS:

NEW YORK—Irving Plaza Hall,
15th Street and Irving Place, City

EAST NEW YORK—568 Sutter Ave.,
near Georgia Ave., Brooklyn

BROOKLYN—Flushing Mansion,
1088 Flushing Avenue, Brooklyn

BRONX—Bronx Hungarian Workers
Club, 642 Southern Boulevard.

FORWARD TO THE GENERAL STRIKE OF ALL KNITGOODS
WORKERS!

LONG LIVE OUR UNITY, OUR STRUGGLE AND OUR VICTORY!

GENERAL STRIKE COMMITTEE OF THE
KNITGOODS WORKERS INDUSTRIAL UNION

*Strike leaflet in four languages, issued by the Knitgoods Workers
Industrial Union for the 1934 strike.*

Der General Strike
in der Strickenwaren Industrie
IST HEUTE GERUFEN !

BRUEDER, SCHWESTER, A R B E I T E N D E UND
ARBEITSLOSE OB WEIS ODER FABRIC, OB JUNG
ODER ALT — ARBEITER IN DER STRICKWAREN
INDUSTRIE:—

MECHANIKER, STRICKER AN HAND UND MOTOR—MASCH-
INEN, SPUHLERS, WARPERS, MENDERS, LOOPERS, OPERA-
TORS AN SAEMMTLICHE NAEH MASCHINEN, WIE MERROW,
SINGER, BUTTONHOLE UND DERGLEICHEN, PRESSERS,
CUTTERS, FINISHERS, EXAMINERS, SHIPPING CLERKS,
FLOOR BOYS UND FLOOR GIRLS SOWIE LEHRLINGE ALLER
ART SOWIE ALLE DIE IN UNSEREM GEWERBE BESCHAEFT-
IGUNG FINDEN.

AUF ZUM KAMPF.

Ihr seid ersucht heute Vormittag, die arbeit niederzulegen und
eure Werkstaetten zu verlassen, um gemeinsam, mit eurer Mitarbeiter
fuer bessere Arbeits-Zustaende und fuer eine maechtige Arbeiter-
Genossenschaft in den Kampf einzutreten.

Unserbarmlich haben uns die Bosses, bis zum letzten Tropfen
Blut ausgesaugt.

Wir arbeiten laengere Stunden mit weniger Lohn als irgend ein
Teil der Ladies Garment Industrie.

Der Haupt prinzip unserer Bosses ist Sweatshops oder Company
Unions.

Dieser Knechterei muss ein Ende gemacht werden.
DIE STUNDE HAT GESCHLAGEN.

Die Knitgoods Workers Industrial Union, die in den letzten vier
Jahren durch unerbitterlichen Ringes Tausende von strickerei Arbeiter
verbesserte Lebens-Verhaeltnisse, erkaempfte, fordert euch auf diesen
Ruf zu folgen unud ohne Ausnahme im diesen GENERAL STREIK
einzutreten, um einen Sieg fuer alle strickerei Arbeiter zu erringen.

Die beiligenden Forderungen stehen uns als Ziel.

Dieser General Streik muss sich zu einem gemeinsamen Kampf
ausbilden. Keine auswahl betreffs, Religion, Raase, oder Politiacher
Neigung gemacht werden. Arbeiter vom Linken oder Rechten Flu-
egel, Arbeiter in offenen Werkstaetten, alle muessen diesen Streik an-
stroemen und eine maechtige, geschlossene Kampf Linie bilden, und
dadurch bessere Lebenslage fuer una und unseren Familien zu erzwingen.

Die Fuehrer der International und U. T. W., wollen diesen General Streik spalten um aus einem Kampf, zwei besondere zu foerdern.
Arbeiter laesst dieses nicht zur Tatsache werden.

Sobald ihr diesen Ruf erhaelt, muesst Ihr sofort alle Hebel in
bewegung setzen fuer:—

EIN VEREINTES STREIK COMMITTEE.
EIN VEREINTES SETTLEMENT COMMITTEE.
EIN VEREINTER STREIK ZUM ERZWINGEN ALLER FOR-
DERUNGEN FUER ALLE ARBEITER.

MARSCHIERT IN GESCHLOSSENEN REIHEN NACH DEN
UNTENSTEHENDEN HALLEN:

NEW YORK—Irving Plaza Hall,
15th Street and Irving Place, City.

EAST NEW YORK—568 Sutter Avenue,
near Georgia Avenue, Brooklyn.

BROOKLYN—Flushing Mansion,
1088 Flushing Avenue, Brooklyn.

BRONX—Hungarian Workers Center,
642 Southern Boulevard, Bronx.

GENERAL STREIK COMMITTEE
KNITGOODS WORKERS INDUSTRIAL UNION

IN THIS GENERAL STRIKE WE ARE OUT
TO WIN THE FOLLOWING DEMANDS:

1—The 35-hour working week.

2—The establishment of an Unemployment
Relief Fund.

3—The abolition of all piece-work and overtime.

4—Limitation of machinery.

5—Paid legal holidays.

6—For the following wage scales:

Knitters Mechanics	$65.00
Winders	25.00
Power Knitters (all kinds)	45.00
Warpers	40.00
Flat Machine Hand Knitters and Links and Links	45.00
Cutters and Markers	50.00
Machine Cutters	45.00
Singer Operators	30.00
Merrow Operators	30.00
Special Machine Operators	27.00
Finishers on Sportwear	25.00
Finishers on Sweaters	22.50
Folders and Examiners	20.00
Menders	35.00
Pressers—Sportwear	45.00
Pressers—Sweaters	35.00
Floor Workers	18.00

Lo Sciopero Generale!
Nell'industria dei "Knitgoods"
E'DICHIARATO OGGI !

COMPAGNI E COMPAGNE, OCCUPATI E
DISOCCUPATI!

BIANCHI E NERI, GIOVANI E ADULTI
DELL'INDUSTRIA DEI "KNITGOODS"

Winders, Knitters, Mechanica, Warpers, M e n d e r s,
Loopers, Operators—Singers, Merrow and S p e c i a l
Machine, Preasers, Cutters, Finishers, Examiners, Shipping Clerks, Floor Boys, e tutti gli occupati nell'industria
dei "Knitgoods"!

Siete chiamati a fermare il lavoro questa mattina, e partecipare
come un sol uomo allo sciopero generale per migliorare le nostre condizioni e costruire una potente e militante Unione nell'Industria dei
"Knitgoods".

I nostri padroni ci hanno sfruttato nella maniera piu'vergognsa.
Siamo stati pagati con salari bassissimi e forzati a lavorare piu, lunghe
ore che nelle altre sezioni del "Ladies Garment Industry".

I nostri padroni tentano di mantenere "open sweat shops" e di
stabilire unioni di compagnia in ordine di poter peggiorare le nostre
condizioni fino al livello degli schiavi.

L'ORA E' SUONATA! La "Knitgoods Workers Industrial
Union", che durante i passati quattro anni ha condotto una continua
lotta ed ha con questa migliorate le condizioni di migliaia di operai, ora
chiama voi di fermare il lavoro, di lasciare le vostre fabbriche, e di
partecipare con noi nello sciopero generale per ottenere la vittoria.

IN QUESTO SCIOPERO GENERALE NOI LOTTIAMO PER LE
SEGUENTI DOMANDE:

(Read English Page)

Questo sciopero generale deve divenire la lotta comune di tutti
gli operai dell'industria dei "knitgoods", senza distinzione di razza, di
credo e di colore. Operai dell'ala destra e quelli dell'ala sinistra, operai
delle open shops, senza distinzione di credo politico e di affiliazione di
unione—tutti essione dobbiamo lottare in questa guista lotta per
assicurarsi un decente livello di vita per noi e i nostri dipendenti.

L'attentato degli ufficiali della "International e U. T. W. di
dividere lo sciopero generale in due scioperi separati non deve avere
esito.

Appena questo appello a sciopoerate da voi letto, dovete prendere
tutti i passi necessari per stabilire un comitato sciopero solo, un
"picket line" solo, un solo "settlement committee", solo otsi'e potra'
assicurare un solido fronte che garentira' una sicura vittoria.

LAVORATORI DI "KNITGOODS", MARCIAMO IN SOLIDI RANGHI ALLE SEGUENTI SALE:

NEW YORK—Irving Plaza Hall,
15th Street and Irving Place, City.

EAST NEW YORK—568 Sutter Avenue,
near Georgia Avenue, Brooklyn.

BROOKLYN—Flushing Mansion,
1088 Flushing Avenue, Brooklyn.

BRONX—Hungarian Workers Center,
642 Southern Boulevard, Bronx.

AVANTI PER LO SCIOPERO GENERALE DI TUTTI I "KNITGOODS WORKERS".
VIVA LA NOSTRA UNITA', LA NOSTRA LOTTA E VITTORIA!

COMITATO GENERALE DELLO SCIOPERO
DELLA "KNITGOODS WORKERS INDUSTRIAL UNION"

---

also had the prestige and the resources of the ILGWU behind them. By the summer of 1934, they intensified their drive to organize the knitgoods workers.

They called a big strike in August 1934 for improvement of wages and hours. Now they were too strong to ignore. We had no choice but to call out our shops too. Our strike demands were stiffer than theirs, but ours was a defensive struggle at this point. They really consolidated their position in the 1934 strike.[13]

We maintained our base throughout this period, but we were weakened in our struggle with the manufacturers and the ILGWU dual union. We never recovered our momentum after the 1933 general strike. We paid for it later on when we finally merged with the ILGWU Local 155, not on the basis of negotiation and compromise, but again because of pressure from above.

6. The Soviet Union, 1934

A few months after the 1934 strike I made a visit to the
Soviet Union. I wanted to see my family and friends that
I left behind in the Ukraine fifteen years ago. I remained
a friend of the Soviet Union during those years, and I was
interested to see what developments took place. On November 7
there was to be a great celebration of the revolution. All of that,
especially the desire to return to Stanislavchik, was of terrific
drawing power.

Following the strike was a period of consolidation which
allowed me to be gone for a month. Sheba could not take off from
her job, so we decided I would go alone. I drew upon our meager
savings, supplemented by help from friends.

Because of the approaching November 7 celebration, several
groups of activists from the Communist Party and the trade union
movement also were traveling from New York to Moscow. Although they were acting as official delegates and I was going as an
individual, I joined them. We had a wonderful time on the boat to
France and on the train to Moscow.

We were met in Moscow by a group of Americans who worked
in the English Department of the Profintern. Among them were
people I knew from the days of the National Textile Workers
Union. Those textile organizers came to the Soviet Union after the
Gastonia strike of 1929. That was a famous textile strike in North
Carolina, where the leaders were framed and threatened with
years of imprisonment. Some of them skipped bail to the Soviet
Union and went to work for the Profintern.[1] They greeted me as an
old friend and secured for me a hotel room.

It was evening when I came into Moscow. I just dropped my
bags in the hotel lobby and went to look around. The hotel faced
Sverdlov Square across from the entrance to the Bolshoi Theater.
Even though it was fall, a light fine snow was falling, reflecting the
brilliance of the electric lights. I walked over to Red Square.

Suddenly, there was the Kremlin, St. Basil's Cathedral, the Lenin Museum, and the Lenin Mausoleum.

In my youth, in the Tsarist days, a Jew could not enter Moscow without special privileges. But there I was walking on the cobble-stones of Red Square, once the parade grounds for the Tsar's troops. It was almost empty. I was listening to my own footsteps as I was walking. It was a feeling of elation that I could get to Moscow and have Red Square to myself. It was fantastic!

Other things did not matter. My hotel, the Metropole, was the headquarters of the soviet during the revolution. The decor, the accommodations, the service, the food, the dress . . . all that was of minor interest to me. I wanted to meet people. I wanted to learn about life in the Soviet Union. I started to remember my Russian and pretty soon I had no trouble communicating with people.

The following day I met my old friends at the offices of the Profintern. They introduced me to some of the Profintern leaders, including Lozovsky, the international head of the movement. I also was introduced to Madame Molotov, who had worked as a hand knitter in the years before the revolution. Then they took me out to see Moscow.

At that time Moscow, and all of Russia, was still clearing away the rubble from the devastation of the war and revolutionary days. It was the end of the First Five Year Plan. The city had all the indications of cleaning up, renovation, and building after a great storm. There were tall new buildings going up. There were wide new streets lined with trees. There was the great project of the Young Communists to construct the Moscow subway. I was amazed to see those students marching into the subway to dig, singing as they marched. It was a joy to see them.

Later that day I met up with Solomon Zaslavsky, who had been an activist in our rank-and-file knitgoods workers group in the 1920's. Now he lived in Moscow. In the years after the revolution, there was an appeal by the Soviet Union for the world's specialists to come and help build. There were simple factory people who came with their little knowledge of machinery; there were miners and steelworkers and laundrymen and engineers who came to help out with their American know-how. Zaslavsky brought his knowl-edge of knitgoods manufacture. He was working as a sewing machine operator and going to school to become a textile engineer.

It was a holiday spirit in Moscow for the anniversary of the revolution. The American delegation invited me to join them at a banquet given by the Soviet trade union leaders. It took place within the walls of the Kremlin. It was a real Russian banquet with plenty to eat and toast after toast. I was called upon to give a short speech of greetings from the knitgoods workers of the United States.

There was a great parade in Red Square on November 7, the day of the Bolshevik Revolution in 1917. That parade was a colossal outpouring of humanity marching in organized blocs. I justified that military display, because it was just a short time ago that they got rid of invaders and internal enemies by force of arms. That show of military power in Red Square was to give confidence to the people across the vast stretches of Russia: "We are on the watch. We'll keep the gun ready. You put your hands to the plow. Work! Build!"

While I was in Moscow, my friends introduced me to the Profintern secretary of the international committee of the needle trades. That secretary, Comrade Bober, was preparing to go on a trip to needle trades factories across the Ukraine. Since I was headed in that direction, he invited me to come along with him. My presence as an American trade unionist would be of interest to the workers and would add the prestige of internationalism to his trip.

I was eager to go right to Stanislavchik, to come home to my father, my family, my friends. But my Profintern friends insisted that I travel with Comrade Bober. They knew that his official trip would help me to get around and see Soviet life. The country was still very raw. Space in hotels was limited, the railroads ran irregularly, factories were difficult to visit. Comrade Bober had arrangements for travel and meetings with leaders of industry and labor.

I accepted his invitation and we traveled together for a couple of weeks. The first place we visited was a knitgoods factory in Moscow. There I found some modern mass production machines along with the old type hand knitting machine that I worked. Like the newer machinery in the United States, that mass producing machinery was imported from Switzerland. It was easier for the Soviet Union to introduce the most advanced machinery in light industry like clothing manufacture.

In those days to compare the industrial development of the United States and the Soviet Union, as some people did, was not logical. On top of the backwardness of the old Tsarist regime was the tremendous destruction during the days of war and revolution. It was not as though the wheels automatically started to turn after the revolution. The wheels had to be built and put to work. The operators of the wheels had to learn to use gas and oil to keep them going. The *muzhik*, the peasant, did not suddenly become a machinist.

I was curious to see what would be the treatment of workers under socialism, compared to a profit eager capitalist system where there was no consideration for the welfare or participation of the workers. At that needle trades factory in Moscow, I found the trade union helping to run the factory. Along with the knitting machinery I found many plants growing in tubs, to help create more oxygen when the windows were shut. I found that women who gave birth to a child had their jobs secured and had children's centers in their residential areas so that work would not disrupt family life. These were my first examples of the possibilities of knitgoods work in a socialist society.

From Moscow I went with Comrade Bober to Kiev. We were met at the train station by a delegation with flowers. Hotel rooms were prepared, committees were waiting to meet us, newspapers were reporting our activities. Wherever we went I was introduced as a representative from the national committee of the Needle Trades Workers Industrial Union, which they called a revolutionary American union. I was well accepted.

I had a pleasant surprise at one of the knitgoods factories we visited in Kiev. There were a couple of thousand workers in that factory with their own clubs and cultural activities. We were invited to a cultural gathering of several hundred workers, Jewish and non-Jewish. After they did some songs and dances, I had the surprise of my life when a non-Jewish worker, a Ukrainian, got up and read a story of Sholom Aleichem in Yiddish! The Jewish workers translated into Russian for the non-Jewish workers. It was an indication of the acceptance of Yiddish culture in the Soviet system. I was fascinated to see those Jewish workers assimilating into a life of industrial comradeship with other workers. It was a beautiful moment.

From Kiev I traveled with Comrade Bober to Kharkov and as far as Rostov on the Don. Wherever we entered shops and factories, the machines would be stopped and the workers called together. After we gave short speeches, there would be an exchange of questions and views. I spoke about methods of production and conditions of life in the United States. I reported on the hardships of life for workers and small farmers with the depression. I spoke about unemployment demonstrations, block committees that fought evictions, and the struggle to organize the needle trades workers.

I found that the Soviet Union was building large centralized factories with a lot of new power machinery. I was impressed by the efficiency of production and by the optimism of the workers. There was a willingness to produce, to change, to improve. There were weaknesses and mistakes, but all of that was taken care of within the framework of round table discussion. The workers were represented in the management of the factories through their trade unions. They had shop committees to take up grievances, which were settled through negotiation and compromise. The workers participated without fear of being discharged because of a complaint. They had rights to the job. They felt like it was their own factories. The life of the worker at the factory was so much better than in the United States.

Traveling with Comrade Bober opened doors for me. I learned a great deal about the Soviet Union, and I even got a hint of something that would be new in the United States. He was very well informed on developments in the American labor movement, including my own Needle Trades Workers Industrial Union. During one discussion he said to me, "I know that the leaders of the NTWIU are well accepted by the workers in the fight for improved conditions and trade union democracy, yet you are not winning over the workers of the ILGWU." When I tried to explain the problems of manufacturers' control and gangsterism, he said, "I know all that. I am questioning whether you can win over those workers and organize the trade as long as you are a separate union. Perhaps it is time for the prophet to walk to the mountain." He did not elaborate, but when I was in Moscow again, I learned more about what was behind that statement.

After I separated from Bober at Rostov on the Don, I continued south to Baku, where my sister Ethel and her husband lived. Baku was the location of the oil fields on the Caspian Sea near Persia. I was pleased to learn that Ethel's husband Avrom, who had been a butcher when I left, worked in a technical position at the main electrical station in Baku. He was often consulted on technical matters by electrical engineers who went through formal schooling. I was amazed that he could leave the backwardness of the *shtetl* and rise to an important technical position in so short a time.

I found their spirit good. He had decent wages and security with the job. Even so, they lived in a rotting shack. Baku was one of the last areas to be freed during the revolution. It seemed to me that because the border areas were not yet fully secured, they were not rebuilt as fast and the poverty from the Tsarist past persisted longer.

Avrom's only complaint was of danger on the job. He worked at a key point for the feeding of electricity to the oil fields and refineries. If anything went wrong, it not only would affect Baku, but also the areas where Baku oil turned the wheels. Therefore the electrical plant was a central point of attack for counterrevolutionary forces still active in the country. Avrom told me about acts of sabotage he witnessed—creating fires and breakdowns and accidents. He had threats against his life if he reported them.

It goes without saying that there were acts of sabotage in the Soviet Union at that time. It all was attributed to the supporters of Trotsky, who wanted to create a situation where Stalin would fall from power. But I think there also were acts of sabotage committeed by remnants of the Tsarist regime—the religious movement and the bureaucracy and the military and the landlords—who continued to oppose the Soviet system.[2]

I found my brother-in-law very much changed because of the new attitudes in the country and the opening of doors for Jewish people to enter all industries. But Avrom was not a politically conscious person who would do something about the sabotage. He was both complacent with his good position and scared of the threats.

It was not just sabotage that was happening in the Soviet Union.

While I was visiting another needle trades factory in Baku, the alarm whistle sounded. The workers gathered to hear a report that Sergei Kirov, who was the liberator of that area from the Tsar's Army, was assassinated. Kirov was secretary of the Leningrad Communist Party and next to Stalin in Soviet leadership. Some people have attributed Kirov's death to Stalin, but it did not seem so at the time.[3]

I believe that assassination made Stalin even more fearful that he was surrounded by traitors. Even though the inner struggle for leadership between Stalin, Trotsky, and Bukharin was over, there was a bloodbath in the next few years. It was a beheading of the remaining Bolshevik leadership from the days of the revolution. That bloodbath cleared away leadership from all phases of Soviet life—people who could have helped in the struggle for industrialization and the war against nazism.[4]

I was allowed into that needle trades factory in Baku through my own trade union credentials. I left New York with a statement that I was a member of the national committee of the Needle Trades Workers Industrial Union and any cooperation from Soviet trade unions would be appreciated. In Moscow the Profintern translated it into Russian and gave it an official stamp. That credential helped me reach out to individuals and institutions, to be accepted in confidence.

I learned from my sister that my cousin Itsik was working at a steel mill near Kamenskoe, which was along the way back to Stanislavchik. It aroused my interest. How is it that my aunt Rivka's son, who also was raised in the petit bourgeois atmosphere of the *shtetl*, came to work in a steel mill? And how does he fare? I decided to visit him on my trip from Baku.

When I went to buy a ticket at the railroad station, I was told I could only get a number on a waiting list, and it could take weeks to get a place on a train. I went down to the trade union center, showed my credential, and explained my situation. When I came back to the railroad station, there was a first class ticket waiting for me.

I was placed on a train reserved for top government leaders. I shared a compartment with a general who also was a diplomat representing the Soviet Union in Persia. We had a wonderful two days of travel and conversation. He explained to me how there was not a sharp division between the military and diplomacy in the Soviet Union, how he wore his Red Army uniform with pride at diplomatic functions in Persia. I told him about political developments and trade union developments in the United States. At one point he asked what Americans thought of Stalin. I was frank. I told him that the people I knew, political-minded people, considered Stalin an organizer and Lenin the Marxist theoretician. On this he tried to correct me, insisting that there can be no separation of theory and practice in leadership, that Stalin was a proven theoretician just as Lenin was organizer of the Bolshevik Party and the revolution.

I left the train at Dniepropetrovsk, which was not far from Kamenskoe. The city was once known as Ekaterinoslav, for the Tsarina Catherine the Great. With the revolution and the building of the great dam at the Dnieper River, they changed the name of the city. The Dnieper Dam was designed by an American engineer, who came to help after the revolution, and I went to see it while I was there. But my main purpose was to visit Itsik.

I had to wait for a bus to Kamenskoe. The Ukrainian winter already was in full swing, and there was a snowstorm that evening. At the bus station, they told me to wait out on the platform or I might miss the bus. I began a conversation with the other person on that platform. And while we were talking, in the middle of that tremendous snowstorm, two strangers with collars up and caps down, he cried out, "*Josef, ty zhe v Amerike*, Josef, you are supposed to be in America!"

It was Yankl, the son of the water mill operator in Stanislavchik!

I explained that I was visiting Itsik, and I was amazed to learn that Yankl was the manager of a *kolkhoz*, a collective farm, in that area. He said, "I will see that you get to Itsik tonight. In the morning you come to the farm."

He dropped me off with Itsik and the next morning a horse and sleigh took me to the farm. There I learned what I already knew from following the literature on Soviet agricultural development. The peasants were brought together to work a big chunk of land with modern machinery. A large part of production went to the government for a nominal price. The rest was sold for profit and distributed on the basis of work put in by each person.

Nobody owned his own plot of land on any *kolkhoz* then, but the desire for land was so strong that within time every peasant did receive his own small parcel to operate as he pleased. Even before I left for America in 1919, I saw the beginning of distribution of the landlords' estates to the peasants. A few years later, when Soviet power was entrenched, the land was turned into cooperatives like the *kolkhoz* I visited. That cooperative was beneficial for productivity, but the piece of land was still the peasant's dream, and there was resistance to the establishment of the *kolkhoz*.

In Moscow I already had heard there was a lot of murder of *kulaks*, the rich peasants who were accused as obstacles to agricultural development. I heard remarks and rumors, but I just could not believe the staggering figures of destruction some people told me. At that time, I thought it was a slander. I could not imagine that inhuman devastation of peasants just to save a few years in overcoming their resistance to change.[5]

I did not hear such dissatisfaction at the *kolkhoz* I visited. The people I met were the leaders. After Yankl showed me around during the day, we talked by the fire late into the night. He explained how he went from Stanislavchik to be manager of the *kolkhoz*. He grew up with an interest in agricultural from contact with the peasants who brought their grain to be ground at his father's water mill in the village. After the revolution he had an opportunity to study agronomy. He did express some dissatisfaction about living conditions to me—he came from a well-to-do family in our *shtetl*—but he knew that in the Tsarist days a Jew could not even live on the land. Here he was a respected scientist in agriculture, an *agronom* and the manager of a *kolkhoz*. It was a great accomplishment.

The following day I returned to my cousin Itsik. He told me about his job in the foundry at the steel mill. He was a boy from a *shtetl* and nothing prepared him, physically or mentally, for that kind of heavy work. I was surprised that he could endure it, and in the long run I think he could not. When I revisited the Soviet Union in 1963, I learned that Itsik had died when he lost his balance and fell into an inferno of melted steel. But during my 1934 visit, Itsik told me, "One thing is sure. I do not have your worries about unemployment, and my children will have their education."

There were several young people from Stanislavchik working at that steel mill. When the first one began, he wrote home that more workers were needed. With little work available in Stanislavchik, others came. Itsik was a Party member and he had the added attraction of the idealistic call to build heavy industry under the First Five Year Plan. He did not talk of his past business experience in the *shtetl* or of his youthful flirtation with Zionism. His job as a hard steel worker was a *kryshka*, a cover, over his personal history.

Itsik and his family lived in a poor man's place, a run down hut, but I could not care less. I knew the backwardness of life under the Tsar, I saw the destruction during the war and revolution, I knew that sabotage was still happening. I did not expect to find Itsik living with the comfort of an American worker. It would be sheer nonsense to compare. I saw that he was making a living, that he was optimistic about the new Five Year Plan, that his children went to school. He was resigned to do the best he could under the circumstances and he hoped that a better life could be achieved, if not for him, then for his children. I saw what I saw and I stopped asking questions.

I returned to Dniepropetrovsk the next day. Before my train arrived, a representative of the needle trades union took me to several factories in the area. One was operated by former prostitutes. In Tsarist days, prostitution was a big problem because of hardship and hunger. The Soviet government encouraged those women to go to work and live a normal life. At first, the prostitutes in Dniepropetrovsk were denounced by other factory women, so they were placed together in their own factory. They told me how their life became normal with work and proper treatment and marriage. It was the only time in my life that I found such a group operating a factory.

The high point of the trip was my return to Stanislavchik. When I was in Moscow, I had written to Mayer, one of my old chums that I corresponded with, to let him know that I was coming. I did that in order to prepare my father. Mayer knew from the newspapers when I landed in the Ukraine with Bober. Every day he was waiting to meet the wagon that brought passengers from the railroad station at Zhmerinka to Stanislavchik.

Finally, I was riding on that wagon. Now it was a better wagon on a wider road, but from a distance everything looked the same. From the hills I could see the red tile roofs of the *shtetl* and the thatched roofs of the surrounding peasant village. It was just like I remembered it from fifteen years ago.

At the outskirts of Stanislavchik we passed the cemetery where I spent many days playing with Nisl, the son of the caretaker. The grounds of a cemetery were not well kept in the Old Country. The monuments were battered, and there were gnarled wild cherry trees growing among the graves. It always gave me an overwhelming feeling of fear and respect. My grandfather, my grandmother, and my mother were there.

When I came into Stanislavchik I got off the wagon before the marketplace and walked there. The *shtetl* remained as it was, but it seemed strange . . . older. Sure enough, Mayer was waiting at the marketplace. We met and he went ahead to tell my father I am coming.

My father was living in the same house. It was an excitement to walk there with all the anticipation of seeing him. It was an emotional reunion. He kept on repeating, "I never thought I will live to see the day when you will come home."

As usual, anything new in the *shtetl* quickly spread. People learned that I arrived and came to shake hands. They wanted to hear about my life in America, to learn my impressions about the Soviet Union.

The *shtetl* was strange to me not just because it was older. It shrunk! I remembered that when I had to go from our house to the market as a boy, it was a big chore. Now the distance was less than a city block. The street itself seemed more like an alley, and that big marketplace with a big fair every week was just a tiny open space.

The same buildings remained, very dilapidated, still pockmarked from the gun battles of the civil war. Little was new. I found the same thing in other small towns nearby. Again I had the feeling that this area was not yet secure enough to justify rebuilding. Furthermore, the Soviet strategists were siphoning off young energy from the small towns to develop basic industry in the cities. Most of the young people were gone. The *shtetl* looked half empty.

The revolution had brought difficult changes for the older folks. The homes of the Jewish people were still grouped together—they were not confiscated—but the *shtetl* lost its old role in the local economy. The small shopkeeper who once sold a herring cut up in a dozen places, who sold tar for the squeaking wheels of a wagon, who sold salt for preserving meat, was gone. No longer was there fighting between shopkeepers for that customer who would come around for two *kopeks* of kerosene. Buying and selling goods, which was speculation, was not the Soviet system. The older Jewish people lost their *parnose*, their means of making a livelihood.

My own father no longer worked. He received a small government pension and some help from my sisters. From America the three sons used to send money and packages, which meant a great deal. But he lived very poorly. His life . . . it shrunk.

The religion of the Jewish people, of all the people under the Soviet system, was attacked even more than today. The opposition to religion was expressed throughout the land in the slogan "religion is the opium of the people." Hence the confiscation of churches and synagogues, the strong opposition to the public practice of religion. The older folks still read the Torah and prayed in the privacy of someone's house, but the children learned to oppose religion in the Soviet schools.

Many older folks never made peace with the new Soviet system. But it was a double process, for the young Jewish people found themselves in a new stream of life with new opportunities. This was true in Yiddish education and culture, in Russian education, in the economy, in the government, in participation in the general life of the country.[6]

Even before I left in 1919, I felt the stirring of Yiddish language and literature. During the time I was gone, there was a terrific development of Yiddish culture in Russia. While I was visiting Stanislavchik, some of the kids from the *Yidishe shul*, the Jewish school, heard that a *dyadya*, an uncle, was visiting from the United States. They came around to recite Yiddish poetry and sing Yiddish songs for me. It was a beautiful performance, a much more developed Yiddish than I learned in my schoolboy days. They did it with much enthusiasm, with no feeling that they had to be careful. It was a product of a feeling of freedom.

It was interesting to see the change in the relations between Jew and non-Jew. It was reflected in a trial that I saw, a trial of a former neighbor who was a baker of bagels. That trial was held in a former *shul* that was now used for public functions. It was a People's

Court, where the proceedings were not based on specific application of law, but on the humanism of personal relations. There was a
panel of three judges and one of them was Jewish—something that
was impossible in Tsarist days. (At one point, that baker came
pleading to me, "If you came from America and you are traveling
with government arrangements, it means you are somebody. And if
you are somebody, you can defend me." Of course, I couldn't do
that.)

Most of the young people that I grew up with were now spread
across the Ukraine doing new kinds of work in factories and
professions. My old pal Mayer was still in Stanislavchik. He was
married to Rose, the younger sister of my pal Nokhem. Before I left
for America, she was walking six miles to Zhmerinka, there and
back daily, for higher education. Now she was a teacher in a village
school, something that was unheard of for a Jewish woman when I
was young.

Mayer had started out working at simple carpentry with his
father. In 1934 I found him the head of the bakeries in the area.
There still was limited food and flour. He held a very important
position, which reflected the confidence of the local population in
him.

Although Mayer had grown into the new Soviet system, I could
sense that something was disturbing him politically. I didn't learn
what it was, but later in the 1930's he disappeared during Stalin's
terror. This was the period when Stalin completed the elimination
of other revolutionary leaders, and not just them. Anyone whose
name was linked with opposition to Stalin, whether or not it was
true, was destroyed or exiled. A *landsman* who later came to the
United States told me that Mayer, who was a devoted servant of his
community and his people, was accused of being a Trotskyite and
disappeared one night. The same thing happened to Nisl, the son
of the cemetery caretaker, and other young people I grew up with.

During my visit to Stanislavchik in 1934, I did hear criticism
from the Jewish young people about the removal of Trotsky. He
was a national pride of the Jewish people, even if it wasn't said out
loud that way. For a Jew to be a right-hand man to Lenin in the
revolution, to lead the Red Army against the counterrevolution,
was much appreciated. You could sense a deep criticism by the
Jewish people over his removal. Open sympathy for Trotsky was

impossible, but I came across hints when I was alone with people. You didn't encourage discussion of such things.[7]

Mostly my time was packed with emotion and reminiscence. I was more inquisitive in 1963 on my second visit back to the Soviet Union. In 1934 it was sufficient to learn that the Jewish young people were in higher positions and embraced the Soviet system.

After five days in Stanislavchik, I had a few more days of rushed visits with family and friends in nearby towns. At the train station in Zhmerinka, I was met by a group of young people who were part of the retreat after our village uprising against the Ukrainian Army during the civil war. In Vinnitsa I had a chance to become acquainted with Sheba's family, whom I had met but once, right after I had fought with a Bolshevik detachment and was hiding out from another Ukrainian Army. Between Zhmerinka and Vinnitsa, my train passed near the sheep ranch my father once rented, but I knew there was nothing to see there now. I regretted then and I do up to the present that that choice flock of pedigree sheep was distributed among the peasants to be bastardized.

Then I met up again with Mayer and Rose, and we all went off to visit Nokhem in Kiev. I was not much interested in seeing the city, which I already had passed through with Comrade Bober, but I wanted to spend time with my old pals.

As we reminisced about the days of war and revolution, I learned how they convinced a Jewish official in the *shtetl* to give me an identification card to use as a passport when I was leaving for America in 1919. That official refused to issue the document without higher authority, so I stopped bothering him for it. But just before I left, Nokhem and Mayer turned up with the identification card. At our 1934 reunion they explained what happened: "We didn't do anything to him. We just took out a gun and put it on the counter. He gave us the document." We endangered our lives to defend each other throughout that period.

My friends were envious about my life in America and naturally so. From childhood they heard of America as a land where some of our townspeople became rich. They knew about the families that were sent for, the money that was sent back. They saw people from America who came back to visit Stanislavchik wearing outlandish clothes and the gold chain across the vest. They noticed my fountain pen and my piece of soap. All their experience told them that America is the place to go.

It was not just the wealth. During that visit, Nokhem said to me, "Do you remember the photograph you sent me with the message *freiheit?*" I sent him a picture of me holding the radical Jewish newspaper *Freiheit*, which means "freedom" in Yiddish, to show that I was in the left-wing struggle for freedom and democracy. Nokhem says to me, "I was envious that you were so happy with your freedom in the United States."

My stay in Kiev was full of sentiment. Finally came the moment of parting. Nokhem pulled off his shirt and gave it to me. I gave him my tie pin, which he thought was very American, and I gave Mayer a jacket. Mayer gave me his cap, which I have kept for over forty-five years now.

When I returned to Moscow, I met up with my Profintern friends and all kinds of people. Moscow was a wonderful place for political discussion. I already was politically alert and in a leadership position in the needle trades in New York, but I learned that I was still backwards. That visit to Russia, especially Moscow, was like swimming out of a river into an ocean—the ocean of international political life. The trip didn't make any basic changes in my life, but it strengthened my feeling about the struggle for building unionism and socialism.[8]

While I was in Moscow at the end of 1934, there already was talk about a new direction in the international trade union movement. Comrade Bober's comment to me about the prophet moving to the mountain reflected new ideas being discussed in the higher levels of the Communist Party and the Profintern. Even before I left, my Profintern friends said to me, "Joe, how long can there be a separate Needle Trades Workers Industrial Union competing against the ILGWU? The orientation of the world has to be towards unity for the purpose of peace and defeating fascism."

My friends urged me to remain in Moscow for the Seventh Congress of the Comintern. I was not ready to remain for a few more months, but at that congress Georgii Dimitrov delivered his famous speech dealing with the threat of fascism to world peace. He argued that despite disagreements there must be a Popular Front, a united resistance by the broad masses of people against the fascist threat.[9]

I left the Soviet Union before Georgii Dimitrov's speech, but already I felt the urgency of merging back into the main body of American labor. I fully agreed with the idea of unity to strengthen

The picture Joe sent to Nokhem with the word freiheit.

the people's fist against the onslaught of fascism in the world and the onslaught of industrialists against the growth of unionism in the United States. But the hints I got about the change that would take place started to bother me about the knitgoods industry. After our struggles to form a radical union, after our bitter fight with the dual union of the ILGWU, what was to happen?

Mayer, Nokhem, and Joe at 1934 reunion in Kiev.

7. United Front, 1935-41

*A*ll that I heard in Moscow from my Profintern friends was the forerunner of things to come. After I returned from the Soviet Union, I continued my work as organizer for the knitgoods department of the Needle Trades Workers Industrial Union (NTWIU). We were still fighting the dual union of the International Ladies Garment Workers Union (ILGWU). But within a few months, we started to feel the new orientation toward a United Front. In the trade union field, it meant giving up the radical industrial unions and merging back into the AFL, the mainstream of the American labor movement.[1]

The greater reason for unity was international developments—the growth of fascism, of nazism. In Germany and other countries, there was a complete oppression of liberal, labor, and radical movements and the start of aggression against neighboring countries. In the United States there was a growth of reactionary political organizations and strike-breaking agencies. The Soviet Union appealed for labor to unite with all other popular forces to stem the growth of fascism. At the Seventh World Congress of the Cominterm in 1935, Georgii Dimitrov gave a ringing call for unity of the people against the reactionary forces of the world. To my way of thinking, this was the most important reason for the United Front.

That international development coincided with the need for unification in the American labor movement. Roosevelt's policies encouraged a spirit of unionization among American workers, especially in basic industry, but there was a new onslaught by manufacturers against trade union organization. At this time, the left wing had separate militant trade unions, federated in the Trade Union Unity League. The TUUL made important contributions to the development of industrial trade unionism, trade union democracy, and improved conditions of work. It formed a group of experienced, devoted trade union activists. There was much quality in that organization, but our industrial unions were never more than splinters of the general labor movement in the AFL. We ran too far ahead of the majority of American workers, like a group of officers running ahead of their army, leading only the advanced group. Now it was time to join the general movement to organize the unorganized.[2]

There was a great need for unification in the needle trades. The ILGWU and the NTWIU were mainly fighting each other instead of the manufacturers. Unification was absolutely necessary if we wanted to organize the knitgoods industry and end the sweatshop conditions. Although the left wing had a different approach to trade unionism, it became obvious that we could exert more influence from within the ILGWU.[3]

Thus the question of merging with the ILGWU, of giving up the NTWIU, became the topic of discussion. It was discussed in the executive committee of the NTWIU, in the executive committees of the various departments, and then with the shop chairmen, the shop committees, and the general membership. Should we merge? Should we maintain our independence?

It was a difficult period of inner struggle in our knitgoods department. One side, especially among the rank-and-file workers in the shops, argued for continuation as an independent knitgoods workers union, even if the NTWIU dissolved. They could not forget the terrific sacrifices and hardships that went into building our knitgoods workers organization. They appreciated the democracy of our knitgoods department and the idealism that drew workers into participation. After our bitter struggle with ILGWU Local 155, a struggle we felt in our bones on the picket lines, they did not want to give up a good organization and put their heads in the yoke of the ILGWU bureaucracy.

Others argued that international and national developments demanded a change of view. They argued that the need to organize knitgoods workers and improve conditions in our trade required that we give up our own union. I believed, without wavering, that merger was the need of the times.

The discussions were full of passion. There were accusations of betraying what we fought for; there were accusations of failure to grasp the political significance of merger. The chairman of our executuve committee, J. H. Cohen, an old activist in the trade, actually cried over the idea of joining the ILGWU. But the handwriting was on the wall. Finally, the majority decided to open negotiations with ILGWU Local 155.

Since United Front was in the air, there was a growing cooperation between Communists and Lovestonites. In the needle trades it became possible for Ben Gold and Rose Wortis to sit down and negotiate with Sasha Zimmerman and other Lovestonite leaders in the ILGWU. The leader of the ILGWU Knitgoods Local 155 was a Lovestonite named Louis Nelson. He had been an extreme leftist in the men's clothing industry in the 1920's, but he split off from the left-wing movement, and he rejoined the ILGWU in 1931. It was natural for Dubinsky to use former radicals, people who were familiar with left-wing methods and phraseology, as a ram to smash the NTWIU. But Nelson was an extremist, even among the Lovestonites. He had been sharp in his fight against us on the picket lines. He had been sharp in his Red-baiting and his false charges that we were a dual union. He was sharp when we came to him for negotiations about merger.

We felt that our union was better entrenched in the knitgoods industry and that we had about equal membership with the ILGWU Local 155. But they were growing with the ILGWU, especially after the 1933 general strike, and we were the ones coming to them for merger. Nelson told us, "You are not doing this on your own free will. It's an order from above. You'll have to accept our conditions for merger."

We negotiated for an agreement like other NTWIU departments were settling upon with ILGWU locals. Our maximum demand was to come into Local 155 as an organization, not as individuals. That meant our people would be accepted as ILGWU members without new initiation fees, and it meant that we would have some leadership participation. We also wanted to continue the thirty-five hour week in the shops where we won it. And we wanted promises of no discrimination against us. That would have been a basis for real cooperation, but Nelson stuck to his guns: no concessions.

The negotiations dragged on for months with all kinds of wild public accusations and denunciations. Then came the time when all the departments of the NTWIU had made arrangements for merger into ILGWU locals, except for the fur workers and ourselves. Because the left-wing fur workers were a majority in their trade, they could hold out for a merger in which they retained majority leadership. But after the disastrous 1933 knit-goods general strike, ILGWU Local 155 had strength and momentum. We could not force Nelson to make a fair settlement. If it had been just a matter of industrial issues, we might have continued as an independent knitgoods union. But there was a change of policy on a national and an international level. Nelson's argument that we were forced to join Local 155 was essentially correct.

We finally settled on the basis of our minimum demands. Local 155 took over all our shops and contracts, but our elected shop leadership continued. They resettled our shops from thirty-five hours to thirty-six hours, while their shops remained at thirty-seven and a half hours until the agreement expired, and then they demanded thirty-six hours for the entire industry. Just before the actual merger, our shop chairmen arranged for our full-time organizers to return to work in the shops. Nelson promised no discrimination against our activists.

I suspect that even if Nelson did not accept our minimum demands, we would have merged into the ILGWU. Nelson knew we had to join the mainstream. He put up such rigid conditions because he feared our strength and the possibility we would take over Local 155. But he should have recognized our achievement, our contributions; we brought in a large group of good workers with tight organization in the shops. He should have accepted our offer of cooperation by dropping the membership fees and giving us token representation in leadership. Events proved that it would have been in the best interest of all the knitgoods workers.[4]

After the merger of the NTWIU into the ILGWU, there was a continuation of the old struggle by the left wing against the union bureaucracy. We repeated what radicals did in the ILGWU in the 1920's. We caucused in our own locals; we met separately, we discussed union matters, and we mobilized our strength to influence the union.

The knitgoods local was dominated by the caucus of the Progressive Group, which had an inner Lovestonite caucus. The opposition, the left-wing knitgoods workers, was organized in the Rank-and-File Group. Like the Progressive Group, the Rank-and-File Group had a double structure. There was a small inner

Communist caucus that would come to the larger Rank-and-File Group meetings, not with formal reports, but with proposals. There could be fifty to one hundred people at those meetings. Many of the Rank-and-File Group members were good class conscious Marxists—"non-Party Bolsheviks," as they were called at the time—who just would not accept the discipline of the Communist Party. They had their own opinions, and they fought for what they believed. No person, no organization, dominated the Rank-and-File Group. We would discuss matters until we reached agreement on the left-wing position, and then we would try to carry it out as a group in Local 155.

Our Rank-and-File Group was a vocal minority in the local. We challenged the leadership at meetings, we expressed criticism in our own bulletin, and we distributed our own leaflets when the issues were burning. We demanded that the local be more aggressive in the fight for better conditions and in the struggle to organize the unorganized. In all of this the truth was on our side.

Nelson resented the organized opposition within the local. He resented the strong criticism and he feared our support among the workers. He and his followers attacked us as agents of Stalin toeing the Comintern line; their Red-baiting surpassed anything in other locals. They misrepresented our criticism and charged us with weakening the union by undermining the leadership. They limited our participation at membership meetings and they punished us through the grievance board. Some of our activists, myself included, were suspended for months at a time on trumped-up charges. They tried to break our opposition and submerge us to complete domination by the union bureacracy.

At one point we had a conference betwen Sasha Zimmerman, Rose Wortis, and myself, to turn the energies of all the knitgoods workers to benefit the union. But Nelson was not impressed. He was a stubborn fellow. I never associated him with the corruption of being paid off by manufacturers, but he was corrupted by Dubinsky's deal to lead the knitgoods workers. There is a Jewish saying for it: "*A gemakhte makhsheyfe iz erger vi a geboyrene*, a created witch is worse than a born one." As a former left winger, Nelson forever tried to prove himself to Dubinsky. In doing that he went farther than the logic of the time to exclude us from constructive union participation.[5]

But this was the time for unity of knitgoods workers. The conditions in the industry demanded maximum pressure for the renewal of our agreement with the manufacturers. During that period New York knitgoods shops were beginning to move to different towns and states to avoid the union. The unionized manufacturers felt they were at a competitive disadvantage with the run-away shops and the New York open shops. It also was a time when the economy was turning down again. The unionized manufacturers, who had their own organization, made a harsh decision in 1936—that they would not negotiate a renewal of the unified agreement with ILGWU Local 155. They received encouragement from the large manufacturers association, which saw those organized shops as a threat to the open shop conditions that prevailed in most of the trade. The struggle to renew the agreement shaped up as a fight for the life of Local 155.

At that time John L. Lewis was starting to mobilize forces in the CIO—including the left wing—to unionize heavy industry. It was a period when political factionalism was not so sharp in the general labor movement or in the ILGWU. Under those circumstances and with the pressure of the knitgoods manufacturers' onslaught, our left-wing argument for joint effort of knitgoods workers factions finally broke through. Even then, the Lovestonite leadership in other ILGWU locals had to pressure Nelson to reach an understanding with us.

Nelson and his followers approached us with a proposal to organize a joint strike committee in the fight to renew the agreement with the manufacturers. He asked that one of our people become the general organizer for Local 155 in the New York area. We were elated. It meant we could mobilize our corps of activists to fight for the union. It brought us closer to the very idea behind our merger into the ILGWU. It was not a question of whether we would accept the offer, but of whom we would choose as organizer. Nelson said that he preferred me, but the choice was left to the Rank-and-File Group. Two names, Alex Kolkin and myself, were placed on the ballot. By a secret vote I was selected for the job.

We understood that such an appointment could not be considered permanent. It was not an elected position; an appointed person could be discharged at any moment. All the elected officials of the ILGWU had to sign an advance statement of resignation, so Dubinsky could get rid of anyone—without membership approval —if he stepped out of line. But no signature was necessary from me. It was just assumed that I could be discharged.

We accepted Nelson's offer without any strings attached. I simply wanted assurance that I could return to my job in the shop when I would be through, and I got that. But I became general organizer just as I was with my ideological baggage on my shoulders. It was a great accomplishment for our radical group.

The only problem was with Willy Shafer, who was the general organizer of Local 155 and a leader of the Red-baiting against us. Turning over the organizational department to me just before a general strike was an insult to him. Shafer was kept on as an organizer for New Jersey—he protested he was being exiled to Siberia—but his followers remained entrenched in the organizational department.

We set about preparing for a total mobilization against the knitgoods manufacturers. The union considered the strike mainly a defensive measure to renew our agreement in the organized shops. But we also considered it an offensive against the open shops—as a general strike in the entire industry. We had to see that every union shop and every union worker was prepared to strike. We had to find meeting halls and form meeting hall organizations. There had to be picket committees, programs for strike meetings, financial support for families, bail and legal help for workers who would be arrested.

It was a terrific mobilization requiring complete support. I placed every left-wing activist worth his salt on the committees already prepared by the union administration. We fully participated in that big diversified strike machine.

When the strike time approached, the union called a general membership meeting in the middle of the day. When you called a meeting after work, even in an emergency, a good proportion of workers would go home to their families. We stopped the shops at three o'clock. Each shop chairman was responsible to see that his shop traveled in a group to the meeting. We warned that it was a preparation for battle. Nobody drops out!

It was a dramatic gathering of the knitgoods trade unionists of New York. For a strike mobilization meeting, if the hall is larger than the attendance and there are empty seats, it dampens the spirit of the people. When you pack a hall, there is greater enthusiasm, especially when it is a mobilizing meeting for the very existence of the union. Cooper Union Hall was packed to the rafters that afternoon. People had to listen from outside that large auditorium.

The national leadership of the ILGWU, including Dubinsky, was up on the platform. Thomas McMahon from the United Textile Workers Union and other labor leaders were there. Every speaker promised complete organizational and financial support. Of course, there was quite a bit of exaggeration, but it helped to create solidarity and militancy. That meeting was a declaration of war against the oppressive measures of the manufacturers. It was a rising demonstration of support for the union at a time of crisis.

I was up on the platform too. At that historic meeting Nelson announced my appointment to lead the organizational department. It symbolized that we would stop bickering and we would turn our united strength against the manufacturers. The response was enormous. It was an outpouring of applause, an emotional demonstration of support for the union.

It was a moment of victory, not only for myself, but for our entire radical group. We put in years of work to organize the knitgoods workers. It was not long before that some of us were suspended from the union by Nelson's grievance board. Suddenly, I was the person they gave organizational responsibility for the general strike. It was a prestige that I never experienced before. It was a historic moment for the development of trade unionism in the knitgoods industry.

We called the strike in a couple of weeks. We kept the strike time a secret, so the manufacturers would be in a state of uncertainty. On the designated day, the workers came into the shops and began working. At mid-morning our shop chairmen gave the order to pull the power switch and walk out of the shops. Each shop group was responsible to see that all its people participated in strike activities instead of going home. Over eight thousand strikers reported to the strike halls in Manhattan, East New York, Brooklyn, the Bronx, and New Jersey.

At the strike halls we designated workers to picket their own shops in shifts all day. In shops where all the workers struck and it would take less effort to force a settlement, we could assign some of those workers to other picket lines. We needed larger numbers on the picket lines at open shops. We issued our strike call to the entire industry, but, as we expected, only small groups of workers from the open shops came to the strike halls.

On the picket lines, we faced hired gangsters and private police from the strike-breaking agencies. The worst conflicts were at the big open shops, where larger blocs of people remained working. Brooklyn, with its reactionary chamber of commerce, was a haven for open shops. It was the hardest area to tackle, and I spent much of my time there during the strike. We met the situation through large mobilizations of our special union defense committee. The gangsters and the hired police and the scabs were not very brave when they faced hundreds of militant workers on a picket line. The greater the number of pickets the easier to close the shop.

We used these tactics at the New York Knitting Mills, a large shop with a stubborn owner. It was in an area close to Tenth Avenue, where the farm produce was brought in to the markets. That neighborhood was tough. It was packed with racketeers, who were hired by the manufacturers during the strike. Those gangsters would pack their limousines with scabs, drive up to the shop, and form a tunnel for the scabs to reach the entrance. The police in that area were tough too, and they helped the gangsters chase us away.

We mobilized the union defense committee. We had several hundred workers who were tested in struggles on the picket lines. We told them to bring heavy tools for defensive purposes. That morning, when the gangsters started to push through the picket line with the scabs, some of those tools ended up smashing windows. In the confusion of falling glass, with everyone running for protection, we chased away the scabs.

In the skirmish on the picket line that morning, I almost became the victim. There was a knitter in that shop whom many of us worked with in different shops over the years. He was part of the craft, working together with other knitters, helping on the job, sharing food at lunchtime. And here that knitter was scabbing! He would come to the strike hall in the morning, leave secretly, and sneak into the shop through another building. He was seen scabbing by a union conscious worker we left inside that shop to report what was happening.

We discussed what to do about Frank. We could send a committee to meet him at his home, as was done with some scabs, to influence him. But in this case I went to see the guy by myself. I traveled up to the Bronx and faced him with the fact that he was betraying the other workers. I reasoned with his wife and children, showing the fallacy of his working against the long-range interests of the family. He promised not to scab anymore.

The next day he came with the gangsters right out in the open! Since it was known that he was scabbing, Frank did not have to hide himself anymore. Not only did I not convince him, but he started to scab openly!

That was the morning of the skirmish on the picket line. Even before the gangsters and the scabs arrived, we were picketing back and forth in front of the building, shouting slogans and singing songs. The police, knowing that a conflict was approaching, picked out the leaders on the picket line. I was arrested and held in the hallway entrance to the shop.

I was standing in that entrance when the scabs and the gangsters arrived. There they came and there was that scab Frank with them! I do not consider myself a fighter. Politically, yes; physically, no. But my anger was so aroused I could not hold back! When that scab came by, surrounded by gangsters and the police, with glass falling around us, I swung at him with all my might. We both went down with gangsters and police on top of us.

The pickets came to my rescue, especially the girls. They dared more, expecting to be treated less rough than the men. One of my best friends on the organizational committee, a class conscious working girl, Irene Mason, started to pull me away by the tie! She almost choked me to death! I told her later, "If I have such friends, who needs the gangsters?"

We were arrested. The most militant—those who are in the forefront and give direction—were always arrested, and in the process we were not so gently handled. But from the picket line to the police station, we sang our militant songs. We had a spirit of courage, a feeling of victory, even though we had to go through the fight and arrest. We were out of jail the next morning and back on the picket line. And when the strike ended, the New York Knitting Mills settled with the union.

I was arrested several times during the strike, and so were others from the Rank-and-File Group. There was one case when I was arrested together with Nelson. We were accused of kidnapping scabs!

There was a large textile trimming shop, the Hornick Knitting Mills with a good group on strike and a substantial number still working. Gangsters were meeting the scabs early in the morning at a different location and then escorting them to the shop. We got the information from a union person we kept working there. We knew the gangsters came to that spot early, parked their cars, and went in for coffee as the workers gathered.

We prepared a surprise! We drove over in several cars to that spot at their meeting time. While the gangsters were drinking coffee, we encouraged those scabs, gently but firmly, to come into our cars. We took them to the strike hall for a meeting with some of the strikers from their shop. Some of us went back to the picket line at that shop. The gangsters came, all riled up, and a fight took place. Of course, we were arrested.

Five of us were charged with kidnapping those scabs. There were front page reports in the New York newspapers: "Workers Kidnapped by Union." It seemed like a serious thing at the time. Our lawyer, a well known criminal attorney named Samuel Leibowitz, asked Dubinsky to appear as a character witness at the grand jury investigation following the strike.

The press was interested in the case, and when Dubinsky came to court, they asked him questions: "Are you going to appear as a character witness for Nelson?"

"Yes."

"Are you going to appear as a character witness for Rapoport?"

He hesitated for a moment—the ideological differences were there and the newspapers were Red-baiting the ILGWU during the strike. So he says, "I'll do what the lawyer advises me."

He did testify for me. That case dragged on for a long time before the charges were dropped.

The strike was mostly the routine work of keeping up the mobilization and maintaining militancy. The manufacturers association continued to oppose a union agreement. Some of us had the feeling that we could break the association's unity by signing agreements with individual manufacturers who would accept our conditions. Others warned that if we sent workers back to the shops we would weaken the picket lines. But we did begin to settle with individual manufacturers, and some of them agreed to permit the workers to start late and leave early, so they could help on the picket lines at the striking shops.

That helped bring about a settlement with the smaller organization of unionized manufacturers. We did not organize many new shops during the strike, but we did force the unionized manufacturers to renegotiate the agreement and remain with the union. At the union meetings after the strike, some people questioned whether there was a victory when only a few new shops were organized. I expected that unfriendly attitude from Shafer, whom I replaced as general organizer, but some of the left-wing activists in the Rank-and-File Group took a similar position.

I looked upon the settlement as a victory. Before the strike the manufacturers association refused to deal with the union at all. It tried to smash Local 155 and it failed. I never liked to exaggerate accomplishment; to my way of thinking it placed you in a defensive position. But that nitpicking by left-wing activists over whether the strike was a victory minimized our contributions to the gains that were won. That strike broke the resistance of the manufacturers to the union. There was struggle ahead, but it always was to strengthen the union. That 1936 general strike insured the union was here to stay.[6]

I continued my work as general organizer after the strike. That's when we sharpened our attack against run-away shops. Whenever there was a rumor that trucks were coming for a shop's machinery in the middle of the night, or when workers were told not to come in the following day, we placed a guard to watch and follow. Then we went after that shop in the new location.

We went after run-away shops with the workers who lost their jobs. We would not go direct to the manufacturer. First we would visit the churches, talk to the newspaper, even see the chamber of commerce. We would explain that we did not come as enemies, but that we needed their understanding. Then we'd go to the manufacturer. Sometimes we forced the shops back to New York, and sometimes we organized the shops where they moved.

Usually, the manufacturer had to move back to New York anyhow for the supply of skilled workers and to be close to the market.

The general strike was in the New York area only, but it echoed in other places where there was a movement for unionization of knitgoods workers. Soon after our strike the general organizer for Philadelphia came into New York to get approval for a general strike. Dubinsky called in Nelson and myself for consultation. Nelson sympathized and promised help. I expressed another opinion: "General strike? Of course. But not now. Go back, organize more groups, organize a shop here and there. A general strike is the easy decision, but it is not certain to be effective under the best of circumstances. Preparatory work is as essential as plowing in order to have results. Strengthen your roots."

Dubinsky shared this view. He said, "We have more at stake than losing a strike. It's the prestige of the national office. And if it is not done right, it will be much harder to pick up the pieces."

Soon after the strike, we in the Rank-and-File Group clashed again with Nelson and the ILGWU leadership. Our break with Nelson began over support for the CIO. In the very early days of the CIO, the Lovestone group opposed John L. Lewis's policy of separating from the AFL to organize industrial unions in basic industry. When the CIO was expelled from the AFL and when the ILGWU went along with the CIO, the Lovestonites changed their position. Only Nelson continued to denounce John L. Lewis and opposed the knitgoods workers joining the CIO.

Because of that, the Lovestonites in Local 155 decided to oppose Nelson as manager in the coming election. The Rank-and-File Group supported the CIO, so some of those Lovestonites approached us to nominate a joint slate and get rid of Nelson.[7] We hesitated to become involved in their maneuvering, but we accepted their offer with the hope to get rid of Nelson as the greater evil. Instead, Nelson packed the caucus meeting of the Progressive Group, took it over, and won the nomination. It was real Tammany Hall tactics. Then he was clever enough to let them keep their union jobs and support him for reelection.

After that, Nelson resumed his policy of Red-baiting the Rank-and-File Group. With the general strike over and the contract signed, he no longer needed the United Front and he turned on us. And so, in the left-wing tradition, our Rank-and-File Group selected

an election slate and came out as an opposition again. I was
nominated to run for manager of the local against Nelson.

When I came to work the day after we began distributing
election literature, I found my name wiped off the glass door of my
office. Shafer's name was on it. I went to Nelson and told him,
"Louis, I expected to be fired from my appointed job as soon as my
name appeared on the slate of the Rank-and-File Group. But to
arrive in the morning and find my name erased! It is not fitting."

I was ready to return to the shop from the moment I took that
appointed position as general organizer. I never was attracted to
Dubinsky's and Nelson's *shmaltstop*, lardbucket. I never was
impressed by maintaining a full-time organizational position with
all its prestige and economic benefits. My happiest days were
working in the shop and participating in union activities as a
volunteer. I had no hesitation about returning to that, but I was not
happy about starting up the old clash of the left wing against
Nelson, the Progressive Group, and the ILGWU bureaucracy.

I did not have a theory about it. I had a feeling ... the same
feeling I had when I fought for merger and unified effort among
the knitgoods workers. The cooperation during the 1936 general
strike was the very reason for the merger—to strengthen the
workers against the manufacturers. Resuming the factional fight
was not in that spirit.

However, we were placed in a position where we had to resume
our oppositional activities. Without hesitation, I carried through
the decision to run on a separate slate and return to my job in the
shop. We lost the election, and we continued our old fight against
the union administration.

In the months and years that followed, our Rank-and-File Group
criticized every weakness we could find in the knitgoods union ...
weaknesses which existed of necessity in a new union. We charged
that the leadership did not make good enough settlements with
the manufacturers, that it did not do enough to organize the entire
trade, that it did not give enough help to unemployed workers,
that it was not competent. We published our own union bulletin,
issued our own leaflets, and mobilized knitgoods workers outside
official union meetings. We became a permanent opposition group
within the union.

Was it right? Was it in the spirit of Georgii Dimitrov's call for unity against the forces of reaction? Was it in the spirit of the knitgoods workers merger? Was it effective? The average worker was not sympathetic. Even if he thought we were an honest bunch fighting for improvement, he did not want to join this kind of opposition. The workers felt it was not constructive to meet outside union channels and constantly attack the leadership.

Today I question those oppositional tactics, but at the time it seemed like we had no alternative. Instead of an open discussion of issues, the administration answered our criticisms with a murderous Red-baiting attack. They charged us with undermining the leadership and splitting the union on orders from Moscow. Nelson and his supporters forever warned the membership that communism was a danger to world humanity. Maybe some of their arguments about "bloody Stalin" were correct, but it had nothing to do with the problems of the knitgoods workers. When the leadership attacked like that, there was nothing we could do but hit back as hard as we could.

Nelson was wild in his public statements, unpredictable and egotistical in his behavior. But he was no fool. He was dancing to the music of Dubinsky, giving up his old radical conceptions to be accepted in the ILGWU bureaucracy, as did Sasha Zimmerman and others. Dubinsky made him a vice president of the ILGWU, with all the financial rewards, but it was never financial corruption with Nelson; it was power and prestige that he cherished. He couldn't tolerate our independence, and he was determined to break our resistance. But at the same time he used our opposition to insure his own position of leadership. A friend once told me, "Joe, don't you see that by hammering away at the leaders, you are strengthening them?"

As we criticized over the years, the union grew and our Rank-and-File Group dwindled. The workers felt—and historically they were proved correct—that the union was steadily strengthening. After the 1936 general strike, the New York manufacturers gave up resistance to union recognition and collective bargaining. With each yearly settlement came an improvement, a *small* improvement, but improvement it was. The knitgoods union spread out nationally, and the ILGWU offered benefits like medical care, a theater show at low cost, a weekend at the ILGWU summer camp.

While the knitgoods union moved ahead, we, the vanguard,

ALL OUT TO VOTE!

on
Thursday
March
23rd

· JOE RAPOPORT
For Manager

J. H. COHEN
For President

For an administration that will build the Union;

That will enforce conditions and defend your interests in the shops;

That will keep the jobbers responsible for uniform union conditions in the shops;

That will give full democratic expression to the membership;

That will aid the unemployed.

FOR BUSINESS AGENTS

ALEX KALKIN   IRENE MASON   SOL REEVE

ELECT THE RANK AND FILE SLATE

Joe heads the Rank-and-File Group slate in opposition to the union leadership after the 1936 general strike.

remained in the rear repeating the same old criticisms. Within
time there was less chance for us to do that. The elections in our
local were called every two years instead of every year. Union
meetings were called every few months instead of once a month.
Nelson further limited our participation at meetings, allowing the
Rank-and-File Group only one short speech on an issue, and the
ILGWU prohibited day-to-day caucus opposition. There was less
discussion of issues as union business became more routine.

When we did offer to help out the leadership—to join a picket
line, for example—the reply was, "We are doing fine, thank you." If
one was a cynic he said, "You had your chance in the 1936 general
strike." But that was not said in public, because it would have given
us credit for helping to save the union. They were pushing us off
the historical record.

I worked at the Tudor Knitting Mills for most of those years after
the 1936 general strike. How I got that job is an interesting story.
Before the union was established, I always had a hard time finding
work because of my participation in the fight for trade unionism. I
would not be hired, or I would be fired after a short time, when
the boss connected my name with the blacklist. With the establishment of the union, however, you could find a job by putting your
name on the union list of unemployed. That is what I did after I
was released as union organizer, after I was laid off from the shop
where I returned to work. And once again I found myself
blacklisted. I was tipped off that people who registered on the
unemployed list after me were being sent out for jobs before me. I
complained, but there always was some explanation and no job.

The workers in the trade knew that I was looking for work.
Some old time knitters in the Tudor Knitting Mills checked with
the boss to see if there was need for another knitter. All the
machines of the shop were working, but the boss agreed to pick up
a man with his own knitting machine.

This was an old practice in the trade. Some knitters used to own
knitting machines, which they brought to the shop when they got a
job. It helped them find work—they would advertise themselves in
the *Morgn Zhurnal.* One of the fights of the knitters, and of the
needle trades generally, was to abolish this practice. So I went to
Nelson, explained that it was against my principles to peddle

myself with a machine, but that the office wasn't finding me a job and here was a chance. He allowed it.

I did not own a machine, but the workers of the Tudor Knitting Mills knew a small manufacturer who had been a hand knitter, and who now had an extra machine in his shop. He was no friend of mine—I had been instrumental in organizing his shop—but he had a feeling for union tradition and did lend my friends the machine.

Those workers did not tell the boss who was coming for the job. When the foreman saw me walk in as the new knitter, he almost had a *conniption*! That foreman once worked in a shop where I organized a strike. There was an unwritten law that the foreman could cross the picket line into a striking shop because he was not a worker, but when he started working on a machine during a strike then he was scabbing. That foreman scabbed, and he was treated like a scab. He blamed me.

The manufacturer did give me a chance to work. That first day the foreman actually sabotaged my production by giving me weak yarns, which kept breaking on the machine, and by setting the machine wrong. In all my years as a knitter, I never was fired because of lack of quality in my work. At the end of the day, I told the boss what happened. I said, "I understand your feeling about me coming to work in your shop, but it is not right to fire me without a fair chance at doing a day's work."

He gave me another chance, and I remained working there for years. In fact, I became chairman of the shop. The first day the foreman and the boss were afraid that with me in the shop, there would be strict enforcement of the union agreement over prices and hours. And I was strict as shop chairman! But never did I forget that an agreement, whether it is a written contract or an unwritten tradition, must be lived up to by both sides.

The shop chairman or chairlady was responsible for enforcing union conditions in the shop. In a union shop, a worker could not be fired just for complaining, but complaining did not necessarily mean anything would be done. At times the ILGWU representatives would gloss over a complaint. So the protection for the workers in a shop came from a good shop chairman and a good shop committee.

Even under the best union conditions, there were all kinds of ways a foreman could manipulate workers against each other. This is where you knew the quality of the workers in a shop. You may talk socialism, you may talk communism, you may talk revolution ... but do you grab the better work order? Do you complain that the way the foreman is feeding you the best orders is not the union way? How do you divide the work between seasons, when the shop is not working at full force? This is where your mettle as a worker and as a person was tested. This is where a good shop chairman would settle the matter at lunchtime between union conscious workers. The more solidarity among the workers, the better the conditions of work in the shop.

We had an interesting case at the Tudor Knitting Mills. There was a small, white-haired old man with a long white beard like from the Old Country. Mendel was the slowest producer in the shop. On top of that, he was a religious man who went to *shul* every morning. He tried to come to work on time, but often he had a *shnaps* after prayer and came late. His production was half that of the next slowest worker in the shop.

There was grumbling on the part of the manufacturer against Mendel, but the other workers sort of protected him. We complained to the union, and finally I asked permission from the union for Sam Steinhart, myself, and the other knitters to put in half an hour on Mendel's machine at lunchtime. The union generally insisted that the hours of rest should not be cheated on, but we got that permission. For years we helped boost Mendel's production at lunchtime.

So when it came to choosing a chairman, the workers of a shop wanted somebody who would serve their best interests. Even though the Lovestonites won the general knitgoods union elections, we of the Rank-and-File Group gave leadership in many shops. The administration did not like it. They repeatedly tried to get rid of me as shop chairman. But in my shop there was a group of old-time knitters who would not let anybody—the boss, the union bureaucracy, the shop chairman—get away with anything they considered wrong. Time and again they reelected me shop chairman, and so it was with the other Rank-and-File Group shop chairmen. We were known as a group who served the best interests of the people.

It was as shop chairmen, in the monthly meetings of all the shop

Sam Steinhart, Mendel, and Joe posed for this picture on the roof of the Tudor Knitting Mills.

chairmen, that we in the Rank-and-File Group tried to exert some influence over the years. The meetings were small and we had more chance to talk, to win concessions. But we never broke through the wall of isolation that Nelson built around us in Local 155.

Looking back today, I wonder if our radical group could have participated in the struggles and acknowledged the accomplishments of Local 155, even while we disagreed with the leadership and advanced better positions. Even under the reactionary leadership of the AFL, from Gompers to the present, workers have fought the bosses for trade unions, for higher wages, for better working conditions. That historic conflict has been a class struggle, even if it has not always been expressed as a politically conscious socialist movement. It has been a training ground for political consciousness of the workers. It has been a struggle for improvement which has demanded participation by the radicals.

Was there room for us during the 1930's? In the CIO, in the organizing of the unorganized, ideological diferences were put aside to establish labor unity against the corporations. John L. Lewis, a fierce Red-baiter from way back, opened the door for all political elements to help organize basic industry. He recognized left-wing organizers as militant people with ability, stamina, and honesty. We participated. We contributed. That outburst of organization was and still is the greatest accomplishment in the history of American labor.

Today, young left-wing historians and activists are charging that we forgot our purpose, that we did not advance the goal of socialism at the time. They charge that we were too much fighting for immediate improvements, that we were too much in support of John L. Lewis and Franklin Roosevelt. It is easy to look back and be superrevolutionary. There is a Yiddish expression for such people: *frazn-shiser*, phrase-shooter. They use revolutionary rhetoric that is not based on reality.[8]

I do accept the criticism that in our conception of socialism we looked too much to the Soviet Union. We forever glorified the accomplishments of Russian communism—the full employment, the new housing, the improvement of food and clothing. We defended the Soviet Union against all charges. Stalin's destruction of the old Bolshevik leadership was disturbing—it never set well

with many of us—but we did not express our doubts in public.
There were reports of mass murder committed by Stalin, but how
could we believe the lying capitalist press, the enemy of socialism?
We glorified the Soviet Union, right or wrong. That kept us too
isolated in America, too much a sect.

Nevertheless, our policies and actions reflected the realities of
American life. It is true that the Soviet Union called for Popular
Front, for cooperation of the left wing with all antifascist forces.
But when the charge is made that the radical movement did not
place socialism on the agenda in America, the question must be
asked, was the 1930's a revolutionary period? True, the capitalist
system got a terrific jolt, there were cracks, but there still was
plenty of power to patch it up. There was great suffering, there was
great confusion and anger, but the workers were not yet ready to
accept socialism as a solution. The country had the juice to bounce
back, and it was not because of Roosevelt alone. The rank-and-file
workers and the trade union leadership supported Roosevelt, who
opened the door to trade union organization, while big business
fought his reforms. Radicals had to join that struggle on the side of
workers and reform.

For the left wing it was a question of building a Popular Front to
fight the evils of the depression—the unemployment, the evictions, the hunger, the lack of security, the weak trade union
organization. The Popular Front position, the position set out by
Georgii Dimitrov, was not to weaken the fight for socialism, but
rather to provide a broad popular base for the defeat of reaction
and the advance of socialism. The radical movement did put forth
the idea of socialism, but we could not go too far without
destroying the accomplishments of coalition. We were able to
push things to the left, to help build unions, to win improvements
and greater security, to make the trade union leadership more
responsive to the rank and file. But anyone who thinks that John L.
Lewis would have tolerated a Communist opposition movement
within the CIO is living under an illusion.

There were some superrevolutionary groups that aggressively
came out for socialism at the time, but they did nothing else. I
knew a knitter who was a member of the Socialist Labor Party.
When I organized a strike at his shop, he denounced me as a traitor
to the working class. "You are fighting for another dollar, for an

hour less of work," he said. "You create illusions that the workers can win reform. You are dulling the political consciousness of the working class."

But the value of the struggle in those days was in doing something for the people . . . in improving conditions. How could you advocate socialism as the answer for people whose furniture and children were put onto the sidewalk on a winter day? You didn't talk socialism; you moved that family back into the apartment! How could you fill the "shrunken bellies" with "pie in the sky"? The promise of socialism tomorrow with no fight for improvement today is just that—"pie in the sky."[9]

8. "Evreiskii Vopros," The Jewish Question

*I*t is difficult for today's young people to understand the idealism of radicals in the 1930's. We took seriously the idea of changing the world. We believed in the dream of socialism. As a matter of fact, some radicals had a timetable for when to expect the destruction of capitalism and the building of socialism. I expected to see socialism in America in my lifetime.

For some of us, it was not enough just to contribute our time and money to the radical movement. We also imposed upon ourselves a taboo against raising children. It was a question of giving our full attention and resources to the movement ... of being prepared to face the blacklist, arrest, and persecution. These were the reasons for our imposed control for many years. Later, when it became clear that our timetable for revolution did not go according to schedule ... when times improved and we had a chance for a more solid income ... by that time it was too late for many of us to have children.[1]

The devotion of radicals at that time went farther than just theoretical ideas. My own contribution to the building of socialism was as a trade union activist. I was accustomed to mobilizing, to organizing, to participating in the struggle to build trade unions. But with Nelson's iron control over Local 155, with the isolation of our Rank-and-File Group, I had to face the question of what else to do.

I never was one to wait for the Messiah. I became more involved in political activities of the radical movement and in support work for other striking workers. If something came up I did my share. My life was full, but I did have time on my hands.

During those years, Sheba and I traveled more than before. We would take a weekend trip to the mountains of New York or to one of the summer camps of the left-wing movement. We dipped more deeply into the cultural life of New York. Sheba did not share my taste for the classical Yiddish theater, but we would go to the symphony, the opera, the classical ballet, and expressionist dance. I even read more during those years. I liked the poetry of Walt Whitman, the historical novels of Howard Fast, the short stories of Mike Gold. We led an active social and cultural life.

Sheba worked at different office jobs through the 1920's. She never had trouble finding work. As a skilled worker, I earned higher wages, but she did not suffer the interruption of seasonal employment. In 1930 she got a job with the Fur Dressers and Dyers Union, which she stayed with for years. She developed and administered their medical insurance program. She started from scratch and became a real expert.

With both of us able to work and with no children to support, we never were desperate about running out of money during the depression, even when I worked for pennies as a full time NTWIU organizer. For economy reasons, however, we were forced to share unheated low rent apartments with others through the 1930's. Sometimes we lived with people from the knitgoods industry, sometimes we lived with office workers Sheba met, sometimes it was strangers. We preferred the privacy of having our own place, but we adapted our living arrangements as economic conditions demanded. In almost every place we stayed, we became lifelong friends with the other people.

The best arrangement was a house we shared with two other families, including the Rabinoffs, whom we knew from our year in Los Angeles. Each family had its own little apartment in that big house. We shared the big kitchen and the living room. We shared the shopping, a lot of the cooking, and the cleaning. It was a communal sort of life. We lived together, we ate together, we socialized together. We shared a lot of good times. Of course, there were conflicts, but it was the conflicts of a family.

In those years, purely by accident, Sheba and I started building a country bungalow. During the war, when I worked with the Jewish Council for Russian War Relief, I once went on a fund raising visit to a Jewish left-wing colony in upstate New York. There were fifty families who had built their own bungalows on one acre parcels in that Golden's Bridge Colony. Those homes would have been the pride of any middle-class community. They had their own elected administration to take care of roads, water, use of the lake, and building regulations. There was a social hall where they had all kinds of concerts, lectures, and parties. On the weekends and during the summers, when the people would take a vacation from the city, there was a bubbling social and cultural life in that community.

I met there people I knew from the knitgoods trade. One of them, Ben Fenster, took me to see the home he built. He said, "Joe, do you see that lot across the street? Why not buy it and build a bungalow for yourself? The people here will show you how to cut a board and drive a nail."

Sheba and I accumulated some savings during the war, so we did buy that lot and start building a bungalow. This in itself was quite a story. We had to design the structure, the plumbing, the electricity, everything. After we got permission from the county, we began building. First, it was cement piers and joists for the base—it was a new language I was learning! Then it was a floor, walls, a ceiling . . . a room one summer, another room the next summer. I had help from my brothers Morris and Herman, who were excellent mechanics. All kinds of friends participated—some were a great help, some were a real nuisance. We had a hell of a good time.

For years we worked at that bungalow on the weekends. After a couple of days at that hard labor, I would come back to rest at my knitting machine on Monday. It was much lighter work in the shop, but I preferred the heavy construction work outdoors on our own bungalow. We appreciated the skills we developed with tools, and we were proud of how the bungalow turned into a good looking place.

My participation with the Jewish Council for Russian War Relief, which led me to that Golden's Bridge Colony, began during World War II. It opened up a whole new field of activity. It involved me in the special problems of Jewish radicals working with the general American Jewish population. At that time, our Jewish radical movement was separate from the general Jewish population. We were aloof from the real problems of the Jewish people in the world. All of this came up in my wartime relief work, and especially after the war when there was the question of establishing a Jewish state in Palestine.

One great problem for the American Jewish radical movement was our historic opposition to Zionism. In the 1930's Israel was still only a hope, but that hope was raised in the years following World War I. On my way to America in 1920, I met up with many young Jewish refugees who were going to *Eretz Yisroel*, the Land of Israel. After the devastating pogroms during the war and revolution, after the insult of anti-Semitic attack, they had a strong feeling about building a new Jewish life. They were encouraged during World War I by the Balfour Declaration, which promised a Jewish homeland in Palestine. Of course, the British spoke out of both sides of their mouths—promising a homeland to the Jews and the Arabs in the same place—but the promise vibrated among the Jewish people. There was a new influx of Jewish settlers in Palestine. They were not the older folks coming to pray, to live and die near the Western Wall of the Temple. It was healthy idealistic young Zionists who were determined to build a new country.[2]

We in the radical movement considered Zionism a bourgeois nationalist movement. We believed the Zionists gave up the fight for a better Jewish life in the Diaspora. Zionism was not a call for Jewish participation in the class struggles where Jewish people lived. The Zionists wanted the Jewish people to separate themselves and establish a Jewish nation. We considered that counterrevolutionary.

The Jewish radical believed that the Jewish question—*Evreiskii Vopros*, as Lenin called it—could be solved only through the establishment of socialism. We thought anti-Semitism would end only in a socialist society where there was no competition for property and where no religious poison was spread. We saw that salvation on the horizon in Russia.

The American radical movement glorified the development of Jewish life in the Soviet Union. When I visited Russia in 1934, I saw how my old friends found new opportunities, how Yiddish culture blossomed, how there was fraternity between Jewish and non-Jewish people. The establishment of a Soviet Jewish homeland in the Siberian province Birobidzhan, which I read about all through the 1930's, suited our feeling of the need for a territorial solution to the Jewish problem. It was with pride that we pointed out how Jewish life could be improved and Jewish culture could be developed not just by selling another herring in the marketplace.

The Soviet Union was living proof to us that under socialism the Jewish question could be solved.

The general American Jewish population, however, looked at the Soviet Union like the older people in Stanislavchik. They saw a proletarian dictatorship which made an undemocratic attack on the private property and livelihood of the Jewish people. After the Jewish people stayed with their religion for over two thousand years, spread among the nations of the world, along came the Soviet Union and abolished religion with the stroke of a pen. The American Jew would not accept it.

To a certain extent, these political differences were based on class divisions among American Jews. The Jewish middle classes and those who aspired to the middle classes were antagonistic towards Jewish radicalism. They knew there was a Jewish problem in the United States. Jewish people had to fight for jobs in heavy industry, on the subway, in government and big business. Jewish people were banned from all kinds of restaurants and hotels. The Christian people considered us strange and kept their distance. Sometimes they were outright unfriendly. Here too there was anti-Semitism. But the radical argument that the American Jewish people needed socialism did not sit well with the Jewish middle classes. They wanted to be accepted in the American system, not to fight the injustices.

Although I participated in the radical movement and believed in the socialist solution to the Jewish problem, I never closed off contact with the general Jewish population. Quite the contrary. When I first came to America and met up with *landslayt* who came to hear about Stanislavchik, I asked why they only met on a special occasion like my arrival. I suggested they start a club. I forgot about that suggestion, but within time they organized the Stanislavchik Podolskaia Guberniia Society. Even though it was middle class and Zionist oriented, from time to time, I came to meetings and clarified the radical position on various Jewish issues. In that *landsmanshaft* I was introduced as the grandson of Alter Khaskel and they would say, "Yosl was the first to suggest organizing the Stanislavchik Podolskaia Guberniia Society."

My participation in that society was unusual. In the 1920's and 1930's the radical Jew did not associate with his own *landslayt*. We joined the International Workers Order, the fraternal organization of the Jewish radical movement, with its own *landsman-shaftn* branches. We had our own cultural events, our own weekend outings, our own insurance programs. We even had our own cemeteries. We separated ourselves and deepened the division between the radical Jew and the rest of the Jewish populaton.[3]

That division became open conflict with the development of world events. There was one incident in 1929—riots in Palestine—which badly shook the left-wing Jewish movement. Our newspaper *Freiheit* first reported Arab pogroms against the Jewish settlers; the next day it changed positions and reported the riots as a revolutionary Arab attack on British and Zionist imperialism. I accepted the second report, but several well-known left-wing writers quit the *Freiheit* in protest of that insulting reversal. Right-wing Jews denounced American Jewish Communists for following the Comintern line and siding with the murderers of the Jewish people. That incident stays with me, because it was thrown back at us time and again over the years. The criticism was justified.[4]

Our position improved in the 1930's, when the Soviet Union appealed to the Western democracies for an alliance against fascism. During those years the United States recognized the Soviet Union, and there was growing contact between the two countries. But the American people, especially the Jewish people, were terribly upset in 1939, when the Soviet Union made a nonaggression pact with Hitler. This was at a time when Jewish life was destroyed wherever Hitler went. Again people of vision and ability defected from our movement. The Jewish right wing denounced us and even demonstrated against us. There were convulsions right in the knitgoods shops—Nelson was calling us "Communazis"—we hit a new low in the next union election. People were emotional ... scared ... indignant. The day after the pact was announced at noontime, I found my brother Morris at the door of my shop: "Joe, what happened?"

I took a positive position toward that pact, just as I did when the Soviet Union attacked Finland's Mannerheim Line to protect its border against aggression. There was a threat that Hitler was ready to turn his guns against the Soviet Union. The Western capitalist powers encouraged him to head east. More time was needed to prepare for the onslaught. The way I saw it, the pact, that extra time, would help the Soviet Union bring about the downfall of Hitler.

During the period of the pact, the American radical movement almost completely lost its independent identity. When war broke out between England and Germany, the Soviet Union tried to remain neutral. It adopted the position that the conflict was between two imperialist systems. When the United States prepared ships for aid to the English, while England was being pounded by the Nazi war machine, the Communist Party argued against the risk of American military involvement by giving aid to British imperialism. American radicals actually picketed the harbor where those ships were prepared!

I thought that position was cynical. Even though the Soviet Union had to protect its national interests by making a pact with the Nazis, American radicals did not have to take the exact same position. I still accepted the analysis of Georgii Dimitrov, who distinguished fascism as the most aggressive form of imperialism and called for Popular Front coalitions to fight it. I thought there was a hell of a difference between English imperialism and German fascism.

When the knitgoods workers met to discuss this question and one of my comrades gave the Communist Party line, I felt so strongly opposed that I asked for the floor to explain my views. Such public ideological disagreement could be a costly step, because you could find yourself outside the ranks of the radical group. But I did not learn the consequences of public disagreement, because Nelson said the Rank-and-File Group spokesman already advanced our position. When I insisted that I had an independent view, he threatened to call me before the grievance board. My friends pulled me down, and I didn't get to speak my mind publicly.[5]

There were other times when we should have been more independent of the Soviet Union. One that I never forgot was the case of Alter and Ehrlich, two Polish Jewish Bundist leaders, refugees from Poland, who were accused as anti-Soviet spies during the war. They were labor leaders, people of the sort who would speak up for democracy against Stalin's oppression. They were executed in 1943.

When Nelson held a meeting to condemn the executions, the Rank-and-File Group called upon me to defend the Soviet Union. I publicly justified those executions as punishment for anti-Soviet conspiracy. I was followed by "Duke" DeLeo, an Italian business agent, who got up and accused *me* of delivering an anti-Semitic speech! At that meeting I was hit hard, the hardest ever as a member of the opposition.

The atmosphere of that meeting penetrated something in me that I was uneasy about. Usually, when I was denounced by the union administration, I felt it was part of my struggle. After such a meeting, the workers going out would surround me, one would shake my hand, another would touch my shoulder in support. But it did not happen after that meeting. I felt that maybe my accusation was not justified.

As time passed in the 1950's, I always checked to learn if Alter and Ehrlich were innocent victims of Stalin's brutality. After Khrushchev came to power, they were expected to be vindicated, but nothing was heard. I never felt too good about my 1943 condemnation speech, up to the present. I made a wrong statement; I came to the defense of the Soviet Union right or wrong. It doesn't sit good with me now, and it did not sit good with the knit-goods workers then.[6]

After Germany attacked Russia, after the Soviet Union came forth as a fighter of fascism and the ally of the United States, it was much easier for the Jewish radical to talk with the rest of the American Jewish people. When America entered the war, we in the radical movement answered the patriotic call for additional production efforts. It was a paradox, in fact, that the most radical organization, the Communist Party, called upon the workers not to strike or to ask for large wage increases. This was at a time when the cost of living was spiraling and big business was profiteering on the war. Again, when the Soviet Union was threatened, the radical movement went overboard to help, to the point where we were criticized by the workers.[7]

I was really jarred in the early days of the war, when there was a danger of fascist victory. I became more patriotic than at any time since I came to the United States. It was then that I applied for American citizenship. Later in the war, when I already was a citizen, I applied to work in heavy industry at Bethlehem Steel in Boston. But by the time I was cleared by the FBI, the war was ending.

(It is interesting that two FBI agents came to the Tudor Knitting

Mills to inquire about my patriotism for work in a war production industry. The manufacturer's secretary told me about their interview with that foreman I always clashed with. He told those agents, "I don't like Rapoport. I think he is a Commie. But if everyone was as honest and as just as him, we would have a better country." He testified for me!)

During the war, I also became more Jewish conscious than anytime since I left Stanislavchik. With the Jewish people marked out for destruction by the Nazis, I felt an identity and a pride of being Jewish. I remembered the days of the First World War in Russia, when young Jewish people crippled themselves rather than fight for the oppressive Tsarist government. In World War II, I was proud to see the children of American Jewish people going off to fight with the full sense that they were defending their country— defending the Jewish people—against oppressors. As part of the radical movement, I had become largely disconnected from the main body of American Jewish people over the years. But that changed during the war when I threw myself into relief work.

I started with the Jewish Council for Russian War Relief. As the war developed, it became clear that the German Army with all its modern power received a staggering blow inside Russia. In just two decades, starting from the devastation of the war and revolution, the Soviet Union had developed enough heavy industry to face the German war machine. There were weaknesses in the early Russian war effort, but they were able to turn the tables in a remarkably short time. When the German Army invaded, there was a tremendous mobilization of the Russian people to defend "*matushka Rossiia*, mother Russia." In the great battles at Leningrad, Moscow, and Stalingrad, they turned the war against the Nazis. No matter what happened in the years to come, no matter what we heard about Stalin's bloodletting, I never stopped appreciating how he led the Russian people against fascism. It was a great inspiration to me at the time.[8]

The Soviet Union fought with the help of American supplies, but more was needed. There was a need for American popular support, for people's participation in meeting the war needs of the Soviet Union. Thus, Russian war relief was organized on a national scale, cutting across the American population, under the honorary leadership of Albert Einstein. Since Jewish losses were so great in

Europe, there was growing Jewish participation in Russian war relief. There still was hesitation after the Nazi-Soviet Pact of 1939, but the American Jewish people began to feel that Hitler could be defeated in Russia with American help.

One action that quieted American Jewish hostility against the Soviet Union was the heroic Soviet attempt to evacuate the entire population of the Ukraine, including the Jewish people, when the Nazi Armies invaded. When I revisited the Soviet Union in 1963, I learned that government warnings helped save part of my family in the Ukraine. My father already had died, but my sisters Ethel and Sorke lived in Bar at that time. When the German Armies first approached, when the first bombs started dropping near Bar, there was great confusion. My brother-in-law Mikhl just grabbed a horse and wagon, rushed home, and told Sorke, "We must run now." Sorke reached Ethel to come along, but Ethel replied, "You are victims of Bolshevik propaganda. I had experience with the Germans during the revolution. They are civilized people with whom you can deal. Run if you wish. I am staying here." Ethel and her family died in that first onslaught of the German Armies.

Mikhl and Sorke fled with their daughters in the direction of Azerbaidzhan. They almost were overtaken by Nazi Armies. They had to cross fields and forests by night to avoid being spotted. Mikhl led the horses on foot until they reached the designated safety area. He saved his family because he was sensitive to those Soviet warnings and because he was willing to take chances. I always think of him with great respect.

The Soviet Union's effort to save the Jewish people, the Russian willingness to stand up against nazism, the terrible Russian loss of life ... it was a convincing demonstration that out of the lion's belly can come honey. The American Jewish people began to send what aid they could to the Soviet Union.

I responded personally to the appeal for relief. I went to the Stanislavchik Podolskaia Guberniia Society to ask for help. They responded with a contribution to the Jewish Council for Russian War Relief, but they did not stop there. They suggested we organize a Podolskaia Guberniia conference, composed of all the *landsmanshaftn* from the towns and cities in our Ukrainian state.

To prepare for that conference it was not enough for a Joe

Rapoport to sign a letter. I was advised to meet with Abraham
Goldberg, a well-known writer for the *Morgn Zhurnal*. He had
been a leader of Ukrainian relief in the First World War. We spent a
couple of hours together one Sunday morning, exchanging experiences about the Ukraine. He offered to cooperate, and he suggested that I contact a Rabbi Avrom Bick, who also came from
Podolskaia Guberniia. He told me that Rabbi Bick had a very
unsound political philosophy, but that he was a good writer, a
good speaker, and a good person.

I asked what he meant by "unsound." He said, "Rabbi Bick is
trying to find a bridge between religion and socialism. That is
impossible."

I went right down to that orthodox *shul* in Manhattan where
Rabbi Bick was practicing. I found him, and he turned out to be
quite a guy. He was the tenth generation in a consecutive chain of
rabbis in the Bick family. He was a learned man who wrote a
number of books. He also wrote a weekly political column for the
Tog, which was a liberal Yiddish newspaper, but his writings
were sympathetic to socialism. I was fascinated by his attempts to
reconcile the teachings of the Prophets with modern socialism; it
was completely different from what I learned about the Prophets
in Stanislavchik. I found Rabbi Bick to be very sharp, very clever,
very articulate. He agreed to speak at the conference.

Then I approached the Russian consulate for a speaker. During
the war, the Russian government was accepted as an ally by the
American establishment and the American people, so a Soviet
representative would strengthen our conference. Again I made
contact directly. Over the telephone you can be discouraged; in
person you can talk and be persuasive. I met with the first secretary
of the consulate. We got to talking about the war, the Ukraine, and
the Jewish people. I found a very sympathetic response. He agreed
to speak at the conference.

When we issued that call to the Ukrainian Podolskaia *landsmanshaftn*, it already sounded like a growing organization. By that
time I had become a member of the Stanislavchik Podolskaia
Guberniia Society; I couldn't organize as an outsider. I soon
discovered that the Stanislavchik society had contact with other
landsmanshaftn. It was like a chain—when you pulled one, the

others followed. We had a large response, a packed hall. Forty organizations showed up from one *guberniia*, one Ukrainian state, including quality like the big city organizations from Odessa and Kiev.[9]

It was a well-prepared conference with speakers, songs, and, of course, an appeal for financial support to the Jewish Council for Russian War Relief. Once again the people showed us the way to leadership. The question came up, "Why just this *guberniia*? Why not an all embracing relief organization of Ukrainian Jews?" Some remembered such an organization from World War I.

That opened a new page of activities for me. In March of 1943, we held a much larger conference of all the Ukrainian *landsmanshaftn* from the different areas of the United States. There we established a permanent national Ukrainian war relief organization —the Ukrainian Committee of the Jewish Council for Russian War Relief. Rabbi Bick became the president. I preferred to work behind the scenes, but was made secretary.

We organized a staff with paid workers, rented some space, and went to work on a large scale. With help from the Soviet consulate, we worked out a small package with flour, sugar, hard candy, needle and thread, soap and towel, and other things. We bought in quantity, which was not so easy during the war; Sheba turned out to be our most resourceful buyer. We packed it ourselves. We became like a small mass production factory, putting together tens of thousands of those packages and sending them to the Ukraine.

We sent each package in the name of the *landsmanshaft* that raised the money for it. We sent the packages, as American Jews, for relief of all the people in the Ukraine. This included the Jewish people of the Ukraine, but not just the Jewish people. There were some strong opinions against helping the Ukrainians, because a large number of them had a record of anti-Semitism. A former leader of Ukrainian Jewish war relief during World War I, M. Usherovich, carried on a campaign in the *Forward* against our approach. But we just could not send bread to Jews while Ukrainians went hungry. It was a matter of humanism and good neighbor policy.

After that first national conference I contacted Ukrainian *landsmanshaftn* that did not respond to our call. There were several

Joe with Rabbi Avrom Bick at a meeting for Ukranian war relief.

buildings in New York where a hundred *landsmanshaftn* would meet in the evenings. I was able to reach many organizations on a single evening, but not all of them would admit me. Each one had a sergeant-at-arms guarding the door against the hundreds of small charities that came begging from the *landsmanshaftn*. If you did not give the proper membership signal at the door, the sergeant-at-arms would not let you in. So when he opened the door, I just stuck my foot in! He'd get angry at me. But I'd tell him what I wanted and insist that he check with the chairman. Usually it worked. I was organizing!

Our Ukrainian war relief organization required an enormous amount of time and work. Along with sending out packages and contacting *landsmanshaftn*, we started a newsletter and we held regular local and national conferences. As the organization grew, all kinds of people came in. We had manufacturers, merchants, pushcart peddlers, and shop workers. We got religious people, Zionists, and all kinds of socialists. A group of left-wing activists from the needle trades joined in the organizational work. It was quite a task to maintain cooperation. It really kept me going.

While I was working for Ukrainian war relief, I received a personal report on what happened in my part of the Ukraine during the Nazi occupation. I met up with Itsik Kupetz, a young man of Polish Jewish descent who was the first Jewish refugee to reach the United States at the end of the war. He had retreated east into the Ukraine when the Germans invaded Poland after the Nazi-Soviet Pact of 1939. Although Stalin agreed to German occupation of western Poland, he opened the borders of Soviet occupied Poland and the Soviet Union to Polish Jews. Thousands of them fled into the Soviet Union and were saved from the Nazis.

That youngster Itsik Kupetz caused a sensation in the New York Jewish newspapers when he arrived. His story was printed in long installments in the *Tog*. When I saw that the articles mentioned towns and even people I knew, I contacted him immediately. I wanted to get a personal report on conditions in the Ukraine, and I wanted him to tell the story at a meeting of the Ukrainian Committee of the Jewish Council for Russian War Relief.

I caught up with him one evening and heard his story. It seems that he remained in the Ukraine after the Nazi occupation of

Poland—instead of going farther east into Siberia—with the hope of returning to Poland later. When the Nazis invaded the Ukraine, he landed in a concentration camp in Zhmerinka. The Germans rounded up the Jews with the help of a segment of the Ukrainian population. I do not know if their collaboration with the Nazis was a question of robbing the Jews or if they understood that this was complete destuction of the Jewish people.

I asked Itsik Kupetz if he met up with any of the Stanislavchik people in that concentration camp at Zhmerinka. I learned that some of my family and friends were there.

The Zhmerinka concentration camp was under the control of the Romanian Army, allies of the Nazis. According to Kupetz the Romanians treated the Jews terribly—not feeding them, demanding bribes, giving brutal beatings—but they would not commit mass murder. When the Nazis were about to retreat from the area, they ordered the Romanian Army to destroy the Jewish population. The Romanians refused! So the Nazis came to do the destruction themselves.

The Nazis told the people in the concentration camp, "We are preparing to fight the Red Army. You will come with us to dig ditches for our soldiers. All you need is shovels, which we will supply. You are coming back."

The inmates of the camp already had contact with the outside resistance movement in the Ukraine. A resistance fighter in the camp warned, "The shovels are not to dig ditches for soldiers, but to dig our own graves. When we leave the camp, we will have a large number of people in the streets of Zhmerinka. At my signal, begin running in all directions. Yes, we will be shot at, but some will escape. That is our only chance."

And the people in the camp replied, "You are worse than the Nazis! Maybe you are right, and they will do what you say. But if there is one spark of possibility that we really will return after digging ditches, your plan will extinguish it."

How did Itsik Kupetz survive? He explained to me, "I figured out what to do. If the man who told us to run started running himself, and put his own life on the line, I would run with him. And so it was. We broke away in the streets of Zhmerinka. They fired shots and we zig-zagged. We ran around a few corners and we were whisked inside a Ukrainian house. That is where I remained till the end of the war."

The other people from the concentration camp didn't run ... the rest is a matter of record.

Since the war some writers—Jewish writers—have pointed a finger of accusation against the Jewish people for submissiveness, for allowing themselves to be slaughtered like sheep in the Holocaust. I am talking especially about Hannah Arendt and her book *Eichmann in Jerusalem*. That kind of history ceases to be the property of her own understanding when it is published, and it becomes ammunition for the enemies of the Jewish people. She aroused the wrath of the Jewish people with that book. I have not read it ... I saw the reviews ... and with all my heart I condemn those opinions.[10]

Throughout the centuries, the Jewish people lived through shattering experiences: the Roman conquest, the Spanish Inquisition, anti-Semitism in England, pogroms in Eastern Europe. Hundreds and thousands of Jewish people sacrificed their lives to remain loyal to their God. Always we were a small minority surrounded by a sea of humanity. How could we fight the attacks? What were out tools of resistance? A *shoyfer*, a ram's horn? A tailor's shears?

When you live as a people under such circumstances for centuries, you learn to defend yourself with passive methods. You do not pick up a weapon. You sharpen your mind for maneuver. There was a background of cooperating for survival, of adapting and compromising with a hope for the best. Thus the *Judenrat*, the Jewish leadership councils established by the Nazis in the European ghettos, gave lists to the Nazis of who would be taken away; they collaborated, they said, in order to save some Jews. One must have compassion. One must understand the conditions. They faced overwhelming power.

And the Nazis were cunning. They never said where the Jewish people were being taken. They never left anyone to come back and tell the story. All along the way to the gas chambers they offered reassurances ... always some hope. The Nazis were insidious.

When the Jewish people did have weapons, when they did see what was happening, they were excellent fighters against the Nazis. There is the example of the great uprising of the Warsaw

Ghetto, when a handful of Jews held off the German Army longer than it took to conquer France. When he has a gun and when he joins together with others, the Jewish soldier ranks among the best fighters in the world. We have seen this after the Holocaust in Israel.

Those who criticize the Jewish people for walking into the gas chambers should ask the question, "If I would be in such a position, how would I act?" And I say that the person who answers such a question is an idiot or a faker. Because until you face that situation, you just don't know. You *never* know what you will do until you actually feel the knife at your throat.

When the wound was fresh, I condemned the Germans as a people. It is correct, of course, not to equate the German people with the German government, to separate a bad government from the people. And yet, in spite of rationality and understanding the Nazi tyranny, I cannot whitewash the German population. There were resistance movements against fascism in other countries. There were resistance movements when the Nazis invaded. There were resistance movements throughout history when a people was oppressed. Even the superoppression of the Roman Armies did not kill the spirit of Jewish resistance in ancient Israel. This is the nature of a people. But there was no resistance movement by the German people against Nazi rule.

I no longer carry the hatred that I did during the days of Hitler. Nevertheless, when I traveled through Europe in 1963, there was no country I so eagerly wanted to pass without stopping as Germany, even East Germany. I stopped in Poland and thoroughly enjoyed it, even though a great number of Poles were not exactly innocent bystanders in the anti-Semitic activities during the war. But Polish anti-Semitism was different than the genocidal German attack on the Jews.

I also can say that I never bought and never will buy a Volkswagen, which was created under the Hitler regime. When I observe the high area which forms a forehead, the hood which forms a nose, and the license on the spot of the mustache, I can see the mask of Hitler. Whether anyone else sees it, I don't know. I see it! Maybe this reflects a wrong attitude, but this is how I feel. How can you reason about genocide?

As we went along with our relief work, there came up the

question of laying a base for a permanent national Ukrainian Jewish society, a *farband*, that would function after there would be no need for war relief. We stepped up our relief activities right after the war when we were able to reach the Ukraine direct. But it became obvious that the Jewish people faced new problems after the war. Many of our members thought that the Ukrainian *landsmanshaftn* had common interests and that by uniting we could play a larger role as part of the Jewish community of the United States.

At first I was not ready to become involved in a Ukrainian *farband*, but I listened with interest. I consulted with leaders of left-wing Jewish cultural organizations and with other left-wing activists working for Ukrainian war relief. Some thought the *landsmanshaftn* were basically reactionary . . . bourgeois and Zionistic. They opposed turning the relief organization into a Ukrainian *farband*. But I disagreed. I decided that a permanent Ukrainian Jewish organization could be a progressive force. I joined with those who wanted to build such an organization.

The development of that *farband* was encouraged by, and ultimately destroyed by, the question of an independent state for the Jewish people. At the end of the war, the Jewish survivors in Europe needed more than relief. They needed a home in a place that was not devastated. The Soviet Union did not, could not, do enough; the United States locked its doors to most of them; the British were outright unfriendly. It pointed toward the need for an independent Jewish state in Palestine. But with that came another problem. The Palestinians, the Arabs in Palestine, were viciously opposed to the establishment of Israel. And they had support from the British colonial rulers of the area.

As the months passed after the war, more and more Jewish refugees made illegal entrance into Palestine. They stole their way in, they manipulated their way in, they fought their way in. It was a struggle for survival, for the life and dignity of a people.

Their appeal to world conscience was a settled question for the American Jewish people as a whole: the United Nations should open the doors of Palestine for the Jewish people, for a Jewish state. But even while the Zionists were fighting to establish Israel, the American Jewish radical movement hesitated. Our movement still believed that the basic solution to the Jewish problem was the creation of international socialism. Our movement could not recognize that, even though the Zionists paved the way for Israel, it was a popular struggle of the Jewish people after centuries of dispersion and oppression. It was a struggle of liberation that went back to our roots, back to the attempt by the Jewish people to return home after the Babylonian Captivity. To deny this ... after the Holocaust ... was not radical! What was wrong with supporting our people's struggle for independence?

There were all kinds of radical meetings on this question. At one public gathering Alexander Bittleman, a Jewish leader in the Communist Party, expressed the majority view of Jewish radicals. He took the position that there should be a Jewish state, but it should be created slowly and peacefully, through negotiations with the Arabs. Bittleman was not somebody you would want to tangle with in public, but at that meeting I did state: "If we wait for the Arabs to agree, we will be waiting until there are no Jews left to settle in Palestine."[11]

I could not accept the cool reasoning of the radical movement on this question. When you separate mind from feeling, neither works very well. I grew up with the religious yearnings of my grandfather and my mother, the religious yearnings of a return to Jerusalem that existed long before modern political Zionism. Many of the Jewish radical leaders came to the United States before the First World War, but I lived through the pogroms of the Ukrainian nationalists. I felt the pain and insult of anti-Semitic attack. During the Second World War, I participated in relief activities; I heard stories from refugees of what happened; I heard a report from someone who reached Babi Yar after the massacre, who saw the earth moving from wounded people who were buried alive![12] While I never was a nationalist, I never was a Zionist, I was a son of the Jewish people. That was my yardstick of measurement. The Jewish people appealed to world conscience to open the doors of Palestine—my sympathy was with my people.

This issue came up when we called a national conference to establish a Ukrainian *farband* in 1947. There were representatives from over two hundred *landsmanshaftn* in a dozen American cities. We agreed on a resolution to establish ourselves as one *farband* of Ukrainian Jews, but then a resolution was introduced by my ideological comrades who earlier opposed setting up a *farband*. Their resolution called for the establishment of the state of Israel only with the consent of the Arab people.

When that resolution was introduced, the conference just jumped on its feet! Many didn't even wait to vote it down. The mere fact that there were elements of leadership in the organization who would take this position, who would try to impose it on the organization, was not acceptable. They condemned it not with words, but with their feet. They walked out! Most remained, out of politeness for our contact over the years, out of respect for the people on the platform. But I could feel the reaction oozing from person to person in the hall. I could feel that something was very wrong.

Later a comrade who agreed with my views on Israel asked, "Joe, how could you permit such a resolution to reach the floor?"

I had an idea they would do it, but I didn't anticipate the sharpness of their challenge and the reaction of the delegates. Looking back, knowing my position on this question, knowing my contact with the people, I regret that I did not get up and dissociate myself from the resolution. It might have had an affect—people knew I was one of the organizers of the conference—but I hesitated. The result was disastrous. After that, our Ukrainian *farband* deteriorated quickly. I felt the disappointment very sharply. I feel it to this day.

Not long after that conference, in May of 1947, I was richly rewarded for my feeling about Israel. That was when Andrei Gromyko, the foreign minister of the Soviet Union, got up at the United Nations and gave his reasons why Israel should be made a nation. It was a sensible resolution, which designated an area for a Jewish state and an area for a Palestinian state. The only thing that upset the dual state compromise was an attack on Israel by the multitudes of the Arab world with the aid of British imperialism.

Years later, when I visited Israel, someone who had participated in the War for Independence told me, "Some people think it is a miracle Israel survived that war. Let me tell you, it was no miracle. It was our guns. It was our spirit. It was our determination. We had no other place to go."

The Jewish radical movement was elated over the establishment of Israel with Soviet support. Of course, even with the Soviet vote for the establishment of Israel, even with the sending of Czech machineguns for use in the Jewish War for Independence, a minority of extremists in our movement continued to hold a deep seated opposition to Israel. The majority of the Jewish radical movement, although we continued to oppose Zionism, took the position that Israel is historically justified, that Israel should be supported, and that Israel should act in a just manner to the Palestinian people and to Arab neighbors. To this day we still believe that socialism is the solution to the problems of all oppressed peoples, including the Jewish people. But time has taught us that you can fight for socialism in a Jewish nation too. We see that struggle in Israel today.

9. Jewish Chicken Ranchers and the Cold War

*L*eaving New York, leaving the knitting trade and the
labor movement, was one of the most difficult decisions
I have made. Twenty-five years I worked for the improvement of life and for the dignity of the knitgoods worker. That
struggle was my first love, my great pride. When I think back over
my span of years, participation in the trade union movement was
the most positive period of my life.

From when I entered the knitting trade in 1922 up through the
1940's, the hand knitter was gradually replaced by automatic
knitting machines. Those electric powered machines produced
cloth incomparably faster than a hand knitter, with no mistakes.
Those machines were responsible for the growth of knitgoods
factories, the increase of unskilled knitgoods workers, and enormous profits. It was a blessing for the manufacturer who survived
the competition.

The old-time hand knitter wanted the union to control the
introduction of the new machinery, so it would be done in a more
human way. But the union had nothing to lose with mass
production. From the viewpoint of the union leadership, the
disappearance of the hand knitter was not such a terrible thing. It
meant that the most union conscious group in the shops—skilled
workers who understood how a union should work, people who
were the backbone of the union for years—were replaced by a few
workers to tend the machines. It meant a huge increase of
unskilled young workers—floor workers, finishers, packers—with
thin ties to the job and little trade union experience.

The hand knitter could learn to operate the power machines.
But you needed union permission to get one of the few jobs as an
apprentice on a power machine in a union shop. I would not have
worked in an open shop, where I would have been hired only on

condition that I made no attempt to organize the workers. So I placed myself on the union list for power machines like anyone else. I received all kinds of promises, but there was delay after delay, excuse after excuse.

There still was some possibility of work for a hand knitter, but I did not just wait around the union office with other idle knitters, hoping a job would be called in. I took all kinds of temporary jobs just to keep going. I also applied to become a fur worker, then a machinist. But I was nearly fifty, an age when I could be hired only to do something like sweeping floors.

I had a few business offers, including one opportunity to open my own knitgoods shop! Harry Kessler, the *landsman* who first suggested I try hand knitting in 1922, the friend whose shop I organized in 1932, had become a wealthy knitgoods manufacturer over the years. At my brother Morris's one evening, Harry offered me fifty thousand dollars financing for my own knitgoods shop. I am not sure if he really was serious, but if I was not ready to compromise basic principles with the ILGWU leadership, I certainly would not go into partnership with a knitgoods manufacturer.

During this period, Sheba was working steady. We were not hurting badly, but how long can one be semi-employed and live off another? Perhaps today, with the movement for women's liberation, a man should not feel bad if his wife is the only steady provider in the family. But I had an old-fashioned streak—it bothered me.

On top of that was the postwar reactionary political atmosphere, which closed off any opportunity for progressive trade unionism in the knitgoods industry. After the war the United States government turned against the Soviet Union and it started a campaign against the American radical movement, with propaganda and investigations and spying. The Red Scare was reflected inside the CIO with expulsion of left-wing leaders and entire left-wing unions. Some radicals went over to the Cold Warriors and became Red baiters. A couple of progressive unions—like the United Electrical Workers, the International Longshoremen's and Warehousemen's Union, the Fur Workers, the Mine, Mill and Smelter Workers—withstood the attack and remained independent. But it was no more the big organizing drives of the 1930's. Organized labor was on the defensive, and the ground gave out like quicksand under the feet of the radical movement.[1]

Within the ILGWU, Dubinsky and the leadership stepped up their Red-baiting. Louis Nelson, of course, felt right at home in this reactionary period. He just sharpened his Red-baiting denunciations of the Rank-and-File Group in the knitgoods local.[2]

The Cold War atmosphere was nothing new for me. Except for the brief period when I was union organizer, I was under continuous Red-baiting attack in Local 155 from the time of the merger in 1935. After I was fired as union organizer in 1937, I became more and more disconnected from union activities. The Cold War attacks just further isolated our Rank-and-File Group as left oppositionists. I would have remained in the industry if I could have found work on the power machines. I would have remained if I saw the possibility of a breakthrough against Nelson and the ILGWU leadership. But developments were in the opposite direction.

That is why, one day, I picked myself up and went to check the situation in Los Angeles. Sheba and I never forgot our wonderful year there in the 1920's; we never completely accepted the hectic pace of New York life. The knitting industry had grown in Los Angeles since then, and I thought there might be work for a hand knitter. After a few weeks investigation, I concluded that the opportunities in the knitgoods industry and outside it were better for me in Los Angeles.

We kicked the idea around after I returned. It was the most difficult decision we faced since leaving the Ukraine. Finally, we decided to go. We left New York in a simple way—little gatherings with friends and family. We sold our bungalow, which gave us a small financial cushion. We knew we faced a big challenge—the move, new jobs, our age, our meager resources. There we were!

Just before we left a friend suggested, "Why don't you try Petaluma?"

"What's Petaluma?"

"It's a town forty miles north of San Francisco. You'll find there a colony of Jewish chicken ranchers living a different kind of life. Ruby and Yeta Venger just moved to Petaluma. Other people from our movement have gone there. Why not stop and look?"

We were taking a northern route, revisiting Yellowstone Park,

Glacier Park, and other places we remembered from our 1927 travels. When we came down through northern California, on the way to Los Angeles, we did stop in Petaluma. We reached our friends the Vengers, whom we knew from our first visit to Los Angeles. They insisted we stay a few days on their chicken ranch.

While we were there, we attended a party with about fifty progressive Jewish chicken ranchers. We were surprised to meet up with all kinds of old friends—people we thought had disappeared into eternity. They were needle trades workers from the radical movement in Los Angeles and New York. And soon we found the party surrounding us: "Why the heck do you go to Los Angeles?"

I answered, "I am a knitter."

"I am a cloak presser," said one.

"I am a fur worker," said another.

"I am a cutter," chimed in another.

"We quit our city jobs to come here. This is the beauty of the country. Life is easier than in the shop. Yes, there is some hard work on a chicken ranch, but you are not a slave to the time clock and the foreman. The time is your own. You work the ranch as you want, even if you rent it, and we have a good radical group doing all kinds of things. Come join us."

"We haven't got the money to start a chicken ranch."

"Credit is easy."

"We don't know how to raise chickens."

"It's easy. We'll teach you."

"We don't like chickens."

"Do you have to like them to raise them? You'll be feeding people."

"No," we said, "our course is set for Los Angeles. Thanks for the invite."

We went on to Los Angeles, but the prospects did not work out. There, too, power machinery was coming into the shops. Where there was work for a hand knitter, the boss already heard of me from New York and would not hire me. At one knitting mill the owner, Andy Wenzel, was a former trade unionist who worked on left-wing committees with me in New York. Not only did Andy become a manufacturer, but he had working in his shop other activitist workers from New York. When I walked into the office, he took me into the shop, pulled the switch on the machines, and said, "Look who's here! We'll have a party!"

When the party was over and we were back in his office, Andy said, "Joe, do you have to start organizing Los Angeles with my shop?" I assured him I just wanted a job like anyone else with no special consideration because of our former trade union relationship. He gave me a flimsy excuse that no machine was ready and he would contact me. That was thirty years ago and I am still waiting for a reply.

We stayed in Los Angeles with our dear friends the Riches and the Rabinoffs, who made a great effort to find a suitable job for me, but nothing worked out. As the months passed, we saw our savings melting away. Sheba and I talked it over. Even though we did not like the idea of raising chickens, there was something attractive about that life on a ranch. We were not afraid of hard work. But would the people in Petaluma really help us get started? After all, it is one thing to offer help while sipping vodka with an old friend; it's another thing when the friend comes for help, especially when he will become a competitor in the same business. I returned to Petaluma to check, and yes, they urged us to come.

We left Los Angeles, moved in with the Vengers, and started looking for a ranch. We learned that some people had come in the last few years with no more than us and borrowed from friends and realtives in order to buy a good ranch. There was prosperity and optimism in the chicken business at that time. But we chose the alternative of buying a cheap run-down place. For that we had the money from the sale of our bungalow. We preferred days of backbreaking labor over sleepless nights worrying about losing the money of friends.

When we bought a run-down place, we did it on a grand scale! A real Hooverville! It was not a house on that six-acre parcel, but a shack. You could sit in the living room, if you wanted to call it that, and watch the rats running below the rotten floor. The water was not connected in the bathroom and the septic tank was useless. There was something you could call a kitchen, but the walls were black with soot from a kerosene stove that had no chimney. The chicken houses were broken down, the windmill did not pump water, equipment was scattered all over, and the utilities did not reach the place. That dilapidated ranch became the talk of the town! People came just out of curiosity to see it! They thought we were crazy for trying to make a go of it there.

But we were confident we could do something with that ranch. The shack was on a hill overlooking a little thicket of eucalyptus and cypress trees. It was beautiful rolling country with chicken ranches and dairy ranches stretching off into the distance. On our property we had fruit trees, berry bushes, and a vine with an unusual white muscatel grape. It was obvious that if and when we did fix up that place, it was a spot where we wanted to live.

Sheba got a job in San Francisco setting up a health insurance program for the Culinary Workers Union. That was our main income for the first two years, while I rebuilt the ranch. When I applied for a loan from the Jewish Agricultural Society, an organization that helped Jewish people leave their hard lives in the city, the representative readily offered support. He explained, "Most of our people who come to live on farms, especially the women, miss the social life of the city, the beauty parlor, the comfortable apartments. They demand to fix up the ranch house right away. You are building up the chicken houses to secure income first. That is the correct approach."

At the very beginning came up questions of how to reconstruct the chickenhouses, of whether to take in meat birds or laying hens, of how to raise the birds. Everbody in the Jewish radical group stopped by with advice, everyone had his own system, and everyone said, "Listen to me, not him." It reminded me of when my father put up that *orn-koydesh*, that cabinet, and then rebuilt our house in Stanislavchik.

We had to be polite and listen to every theory. The effort to help was very beautiful. But I learned there was a county poultry department with a farm adviser and scientific information from the agricultural university in Davis. That farm adviser took me around to different chicken ranches, he gave me sound advice, and he started me reading poultry magazines. He even sent me off for a few days of school at Davis. I drew the best information on the market, and I went about ranching in my own way.

It was not a marriage of love between the chicken and me. The first time I tried to kill one, I did it as I saw others—I took it by the legs and swung its head against the wall. When I let that chick down it just picked itself up, ran away, and I never saw it again!

With my first raise of chickens there was a flood in the chickenhouse. When I walked in and found my chicks swimming for their lives, I was sick! Many drowned, and cleaning up was an enormous job. But I paid careful attention to the chicks that survived. They grew to be healthy, I hit a good market, and there was a large profit. That was great encouragement to continue.

Our friends couldn't understand how we could live in that shack without improving it, but I gave attention to the chicken business first. They thought I was crazy for building chicken houses with half open walls, but I learned that confinement in closed buildings bred disease. I experimented with meat birds and laying hens for a couple of years. Gradually, I expanded capacity and developed a productive flock of laying hens.

Our ranch was in Cotati, a village seven miles north of Petaluma. During the first year, I got a group of neighbors to approach the Cotati town council with a request to extend the water and sewerage lines to our ranches. I had to attend meeting after meeting of that council, reminding them that we were paying taxes without getting benefits, and finally they extended the town services. I also convinced the gas company to come out with its lines. All the while we slowly rebuilt our shack. We started with a corner, then a room, then another room. We put in new floors and a new roof, we rebuilt the bathroom, we even found knotty pine when we scrubbed the soot off the kitchen walls.

After two years work in the city, Sheba quit her job and joined me at work on the ranch. Most of the women in the Jewish community worked on the ranches along with caring for the families. There was so much hard work on a small chicken ranch that the entire family had to pitch in. It was not just the routine jobs of hauling feed sacks, collecting eggs, and cleaning chicken houses. But there were constant disasters with poultry diseases, floods in the chicken houses, and wild animals that would attack the chickens. I once spent three nights in a chicken house trying to find out why some of my chickens turned up with only one leg in the mornings. I spent two more nights catching the racoons who were grabbing those chicken legs.

We went through five years of hard living and backbreaking work to start that ranch. But what satisfaction with the results! We built up a productive, profitable hen ranch. We met all our obligations, and we began pulling ahead financially. And our home not only became liveable, but loveable, with large new picture windows that looked down the hill over the rolling country.

The ranch life was easier for me than for most other people who came from the city. I grew up working under rough conditions on my father's sheep farm in the Ukraine. I preferred rural life with all its hardships to the rush and crowding of the city. I never liked working with chickens—I don't like the smell of the animal! Nor did I like bargaining with the poultry hucksters when it came time to sell my meat birds or my old laying hens. But I took pride in good management of my birds. I enjoyed fixing up old buildings, repairing a pump, sawing a fallen tree, and raising a few steers. I preferred it over work in a shop. Here I went at my own speed, on my own place, outdoors in an area of great beauty.

Joe and Sheba in front of rebuilt chicken houses, 1955.

And then too, it didn't take long before I was involved in community life, in political and cultural activities. From my early days on the ranch, I never was so busy that I could not put down my tools and discuss matters with a visitor. I never felt I had to separate myself from others in order to work my ranch a little faster. It took some time before I made contact with the Democratic Party, the Sonoma County Central Labor Council, the Grange, and other general community organizations. But from the beginning I participated in the radical Jewish movement of the area.

I found two remarkably different Jewish communities in our area—one around Petaluma and one in Santa Rosa, fifteen miles to the north. Santa Rosa, the county seat, attracted a small community of Jewish people who were in business and the professions. It was a middle-class Jewish community with some very wealthy people. They had their own temple and their own rabbi, but they were well assimilated into American life. They considered themselves aristocrats, and they looked down on the Jewish chicken ranchers in Petaluma.

The Petaluma Jewish people were closer to the earth, closer to Jewish tradition, closer to the interests and identity of the Jewish people. The community started before World War I, when a few Jewish people left San Francisco for an agricultural life. They went into chicken ranching, like me, because it didn't require much money or special knowledge. They came to Petaluma because it was the center of poultry production in the West. After that, one heard about it from another—from family, from *landslayt*, from comrades. It was a chance for Jewish people, who were barred from the land in Tsarist Russia, to take up a farming life.[3]

It was a community of idealists ... people who were not so concerned with making a lot of money, people who preferred the agricultural life over the sweatshops and the pushcarts of the city. Many of the early settlers came to learn the chicken business with plans to settle on a *kibbutz* in Palestine. The Zionists in Petaluma maintained close contact with the Labor Zionist movement in Israel, and they gave the Petaluma Jewish community a strong Zionist flavor. There were other Jewish chicken ranchers from the religious tradition, the Bundist tradition, and from the radical Jewish movement.

There were about two hundred Jewish families when we arrived in 1949. It was not a colony, a ghetto with Jewish people consolidated in one spot. The families were scattered on small chicken ranches around Petaluma and the nearby towns of Penngrove, Cotati, and Sebastopol. The central spot was the Jewish Community Center in Petaluma. All the Jewish people and Jewish organizations met there over the years. Petaluma had an active Jewish community life, a high level of Yiddish culture, and sharp ideological differences.

The radical group made up almost half the Jewish community. Where the majority was oriented toward Zionism and the religious education of their children and grandchildren, the radical group was dedicated to a general change of American society. They maintained a Jewish identity, but they were people with a national and a world perspective.

It was an interesting group. Ben and Lena Fields I already knew from New York, where we met at the 1923 conference of the Trade Union Educational League. Yakov and Rachael Levinson I knew from organizational work with the Needle Trades Workers Industrial Union. Gus Wollman had been a leader among the Millinery Workers Union, and Louis Sisselman had been an organizer for the Fur Workers Union in New York; both had a developed knowledge of socialism and Yiddish culture. Zari Gottfried made a great contribution to community life as the conductor of the Petaluma Jewish Folk Chorus. His wife Malke was a widely published Yiddish poet. Sol Nitzberg came from a background of rabbinical study and participation in the 1905 Russian Revolution; he was a political activist who was well versed in Marxism, in Yiddish literature, in mathematics and electrical engineering, even in Torah. Each and every one of that radical group had a big story.

They were well organized and very active. There was a general organization, a branch of the International Workers Order, the IWO, which was the national radical Jewish fraternal organization. Through that IWO branch with over a hundred people attending the monthly meetings, there was social contact, political discussion, educational and cultural programs, preparation of affairs, fund raising for radical causes. There also was a chorus that sang in the Yiddish language, a dramatic group that performed classical Yiddish plays, and a Jewish Women's Reading Circle. These

Yiddish cultural organizations were flourishing when I arrived. The radical group did everything in Yiddish—the meetings, the minutes, the performances, the affairs. They maintained the language, the literature, the culture of our fathers and forefathers.

When I arrived in Petaluma in 1949 at the beginning of the Cold War and McCarthyism, I found the Jewish community divided between the left wing and all the other elements. That was not new to me. The surprise was to find unity for certain common purposes. The board of directors which administered the Jewish Community Center included several left wingers. All Jewish organizations, including those of the left wing, met there. People from all political groups came to community dances and concerts and theatrical performances. I was amazed to discover that the entire community participated in one big campaign to raise money for Israel and for the Jewish settlement in the Birobidzhan province of the Soviet Union. This kind of coalition was unique in the country.

That feeling of cooperation was left over from the wartime unity against fascism. Behind that was the long community history of closeness as a small group of Jews in a largely gentile area. The economy—the chicken business—was an underlying base for unity. All the Jewish chicken ranchers faced the same poultry diseases, dealt with the same feed mills and chicken buyers, belonged to the same cooperatives. There had to be cooperation, despite ideological differences, and there was.

That coalition between the Jewish radical movement and the general Petaluma Jewish community was destroyed by the Cold War. It was a time of sharp ideological conflict and attack on democracy. Anyone could be pointed out to the FBI for friendship toward the Soviet Union, for not accepting the views of Joe McCarthy, for belonging to an organization that was not continually waving the American flag. The Jewish right wing in Petaluma and nationally joined that reactionary attack on American radicalism and peaceful coexistence with the Soviet Union.

After the IWO was placed on the attorney general's list of subversive organizations in 1949, the Petaluma Jewish right wing passed a resolution barring our branch of the IWO from meeting at the Jewish Community Center.[4] They used as a pretext our invitation to Harry Bridges to speak at the Jewish Community Center. There was a bitter conflict with maneuvering of membership shares, stormy meetings, and all kinds of denunciations. Many of our people helped to build the Jewish Community Center in 1925. They contributed for decades, and suddenly they were expelled with Red-baiting! It divided people who were friends and neighbors for decades. It divided families! Even after the IWO was dropped from the attorney general's list, we were not allowed to meet at the Jewish Community Center. Not even after the IWO dissolved and reconstituted as the Jewish Cultural Clubs of America.

The Jewish Folk Chorus continued to meet at the Jewish Community Center for a time after the expulsion of the IWO. The chorus, after all, was not a political organization. It sang the Yiddish song . . . songs that our parents and grandparents sang to us in the Old Country. It sang songs of the Holocaust and songs of the life of the Jewish worker in America. Those songs vibrated with the right wingers at the Jewish Community Center too, but the division became so great that even the chorus was attacked and expelled on ideological grounds.

Why did the Jewish right wing turn on their own friends and family? I can explain with a story about Mendel, the little old white-haired knitter at the Tudor Knitting Mills. He was a religious man, but he had a strong feeling for justice and he did not see evil in the radical movement. Perhaps that was because the left wingers in the shop helped him with production and protected him from the foreman. Once, when Mendel insisted upon donating money to support the *Freiheit*, we kidded him about supporting a Communist newspaper. He replied, "You are right about communism. It's not an easy thing. People don't like it." And he explained it like this: "*Shver tsu zayn a Yid nor tsu zayn a Yid a Komunist, zol Got shoymer umatsl zayn*, it's very difficult to be a Jew but to be a Jew and a Communist, God Almighty save us!"

I am saying, then, that the atmosphere of fear during the McCarthy period touched the Jewish people especially deeply. There was a history of Jewish participation in radical movements in Russia and the United States, there was a history of attacks on Jewish people for their radicalism, real or imagined. The general

Jewish population in the United States was afraid that all Jewish people would be charged as Communists, as friends of the Soviet Union, as enemies of the United States.

The American government played upon this fear very directly in the Rosenberg case. Our left-wing Jewish organizations, like the American radical movement, did not accept the accusation that the Rosenbergs were spies who gave the secret of the atomic bomb to the Russians. There were many statements by scientists, even in those days, that the atomic bomb already was basic knowledge to scientists of the world. The real accusation against the Rosenbergs was that they were Communists and friends of the Soviet Union, and there were undertones of anti-Semitism—that it was Jewish Communists who betrayed the United States. That prosecution was a government attempt to whip up support for Cold War policies.

Our Petaluma radical group participated in the movement to defend the Rosenbergs and Morton Sobell. We had protest meetings, raised money, and wrote letters to the newspapers. It touched us deeply. It was another frame-up in Jewish history, like the Dreyfus Affair and the Beilis Case, where the Tsarist government persecuted a Russian Jew for using Christian blood at Passover. It was another American frame-up, like the jailing of Tom Mooney and the execution of Sacco and Vanzetti. We saw the Rosenberg prosecution as a *bilbul*, a blood lie, and we fought it.

American Jews should have acted as a whole to fight that prosecution, or at least to fight the execution and demand more time for proof of contentions. The promise of justice, of refuge from persecution, was according to every teaching of the Prophets of Israel. It was the promise of America, represented by the outstretched hand of the Statue of Liberty. However, the leadership of the Petaluma Jewish community was as silent as the American Jewish leadership—the rabbis, the Zionists, the social democratic trade union leaders. That Rosenberg case with its Jewish judge and Jewish prosecutor and Jewish victims was a special warning to the American Jewish people. They were not ready to stand up and be counted, nor was the majority of Americans. America carries on its conscience a blood spot for the murder of those two innocent people.[5]

The fear was not just created in Washington, but it was fed by the activities of the FBI in our area. The radical group in Sonoma County, which was mostly Jewish, was active in all kinds of people's causes. The FBI visited our people, trying to learn about our activities, past and present, always looking for left wingers who might become informers. The FBI also visited our opponents in the Jewish community, again seeking information on us. These visits had an intimidating effect on people who went through persecution from the Tsar's government.

The FBI also visited our neighbors, asking what we said, encouraging reports on our activities, warning people to be careful of us. You could always tell when a neighbor received an FBI visit. They behaved different towards you; some stopped talking with you altogether. This was an aggressive persecution, not just for information, but to arouse the civil population against us. It made us nervous and it caused great fear at the Jewish Community Center.

There were other special factors that fed reaction among Jewish people in Petaluma and nationally. At the beginning of the Cold War, Israel, like other small countries, was forced to choose alliance with the United States or the Soviet Union. Even though Israel received great Communist support at its birth, the United States—the Jewish people of the United States—provided the very lifeblood of Israel. With the development of the Cold War there was a danger that Israel would lose support of the American establishment if it did not sever ties with the Soviet Union.[6] Within the United States, there was fear that organized Jewish opposition to McCarthyism and the Cold War might endanger American support for Israel. Thus, the Jewish right wing regarded the anti-McCarthy activities of Jewish radicals as a threat to United States support for the development of Israel as a national homeland for the Jewish people.[7]

The mainstream of the American Jewish radical movement did come around to support the state of Israel. We had extremists who continued the old denunciations of Zionism and Israel, but the majority in our movement helped in the building of Israel through the Israeli left wing. And like the Israeli left wing, we reserved the right to criticize Israeli capitalism, the unwise Israeli break from all contacts with the Soviet Union, and Israeli policies towards the Arab peoples. The mainstream of American Judaism, however, would not tolerate any criticism of Israel. In Petaluma their extremists denounced all Jewish radicals as enemies of Israel and of the Jewish people.

Along with this was the old conflict over the Soviet Union. During the Cold War, the mainstream of American Judaism attacked the Soviet Union and the friends of the Soviet Union more sharply than ever. Our radical Jewish movement continued to defend all Soviet developments as positive. If we had some doubts, we still did not make public criticism for fear of feeding ammunition to the enemies of the Soviet Union and the radical movement. But they already had ammunition. This was a period in Soviet history—I don't know if it ever will be explained—when Stalin turned his guns against his own people, especially the Jewish people, the greatest minority problem in the Soviet Union.

What to do with them? The Jewish people, unlike other minorities in the Soviet Union, did not have a land base where they could develop Jewish cultural and political institutions within the Soviet framework. The attempt to build Birobidzhan as a Jewish province was a fiasco. The Russian Jewish people did not have the traditions to become pioneers in Siberia. They never really found a place in the Soviet system as a nationality group like any other Soviet nationality group. When Israel became a state, with Soviet support, there was an outburst of desire by Soviet Jews to go where they had historic and religious roots. But the Soviet Union would not open its doors for the exodus of so many skilled, educated people, especially with the development of the Cold War and antagonism between Israel and the Soviet Union.

What to do with this minority that refused to go to their province in Siberia, refused to assimilate with ease, refused to rest content? The Soviet Union, which promised justice to oppressed minorities, could not solve the problem of the Jewish people. It seems that Stalin found only one solution. Suppression! He started with an attack on the thinking part of the Jewish people, on the writers and teachers and professionals. This was reflected in the Jewish Doctors' Plot, the false charge—the *bilbul*—that a group of Jewish doctors plotted against Stalin's life. It was a period of destruction of Soviet Jewish cultural leadership.[8]

Many in our movement accepted the charges against the Jewish doctors. As one Polish Jewish newspaper put it: "*Merder in Vayse*

Khalatn, The Murderers in Their White Coats." There were
reports of mass murder in the *Forward*, the organ of American
Jewish social democracy, and in the rest of the capitalist press. But
they had lied about the Soviet Union too many times in the past for
us to believe them now. We still believed in the promise of the
Russian Revolution to solve Russian nationality problems. We
simply could not believe there was an anti-Semitic attack taking
place in the Soviet Union. It was several years before we confirmed
what was happening through our own left-wing sources of information.

So we were denounced, in Petaluma and everywhere else, for
our refusal to join in the Cold War attack on the Soviet Union. We
were denounced as pro-Russian, as pro-Arabic, as anti-American
and anti-Jewish. It wasn't true. Our positions were complex, and
we were shifting our views with the development of history. But all
that was lost in the wave of reaction.[9]

For all those reasons, the political reaction was even stronger
among the Jewish people than the general American population.
There was no lack of anticommunism among gentiles in Petaluma,
but they did not attack the freedom of expression of Jewish
radicals. It is remarkable that after our Jewish radical organizations
were expelled from the Jewish Community Center, we were
allowed to meet at the most respectable institutions in the area—
the churches, the women's clubs, the high school, even the VFW
hall. It was to the credit of the Christian community. It was to the
shame of the Jewish reactionaries.

It seems that it was not enough for the reactionary leadership at
the Jewish Community Center to expel us. They denounced us
publicly to prevent the rest of Petaluma from cooperating with us.
They wanted special recognition from the local establishment that
not all Jews were Communists. The Jewish right wing did the same
thing in New York. This was not just ideological denunciation.
They attacked us an an enemy. They tried to destroy the left-wing
movement.

This aroused indignation in their own ranks. There were people
in the general Jewish community who appreciated the contribution of our organizations. They felt not everyone had to associate
with the left wing ... but to tell the world that Jewish people
cannot live together? That was a shame! That was against the

teachings of the Prophets—that there shall be no enemies in the ranks of Israel.[10]

The expulsions and the public denunciations created a terrific resentment in the radical group, especially among those who had been in Petaluma longest. Some of us who arrived more recently believed that the Jewish radical group should not knuckle under to bitterness and isolation. The Red-baiting attack from the Jewish Community Center did not cut so deeply with those of us who came to Petaluma with organizational experience in the radical movement. The controversy within the Petaluma Jewish community was child's play compared to conflicts within the labor movement. We had a background of reaching out to people of different views. We wanted to find common ground with the Jewish Community Center in raising money for Israel, in fighting local anti-Semitism, in the annual community commemoration of the Holocaust.

The old timers in the radical group were opposed: "You want to approach those *yarmlkes* for cooperation? They spit in our eye! They tossed us out on our ear! They still go along with McCarthyism and superflag-waving!" The idea of walking into the Jewish Community Center and talking with those people was like for a religious Jew to go into church and cross himself. They swore by the beard of Moses they would never again step over the threshhold of that building!

I appreciated the closeness of the people in the Jewish Cultural Club, the money we raised for the radical movement, and the high level of Yiddish cultural activities, but cultural evenings in the Yiddish language by ourselves for ourselves were not enough. A group of us wanted to reach out, to widen the base, to put our left-wing experience to work in the struggles of people around us.

This was not easy. Even though we lived on chicken ranches all over Sonoma County, there was a ghetto feeling that separated the Jewish and non-Jewish populations. We did not play on the American baseball diamonds; we did not pray in the Christians' churches. We were forever strangers, and left-wing strangers at that. There was a veneer of good manners towards us—friendly talk with a neighbor across a fence—but rarely were we invited into a gentile home.

Those of us who had experience working with other nationalities in the shops and in the labor movement did reach out, like joining the Grange. That was a national organization of small farmers which dated back to the nineteenth century. In our area the Grange generally did not open its doors to Jewish people, but several of us responded to a notice that a new Grange chapter was to be organized in Cotati. We joined in the hope that the organization would work to help the small poultry farmer, who was beginning to feel the pinch from competition with big poultry corporations.[11]

We found things in the Grange that did not interest us and that we did not like. It was a secret organization like the Masons with secret signs, special handshakes, and code words. We learned about anti-Semitism in the organization when a Jewish right winger applied for membership and was blackballed. There also was opposition to the labor movement, which Grange members blamed for the high cost of farm labor. And on top of that, there was this business of "the Russians are coming." Our Grange chapter actually built a platform on a hill and established a twenty-four hour lookout for Russian air attack. It was worse than Don Quixote, who at least saw the windmills he was fighting.

Nevertheless, through the Grange I started to appreciate the value of cooperation for the small farmer. I was appointed to a special agricultural committee, where I began to study farm cooperatives. Through that Grange chapter I took a closer look at American agriculture generally. I met up with all kinds of agricultural leaders in the area, and I joined attempts to influence political representatives on behalf of small farmers.

Four or five Jewish Cultural Club members participated in the Grange, but we could not convince the majority to join. Some criticized the Grange as a backward organization. Most just preferred to give their time for more familiar Yiddish cultural activities and radical causes. They would not venture outside the Pale of Yiddish radicalism.

There was a sharper clash in the Jewish Cultural Club on the question of helping food processing plant workers who struck under Teamsters Union leadership in nearby Sebastopol. Some of us proposed bringing poultry and eggs to their strike hall as a gesture of solidarity. There was a record of Jewish left-wing support for labor in the area. In fact, one Jewish radical was tarred and feathered in the 1930's because he helped striking apple pickers in Sebastopol. But now, after the war, these old time activists argued, "The Teamsters Union is rich enough. They don't need our dozen eggs. You want to give away the few dollars we have for our own movement."

Nevertheless, some of us did bring over a couple of carloads of food in the name of the Jewish Cultural Club. The strikers appreciated that gesture, and we began to make acquaintance with organized labor in the area. It turned out that some of the local labor leaders were very forward looking, very progressive. Over time the Jewish Cultural Club supported a Teamsters Union drive to organize local food processing plants, and we worked in the mayoralty campaign of a trade union leader. Out of this contact we became accepted as friends. We were able to mobilize the county central labor council to join the fight against local anti-Semitism, to co-sponsor our Warsaw Ghetto Memorial meetings, to send speakers on contemporary labor problems to our club meetings. For many years it was a good working relationship.

And so it was with county politics. I first joined the Democratic Party after I received my citizenship papers in New York. But not until I came to California did I become involved with candidates, programs, elections, and the inner workings of the Democratic Party. Within a few years, I was out campaigning in the precincts for candidates who advanced programs in the interest of the people. I helped organize meetings and raise money. I mobilized support from the Jewish Cultural Club. Just a few hundred dollars meant a great deal in a congressional campaign in those days.

One of our Congressmen, Clem Miller, became a good friend. He stopped by my ranch whenever he was in the area. I would put down my tools, step inside, and make some coffee. Over the years we thoroughly discussed the poultry industry, the problems of farmers in Sonoma County, and the political positions of the Grange. Inevitably, we talked about the House Un-American Activities Committee, about Israel and the Soviet Union. We could be frank with each other—there was no obligation for complete agreement—but our ideas were close on many issues, especially the needs of the family farmer.

In the Democratic Party, I worked with some people who were very conservative, but people who were honest and just ... people who would fight extreme reaction. One of the Democratic Party leaders I worked with had been among the vigilantes who tarred and feathered a local Jewish radical in the 1930's. He was a wealthy dairy farmer and a leader in the Farm Bureau, the conservative organization for large farmers. But he also had become someone who supported organized labor. He became a conservative constitutionalist, a person who took the Constitution and the Bill of Rights at face value. He was an opponent of socialism, but a defender of the right to free expression. It was this layer of conservative people that stopped Joe McCarthy. Through participation in the Democratic Party I learned to value and respect that conservative element in the United States.

My participation in the Democratic Party was accepted, even though it was known that I had radical ideas and came from a left-wing group, the Jewish Cultural Club. There were people from the Jewish Community Center who complained to the Democratic Party that I was a Communist, a sympathizer of the Soviet Union, a person who danced in the streets when there was a pogrom in Moscow. Clem Miller told me that one of the state Democratic leaders finally told them, "Joe participates, he contributes, he works for our program. Go home and forget about it."

In fact, I was approached several times to become a member of the county central committee of the Democratic Party, but I refused. I did not want to be in a position where I had to endorse everything in the Democratic Party, including the Southern racists and our own Democratic reactionaries in Sonoma County. Had there been a larger left-wing membership, where I could have drawn support for minority positions, it might have been constructive. But rather than be a perpetual loner in the party machinery, I preferred to exert my little influence through participation at my own choice.

I was criticized for participation in the Democratic Party by some members of the Jewish Cultural Club and by others in the left-wing movement. The group had its traditional parties and positions that it supported for years, and suddenly there was a member bringing in new gods to be bowed to. From the extreme Left, I was sharply criticized for trying to win club support for this candidate or that campaign, for working on behalf of the Democratic Party, a bourgeois party. My contention was and is that sometimes we must support a lesser evil to fight a greater evil. A good number of our members recognized the importance of supporting the better candidates and the better programs in the Democratic Party, even though it was not a socialist party.

The most bitter clash within the Jewish Cultural Club came each year over how to organize our Warsaw Ghetto Memorial meeting. We all agreed that the Memorial at the Jewish Community Center, which was limited to a *kaddish* and *El mole rakhamim*, songs of sorrow, was not enough. At our Warsaw Ghetto Memorial, instead of prayers, we talked about the historical forces that created the Holocaust and the heroic uprising that saved Jewish honor. But some of us wanted to go further. We wanted to approach the Jewish Community Center for a joint memorial, and we wanted an English-speaking memorial with participation by non-Jewish people. We thought the Holocaust was not just a Jewish affair, but a lesson for all humanity. If that bestiality could be committed by the highly civilized German people, who could guarantee it could not happen again? We wanted to keep the eternal light burning, not just on the souls of the victims and on the Jewish resistance, but also as a warning of future danger.

That proposal was like touching a hornet's nest! Some club members bitterly opposed a joint affair with prayers at the Jewish Community Center. They said that bringing in gentiles would be an insult to the memory of six million Jewish victims. They played on antireligious, anti-Christian, nationalist feelings. It negated the very idea of our movement. After all, if you cannot get together with other Jews and with liberal gentiles to commemorate the Holocaust, how the devil will you ever build socialist internationalism? With whom?

This question touched deep sentiments. It was our families that we lost in the Holocaust. There was sharp ideological debate year after year. Eventually there was approval by a majority of the club members to broaden out. When our committee approached the Jewish Community Center for cooperation, they made sharp remarks: "The Commies are here with their tricks." They would have nothing to do with us. But over the years we built a small coalition of people and organizations who cosponsored the memorial with us. It was leaders from the Democratic Party, the central labor council, the NAACP, the Unitarian Church, professors from

Sonoma State College, and other professionals in the area. It brought us outside our four walls of Yiddish radicalism, and yet still every year we had bitter discussions before and after the memorial.

These were the struggles within our radical Jewish group. Those of us who came after the war, with big city experience in the radical movement, found ourselves in a small provincial Jewish community with its own ways. I had great respect for the political and cultural knowledge of the established leadership in the Jewish Cultural Club. I appreciated all the Yiddish cultural organizations and activities, but I was a stranger to our progressive Jewish movement by not declaring *"Yiddish iz loshn koydesh*, Jewish is a holy language," like it was said about Hebrew in the Old Country. And for the first time the leadership was questioned about their old groove. Suddenly someone had the nerve to lock horns with them on questions of principle, on issues of broadening the base, on the need for a little fresh air.

The struggle lasted many years. Those of us who wanted change worked slowly, patiently. It was our job to explain, to win over people to our position. We never brought the differences to a point of split. We would come back to the issues time and again at club meetings until a majority accepted our approach. One of the old leaders said to me after I was *roundly denounced* at one such meeting, "Joe, don't be discouraged. It took ten years before they recognized me as a valuable contributor to our movement." It took him that long; it took me a little longer!

The sharpest of all the clashes in the radical movement, the crisis in the struggle, the real turning point came with the Twentieth Congress of the Communist Party of the Soviet Union in 1956. That is when Khrushchev made his famous exposé of Stalinism. Then and only then were we clear about the bestial behavior of Stalin and his entire gang of Communist functionaries.

Here in Petaluma we called a special meeting of the radical group. It was a painful discussion, like a dream, a nightmare. One said it was like when Moses first came down from the mountain and saw the people praying to the golden calf. Moses dropped the first Ten Commandments tablet—it was an ideal that was smashed.

It was not just our idealism for the Soviet Union that was in question. It was a hope that the Jewish people, a suffering people over the centuries, would find salvation through the Russian Revolution and Soviet socialism. We were consistent in that idealism for decades. Now there was a danger some would conclude that Stalin's betrayal was the end for socialism.

I personally stated that the gods were exposed to us naked. That our leaders are nothing more than human beings—mortals who *can* make mistakes and commit terrible antisocialist acts—and it is a mistake to follow them blindly. That you must stay with the idea of socialism, but you must consult your own understanding of the realities around you. The ideal of socialism carries a promise of no more exploitation and no more wars, of freedom and equality for all peoples. But we must criticize developments in the Soviet Union and any other socialist society which do not live up to the socialist promise. In my judgment, socialism had to practice humanism or it was not socialism, even if there was an abolition of the old oppression and private property.

"Never again," I said, "will I act different from what my conscience dictates. *Never again* will I feel morally or organizationally obligated to accept what comes from the top, whether it is from a leader, a party, or a country. The prerogative is mine!"

Most realized our mistake at that time. It was building up over the years. But even after Khrushchev's exposé, there were Jewish Cultural Club members—and not just those who remained in the Communist Party—who maintained the attack on Stalin was exaggerated. I heard it at that discussion of the Twentieth Party Congress, and I have heard it time and again since: "You hurt socialism with public criticism of the socialist states. How can you win over people when you call attention to a few errors in the building stage? Our job is to attack capitalism and imperialism."

I never minimized the achievements of socialism in Russia. It was and still is the great breakthrough against capitalist greed and plunder in the world. No matter what was said, I never stopped appreciation for the achievements of the Stalin period—the rapid industrialization and the victory over nazism. Only people who accept capitalism as the highest form of society would say that the Russian Revolution in its essence was bad for the Russian people and the world.

But I concluded that Jewish radicals must publicly criticize negative developments in the Soviet Union and in other socialist states, especially anti-Semitism. We cannot dissociate ourselves from the problems of the Jewish people. There is nothing wrong with putting the needs of your own people on the first line of struggle. The extreme leftists in the club attacked those of us who criticized Soviet anti-Semitism. They called us bourgeois nationalists, but we attacked anti-Semitism as an *un-socialist* development in the Soviet Union.

We took a similar position towards Israel—praise the positive and criticize the negative. After the Holocaust, after the revelations of Soviet anti-Semitism, I believed more strongly than ever in the need for Israel as the home of the Jewish people. Some club members called us Zionists and attacked Israel as a flunky of Western imperialism. But even as we recognized Israel as the result of the historic Jewish struggle for liberation, we continued to criticize Israel where it did not practice justice.[12]

These were the struggles of our radical Jewish group. These were the struggles of the national Jewish radical movement and of the American left wing. It is true that we lived on chicken ranches in a provincial corner of California, but we did not separate ourselves from national and international developments. We knew we were affected, and we took our stand.

In 1957, after seven years in Petaluma, Sheba and I decided to take a sabbatical from chicken ranching. At that time Sheba started to tire of our life in the country. She wanted to take another look at New York. She thought we might want to live there again.

I did not like the idea. I appreciated the high level of cultural life in New York, but I preferred having a bedroom window that looked out to rolling hills. I enjoyed the outdoor work on the ranch. I had no desire to return to the dirt and confinement of a shop. I was not even sure I could find another job in New York, while in Petaluma I could maintain my dignity by earning our upkeep. New York meant hardship for me.

But in 1949 Sheba quit a good job and took her chances to go with me to California. She came to live with me in that provincial corner on that God-forsaken ranch, but she never enjoyed the ranch work like me. So in 1957 I said, "You came with me this far. I'll go to New York with you. If you want to stay there, I'll try to get back into the knitting industry or find something else."

After years of hard work on that rock pile of a ranch, we sold it for a good price. We more than tripled the resources we had when we arrived in 1949. We could afford a relaxed visit to New York and a good look around.

We stayed in New York with Edye and Phil Lutzker, dear friends from the 1920's. Sheba went her way, checking into work, and I did the same. First thing I looked up my old comrades among the hand knitters, especially Sam Steinhart. They confirmed what I already knew from correspondence—the hand knitter was almost completely wiped out of the knitting industry. A handful of them continued working, including Sam, in a small shop that did specialized work which was too delicate for the power machines. The rest of the hand knitters went into other trades or retired on social security

As for the left wing, it no longer was a voice in the knitgoods local or in the ILGWU generally. It was more of an echo. In the years since I left, there was agreement after agreement with the knitgoods manufacturers, without a real fight for improvement. Local 155 was lax, and the workers may have wanted more, but there was a gradual improvement which the workers appreciated. The left wing almost dwindled out, despite the heroic efforts by activists of the Rank-and-File Group like Sam Steinhart, Sol Reeve, and Louis Cooper.

After a few days I called Louis Nelson at the union office. He said, "I heard you were in town. I was wondering how long it would take you to say hello."

He sounded very friendly, almost like the days when I joined the leadership to organize the 1936 general strike. He invited me to be his guest for lunch. It was noon and I was clear across town, so I suggested we skip lunch and meet in the afternoon. But he insisted he would wait. His eagerness was a little too much for me!

Well, he did treat me to a good lunch, and we spent several hours talking about what happened in the union during the seven years I was gone. He told me a story about a former left-wing knitter, Ben Fenster, the one who convinced me to buy a lot in the Golden's Bridge Colony. Ben was an extremist to the Left when I lived in New York, and later he swung to the extreme Right. After he left the radical movement, he wrote articles for the *Forward*,

the organ of Jewish social democracy, telling dirt about manipulations in the Communist Party. At that time he applied for a job running the educational department of knitgoods Local 155. Nelson
said, "By rights I should have hired him, because he joined me
ideologically. But even if what he wrote in the *Forward* was true, I
hate an informer. I refused him the job."

Nelson said there was no question I could get a union card and
work in a union shop if I could find a job. But he thought there
might be room for me to come in as a business agent or an
organizer. This was just a year after Khrushchev's exposé of Stalin
at the Twentieth Party Congress. The shock of that revelation
caused a mass desertion from the radical movement in New York.
Some of those left wingers ended up going to work for the right-
wing leadership of the ILGWU.

During lunch Nelson questioned my ideological position on the
Soviet Union, on Israel, on American politics and the labor
movement. He sounded as though the differences between us
were not as great as they once were. He was not direct, but he gave
all the indications of offering a union job.

It was a temptation. But I knew Nelson could not assure me of
ideological freedom on the job. The ILGWU staff was under
Dubinsky's domination, and Dubinsky had not allowed such
freedom to other left-wing activists who came into his fold. I still
was not willing to toe the ILGWU line on trade unionism or on
world developments.

Before I had to make any final decision, Sheba settled my
problem. After a couple of days riding the New York subway she
said, "Joe, let's run away from this city!" She didn't even want to
stay long enough to visit all the people we wanted to see.

We returned to California in a few weeks and bought another
ranch in Cotati. This time I raised meat birds instead of laying hens.
Raising chickens was becoming a big business—family farmers
faced competition from huge poultry corporations—and I did not
want to make a larger investment than necessary. The land itself
was a good investment. I decided to continue raising chickens as
long as I could show a small return.

After we returned I just picked up where I left off in my
activities. My life in the community like my life on the ranch gave

To Joe, Beloved Comrade
(June 4, 1960)

By IRENE PAULL

There is singing tonight on the hills of Cotati
Where the sheep graze
And the cock crows
And the blue lupine cools the hot blaze of the poppies
And the mail boxes under the weeping birch read
"Rapoport, Stein, Rosenberg, Bloom . . ."

This is a song of Indian summer
Richer than April, mellower than spring
The time when the mind gathers its harvest
And the heart turns with yearning to ripened fruit

This is the Indian summer of a man.

Joe
Breaker of ground
Farmer, worker, organizer, Jew
Brother of Moses and of Jeremiah
Standing in his grove of eucalyptus
Seeing the moon above the chicken sheds.

I sing the beauty of this man
Who pitched his tent on far horizons
Fought and stood guard upon the outposts
I sing the beauty of a man who plants and sows
And watches the greedy foxes eat the vines
And patiently plants again.

Joe, child of the Ghetto
Manhattan Isaiah
Crying the prophet's cry among the sweatshops
"Hear O ye who swallow the needy
And destroy the poor of the land!"

Beloved countrymen
Gather together
You who came from the Don
The Ukrainian steppes
The Black Sea, the Carpathians
From the Manhattan jungles
To the Valley of the Moon

I sing of you all
Who built your homes upon volcanoes

Poem written in honor of Joe's sixtieth birthday, by friend and writer Irene Paull, printed in Jewish Currents *(September, 1960). Courtesy of Irene Paull and Morris U. Schappes.*

Crying,
"Woe unto them that are at ease in Zion
And stretch themselves out upon couches
Who eat the best lambs of the flock
And are not grieved for the affliction of Joseph!"

I have met you before
Met you in a thousand places
In anguish together we wept for Spain
And a part of us died with the Warsaw ghetto
In victories we have marched together
In different climates and on different coasts
We have lifted our songs together in a common chorus
And our love like diverse rivers has met together in a common sea.

Let us sing with our Joe
For this is the harvest
Hear how there's shouting in all the ravished villages of the world!
New waters are bursting the ancient dams
Sweeping old pyramids before them
New grass is growing upon the mountains
The valleys of man are green
And the time has come for man to dwell upon them.

For this is the century that our flowering tree must bear
From seed we planted on the top of Sinai!

This is the flowering century of Isaiah
When there shall be a highway and a road
Which shall be called the way of holiness
When men shall come singing
And sorrow and sighing shall fade away
For behold! There shall be a new heaven and a new earth
And former things shall not be remembered
When men shall build houses and inhabit them
When they shall plant vineyards and eat the fruit of them
When they shall not build and another dwell
When they shall not plant and another eat
As the days of a tree shall be the days of the people
When men shall enjoy the work of their hands.

Let us sing with our Joe
In the time of our harvest
But let us post our sentries on the hills
To guard our budding vineyards from the foxes
And summon to us all people of good will
To batter the swords to pruning hooks
The shields to ploughshares!

L'hayim, Joe! Sholem, beloved comrades!
To all the world, L'hayim! and Sholem!

me a feeling of accomplishment. My participation followed my personal conviction that no man is an island ... that the struggles of other people must be supported, no matter how small the personal contribution. I tried to follow my conception of a purposeful life. As I recall, Jack London put it this way: "A man is born not just to live, but to create."

10. Travels in 1963: The Soviet Union, Israel, Brazil

I took another sabbatical from the chicken ranch in 1963. It was not for a vacation, but for a pilgrimage to the Soviet Union and Israel. I wanted to see the remnants of my family who survived the Holocaust. I was curious to see how Jewish life was developing in other parts of the world. I wanted to pick up the threads of my own past.

Sheba did not want to make that trip, but she agreed it was important. So at the end of February in 1963, I flew alone over the hump of the globe to England. I spent a couple of weeks in London and Amsterdam with family. I made travel arrangements with Intourist, the travel agency of the Soviet Union, and soon I was on a train going from Amsterdam to Warsaw.

I shared my compartment with a group of Soviet Armenian chemical engineers who were returning from a trip to see new developments in Western Europe. Our conversation gave me a chance to brush up on my Russian. I was interested to know how the Armenian people fared under the Soviet system. The Armenians had been an oppressed people who suffered a holocaust under the Turks during World War I. We discussed the survival of the Armenians and the Jews in the twentieth century. They assured me that the Armenian people had their own territorial republic within the Soviet system, with encouragement of industrialization and Armenian culture. But there were three of them, so I could not have a frank one-to-one conversation about Soviet Armenian life.

When the train reached Poland, I met up with a group of Polish railroad workers who were traveling home for a few days. They too were curious about the *Amerikanets*, about my life in America. I learned they were of peasant stock and still had little farms. I told them that I noticed horses working in the fields the train passed and I asked, "Why the lack of agricultural mechanization?"

They explained, "After World War II the new government gave us small parcels of land to meet the needs of each family in our village. We produce enough for ourselves, and what is left we sell to the government. We don't want any Russian *kolkhoz*."

"All right, you don't want government control," I replied. "But wouldn't it be more productive with a tractor? Why not form a village cooperative.?"

"That sounds like Bolshevik ideas!"

I discussed this question of agriculture with a Polish railroad engineer I met over a meal in the dining car. He said that over two-thirds of the Polish population still lived on the land. It played havoc with the Polish economy, which needed manpower for industry. The government was trying to organize cooperatives, he said, but there was great resistance to any kind of collectivization.

We became so involved in our discussion that we continued to meet for meals until we reached Warsaw. At the railroad station, he insisted, "You are staying in Warsaw for a few days. Come to my home for dinner. I want you to meet my family. I want to continue our discussion. There is more I would like to know about America."

Traveling through Eastern Europe and Russia by train, I have had many such experiences. You meet someone, you share stories from your life, you exchange views. It is that traditional Slavic ease of conversation with strangers. I traveled to Warsaw and Moscow by train for that very reason.

My travels on trains in the United States have been disappointing in this respect. The American traveler minds his own business, and I twiddle my thumbs. Once, on a train from Washington to New York, I did get into a conversation with a history teacher who had been touring the capital. She took great pride in the monuments, the government institutions, the systems of checks and balances. I agreed with her, until the conversation turned to the building of atomic weapons. I questioned whether the Founding Fathers, with their sense of justice, would approve of such instruments of mass destruction. She indignantly replied that America never would use atomic weapons. I said, "Madam, Hiroshima and Nagasaki are not fictions. We Americans—you and I—dropped those atomic bombs. What makes you so sure it will not happen again?" From that moment, till we reached New York, she was deeply involved in reading, and so was I.

I regret that I did not have time to meet again with the Polish railroad engineer. I came to Warsaw for just a few days and definite purposes. I was to meet with George Siskind, who had been an activist in New York and who was forced to leave the U.S. during the McCarthy period. I wanted to learn about Jewish life in Poland and to visit the remains of the Warsaw Ghetto.

George showed me around Warsaw for four days. I already knew there were only thirty thousand Jews left out of millions from before the Nazis. Despite the small population, they had a bubbling Jewish cultural life. After the war, the new Polish socialist government treated the Jewish survivors well and encouraged Yiddish culture. A few years after my 1963 visit there came a period when the Polish government persecuted the remnants of Polish Jewry in an inhumane manner, but at the time of my visit Jewish life was flourishing in Poland.

George took me to the Jewish Cultural Center in Warsaw. It had extensive facilities for printing Yiddish newspapers, magazines, and books. It also printed educational material for Yiddish schools in Poland. Another evening George took me to a performance of the Yiddish theater, with the famous Yiddish actress Ida Kaminska. George introduced me to all kinds of Jewish cultural leaders. It was a high level of Yiddish culture, and it touched Jewish people all over Poland.

The Warsaw Ghetto was what I really wanted to see. George brought me there the first day. I stood in penetrating rain, looking at the rubble of blasted buildings, just as it was at the end of the Nazi destruction. To me that rubble represented the living story of the Warsaw Ghetto uprising. It was a desperate final resistance to nazism. It was a decision to die fighting, with honor, like my Jewish self-defense group in Stanislavchik decided during the Russian civil war. They fought off the Nazis for thirty-three days, longer than it took the German Army to conquer Poland or France. I was moved by that sight—a city square block with the rubble of destroyed buildings and a stirring sculpture as a monument to the struggle. It gave me a feeling of protest against the destruction of my people and a pride in our heroic resistance.

I arrived a few weeks before the twentieth annual commemoration of the Warsaw Ghetto uprising. There were plans for a large ceremony with delegations from all over the world. I arranged with one of the organizers for a telegram of solidarity to be sent to our Jewish Cultural Club memorial in Petaluma, and I inquired, "Will there be a delegation from the Soviet Union? After all, it is not only a remembrance of the Jewish dead, but it is an antifascist demonstration."

He answered, "We received no replies to the invitations we sent to Moscow, to Kiev, or anywhere else in the Soviet Union. You are going to Moscow. Stop in the office of Aaron Vergelis, the editor of *Sovetish Haimland*, the only Yiddish magazine in the Soviet Union. Ask him the question."

I learned more about Poland from my conversation with George. He confirmed what I learned on the train about the Polish agrarian problem in relation to industrialization. He elaborated further on the Polish dislike for the Soviet Union. He explained that Soviet control was not exercised so openly in Poland as in East Germany. He said that Poland, under Russian domination, was rebuilding the cities. But if it was not for the greater fear and hatred of the Germans, he said, there would have been even less Polish tolerance for the Soviet occupation since the war.

What I saw and what I heard in Poland confirmed my ideas about how socialism cannot come about through compulsion from the outside . . . through occupation by the Red Army. It was correct that the Soviet Union should break out of the *cordon sanitaire*, the circle of enemy countries that world imperialism constructed around Russia after the revolution. It was reasonable for the Soviet Union to demand friendly governments in those countries after World War II, but it is not surprising that the Polish people would not wholeheartedly accept the Soviet imposition of socialism. The inevitable result was a growth of Polish nationalism and an opposition to collectivization, especially in agriculture. It confirmed my view that socialism must be established on the basis of popular understanding of its humanism, of its promise of a better life for all.

After four days in Warsaw, I hopped a train for Moscow. Even though I traveled as an individual, rather than in a tourist group, I was met by an Intourist representative at the Moscow railroad station. She took me to my hotel, the Metropole, the same hotel where I stayed in 1934. And sure enough, as I walked into the lobby I saw a familiar face, Sophie Knizhnick, who had managed a left-wing summer camp in upstate New York in the 1930's. She was on her way to Kiev, and we arranged to meet when I got there.

First thing, I made contact with a person whose name I was given by George Siskind. That was Harry Eisman, whom I knew from New York in the 1920's as a young militant streetcorner orator. At the big Union Square unemployment demonstration of 1930, Harry Eisman was arrested and later sentenced to five years in prison for resisting arrest. Because he was just a youngster and not yet an American citizen, arrangements were made for him to be deported to the Soviet Union instead of sent to prison. In 1963 he worked for the Soviet-American friendship organization in Moscow.

I reached Harry Eisman on the telephone. I said, "I am calling at the recommendation of George Siskind. My name is meaningless to you, but we are blood brothers. Our blood was mixed on Union Square in the March 6 demonstration."

"Stay there! I am coming!"

I spent the entire day with this remarkable man. He had a story to tell! When he came to the Soviet Union in 1931, he was carried on the shoulders of the people as a hero. They wanted to send him to school, but Harry did not want to be a burden. So he worked as a machinist by day, and at night he got his education.

Harry married, he had a daughter, he continued his work and his education. Then his life was interrupted by World War II. He enlisted, he fought, he was wounded. The wound was not too serious, and he insisted upon returning to the front lines. He was wounded several times in the war, but he fought to the end. He still had shrapnel lodged in his body at the time of our meeting in 1963.

After the war he returned to his family and his factory, eager to resume his old life. However, he was arrested in the Stalin terror of the late 1940's. He did not know why, but he was sent to a camp for political prisoners in Siberia. Harry told me, "I did nothing wrong. I knew I was innocent. I knew justice would prevail."

Near his prison camp in Siberia he noticed broken down tractors in the fields. The Russian peasants burned out those tractors because they did not understand the need for oil. Harry volunteered to work extra and repair them. The officer in charge of his group refused, but Harry was a fighter and found a higher officer with a better political understanding. Harry repaired those tractors and continued to do that in Siberia. It shows the mettle of the man.

Only after Stalin's death, after the Twentieth Party Congress in 1956, was Harry rehabilitated by Khrushchev. He was a victim of Stalinism, yet he had so much faith in the Soviet system he was not bitter. Even as a political prisoner he overcame obstacles to serve the state and the people. His story explained a great deal about how the Soviet system survived Stalin's bloodletting. Harry told me, "In spite of Stalin's misrule the people worked on the jobs, produced the goods, and defended the country. We believed in the promise of the revolution and the Soviet system."[1]

This was one of the few conversations I had about Stalinism during my visit. People did not like to talk about it, nor about the Twentieth Party Congress. In fact, I detected a certain animosity against Khrushchev for the job he did on Stalin at that congress. But there was no open discussion of politics in the Soviet Union.

The next day I had a less informative meeting with Aaron Vergelis, the editor of *Sovetish Haimland*. I went to learn if a Soviet Jewish delegation would be going to the twentieth Warsaw Ghetto Memorial in Warsaw. He said his wife would go as a private observer, but his magazine would not send a delegation. As far as he knew, there would be no official delegation from any Jewish organizations in the Soviet Union.

He offered no explanation, and I did not ask for one. It would have meant explaining the Soviet Union's attitude towards the Jewish people. He changed the subject to small talk about my trip and his personal life. It was a brief, restrained conversation. He probably felt that I could not tell him anything new about Jewish radicalism in the United States. I knew I could not get anything from him that would deal intimately with the Jewish problem in the Soviet Union.

That editor and his journal represented the end of any Yiddish radical tradition in the Soviet Union. *Sovetish Haimland* did print some good Yiddish literature. It discussed Jewish life in Tsarist

days, during the war and the revolution, and occasionally it had
something on the Holocaust. But it had no real discussion of Soviet
Jewish problems of the day. It did not acknowledge that there was
any Jewish problem in the Soviet Union. That journal just went
through the motions of the official, superficial Soviet positions.[2]

I also spent time in Moscow with my niece's family from New
Haven, whom I met in Amsterdam and who flew into Russia ahead
of me for a long visit. One evening we saw a superb performance of
the Bolshoi Ballet at the Palace of Congresses within the walls of
the Kremlin. I was impressed by that theater, a building of marble
and glass with extraordinary fine construction for sound and
movement of crowds. That supermodern building would do pride
to any capitalist metropolis, but I was dissatisfied with how it
disturbed the architectual unity of the ancient structures within
the Kremlin.

Like my visit to Moscow in 1934, again I found an enormous
amount of building after the destruction of war. I found blocks and
blocks of new multiple story apartment buildings. The archi-
tecture was monotonous, but those apartments came with individual kitchens and bathrooms, instead of collective ones for entire
floors. It represented a great effort by the Soviet Union to catch up
with housing needs after the war.

I noticed a much higher standard of living in 1963 than what I
saw in 1934. The people dressed better, and there was plenty of
food. There was a shortage of fresh produce for which people
waited in long lines even when it was in season, and there were
shortages of consumer goods because the Soviet Union still
stressed investment in heavy industry. But one afternoon, when I
went shopping from store to store with my niece, I found
consumer goods more plentiful, better made, and more colorful in
appearance than what I saw before the war. Those stores were
packed with people buying all kinds of things.[3]

I also was impressed by an experience I had at a hospital the day
I was with Harry Eisman. I needed a vaccination against disease for
one of the countries ahead on my journey. We went to the nearest
hospital and explained my problem. I was accepted and treated.
When I was ready to leave, I asked what I owed for the service.
They said there was no charge for medical treatment in the Soviet

Union and as a guest of the country I did not have to pay either. That kind of security of medical care still does not exist in America, not even for American citizens.

From Moscow I traveled by train to Kiev, where I was met at the station by another Intourist representative. As we rode to the hotel I immediately inquired, "Can I travel around Kiev myself? Can I visit my sister in Bar? Can I visit my home town Stanislavchik?"

The most important reason for my visit was to meet with family, especially my sister Sorke. There always was a special feeling between us. Sorke was the main reason I survived the typhus epidemic during World War I. I joined the self-defense group during the revolution, especially with the idea of protecting Sorke from pogrommakers. Sorke was the one I corresponded with most from the Soviet Union.

I very much wanted to visit Stanislavchik, even though the Jewish people, the Jewish homes, and the Jewish stores were gone . . . even though I would see just the ruins of my former life in the Ukraine. I knew people from America who had visited their *shtetlekh* in that part of the Ukraine and were heart-broken—they only found destruction and a few Jewish survivors with horror stories. Nevertheless, I wanted to visit the cemetery where my parents were buried. I wanted to see the tombstone of Jewish life in my *shtetl*, and if a Jewish person still lived there, it would be so much more interesting to hear his story.

The answers to my questions were as I expected. No restrictions in Kiev, but I would have to approach higher authorities for permission to visit Sorke in Bar, my cousin Khayka in Zhmerinka, and my home town Stanislavchik.

The next morning I went to visit a relative, Khayim, in Kiev. From Cotati I already wrote him that I was coming. I did not telephone from the hotel, because I heard stories of people who were afraid to see American relatives. Not knowing how he would respond, I decided to go there and refuse to take no for an answer.

I took a cab to Khayim's address, which turned out to be half a mile from my hotel. I paid the driver the fare, which I later learned was above the standard rate, but he didn't let me out. He said, "You are an American."

"How do you know?"

"I can tell from your clothes."

Then he began pumping me for information about America. He wanted to compare his income with the income of an American taxi driver. He wanted to know how so many American wage earners could afford to visit the Soviet Union. He wanted to know how long I worked to pay for my clothes. He said the pay to taxi drivers, to all service workers in the Soviet Union, was too low.

I started to explain how the United States benefited from two world wars while Russia was devastated ... how Americans didn't have the security of employment and the social benefits of the Russian people. "And besides," I asked, "how do you know so much about America?"

"We listen, we talk, we know."

Here I saw that the Russian people were not altogether disconnected from the capitalist world. They did not just swallow the *Pravda* editorials. They drew their own conclusions on the basis of information from the Voice of America and from visitors, but a lot of that information was distorted.

I left the cab, walked over to the building, and located Khayim's apartment. He recognized me at the door, and he accepted me with the warm greeting of a lost relative. I spent that day getting acquainted with the family, exchanging experiences, toasting Sheba in Cotati. Khayim survived the war, he said, because he was a soldier at the front, which was a safer place for a Jew than among the civilian population of the Ukraine under the Nazi occupation. Now he worked as a dental mechanic in a clinic in a large factory. His income was good—better than my taxi driver or the factory workers—and they lived comfortably. The children were completing school and one was an accomplished violinist. They had a good life.

However, they were people who lived in fear. When Khayim took me for a walk in the street, he cautioned me against speaking Yiddish. When he learned that I found his apartment by asking kids in the courtyard, he said not to do that again. If I came by cab, I shouldn't stop in front of the building. And no, they would not visit me at my Intourist hotel. Khayim warned that there were government spies at the hotel, watching to see who came and where people went.

It didn't take long for me to learn that Khayim was not typical. That evening at the hotel I ran into my friend Sophie, whom I already bumped into in Moscow. When I stated my experience with Khayim, she invited me to meet her niece and nephew who would visit her the next morning. They were two young professionals, with no fears of entering the Intourist hotel. When I met them the next morning, we conversed in Russian and Yiddish, right in the hotel lobby. In fact, I spoke quite loudly in Yiddish—as I later did in the streets—and there was no reaction.

So there I had a two-sided story. What was fact and what was fancy? During this visit I discovered that a lot of people—especially Jewish people—were afraid of the government. In fact, some relatives in Kiev would not even see me. I attributed those fears to the historic persecution of the Jewish people over the centuries— by the Tsars, by the Ukrainian nationalists, and then by the Nazis. Those fears were revived during the Stalin terror after the war, when Jewish cultural leaders were murdered. That was a period when any contact with a foreigner was dangerous, and the Soviet Jewish people had a lot of relatives and friends in the United States and Israel.

Some people had personal reasons for fear. Those who were not living kosher—those who were dealing on the black market—did not want to call attention to themselves with foreign visitors. Others had denied the existence of any American relatives when they applied for Communist Party membership, and they feared expulsion from the Party when an American relative turned up for a visit. There were all kinds of justified reasons for fear of contact with foreigners, for fear of the government. But I was convinced that a lot of the fear was exaggerated at the time of my visit in 1963.[4]

My second day in Kiev I saw the hotel manager about visiting Bar, Zhmerinka, and Stanislavchik. He said it was impossible. I persisted, so he sent me to see the head of Intourist at the hotel. He too refused, and again I insisted upon speaking to higher authority. This was not like 1934, when I traveled with letters from the Needle Trades Workers Industrial Union and the Profintern. All I could do was push my way through the bureaucracy.

The Intourist manager sent me to the section of the Kiev police department that dealt with passports and visas. There I was referred to a police officer, who became enraged at the Intourist manager: "It is his responsibility to decide!" At my request, and to my surprise, he called the Intourist manager and said just that. When I returned to the hotel the attitude was entirely different: "Mr. Rapoport, we will look into it."

At nine o'clock the next morning there was a knock at my door: "Mr. Rapoport, we have some good news. We just received a telegram from your sister—she is taking the train to Kiev and will arrive at eight o'clock this morning." It was nine o'clock! The other good news was that I could rent an automobile and chauffeur to visit Bar, Zhmerinka, and Stanislavchik.

I dressed as fast as possible. On the way out I checked with the hotel manager to see where Sorke would stay. He said, "We are not responsible for your relatives. This is a hotel for visiting foreigners only, and we are booked up."

I said, "My room is big enough to hold a ball." It was an old hotel, where the rooms weren't built to save every inch, and I had a huge beautiful room. I said, "Bring an extra bed into my room. My sister is sixty-seven years old! Where else will I put her? And why should we separate?"

Again he told me the rules and refused. He gave me a list of other hotels, but he warned there was a convention of Ukrainian writers in Kiev and there was no possibility of finding a hotel room.

I couldn't continue this conversation. I already was late for the train. I hurried the taxi driver, but he reassured me that we were only two hours late and Sorke probably would be waiting for a bus to my hotel!

Sure enough, as we drove up to the railroad station, Sorke was standing in a line, just about to board a bus. I jumped out and ran to her. The reunion I can leave to the imagination ... the hugging and kissing and crying.

First thing, we took the cab to a different hotel, and again I heard the story there were no empty hotel rooms in Kiev. So we returned to my hotel to rest and see what's next. In the lobby the manager called me over and said, "I knew you could not find a room. Even though we are strict with the rules, I accept your reasoning that there can be exceptions. We put an extra bed in your room."

From there passed days of reacquaintance and reminiscence with Sorke and with her daughters who also came to see me in Kiev. It was a wonderful family reunion. We walked in the parks, shopped in stores, visited with family, and just talked. The first evening in the hotel dining room, when the band started playing dance music after dinner, I asked them to play "The Anniversary Waltz." When the other people learned that it was a reunion of brother and sister, they honored us with the dance floor to ourselves.

Sorke spent a week with me in Kiev. We relived all the hardships of the First World War and the revolution, all the joys of my return visit in 1934. She told me the story of how her family escaped the Holocaust by fleeing from Bar to Azerbaidzhan when the Germans invaded. About the Holocaust itself, about the destruction of our family and our *shtetl*, she would not talk. She froze everytime I touched the subject. It was too painful.

When I first told Sorke we could take a chauffeured automobile together back to Bar and Zhmerinka and Stanislavchik, she was happy to hear it. She lived part of the year with her daughter in Bar and part of the year with our aunt Rivka's daughter Khayke in Zhmerinka. The family was drawn closer than ever after the Holocaust. But soon Sorke changed her mind about my visit. "Yosele," she said. "We shouldn't do it. Khayke will be scared."

"Why?"

Joe with Sorke's daughter Rose, Khayim's niece Masha, and Sorke during 1963 visit to Kiev.

Again came the story of fears. Khayke had an incident—a postman asked why she received letters from America for Sorke—and she interpreted it as a check-up rather than curiosity. Khayke was scared to see me, and especially if I came with an Intourist chauffeur, a man who would watch whom I met.

However, when Sorke learned I would be traveling from Kiev to Prague, she said, "That international train stops in Zhmerinka in the middle of the night. I want to see you once more. I will meet you on the platform at the railroad station. I'll try to have Khayke and the rest of the family there. You be on the lookout."

I spent a few more days in Kiev after Sorke left. One afternoon I went to the old Jewish ghetto and the city's only remaining synagogue. It was the first day of Passover and people were pouring out of *shul* when I arrived. The services just ended and the people were talking outside. They were all older folks in their seventies and eighties. I didn't see a single young person among them. It was obvious that they wore their best holiday clothes, but those clothes were worn and ragged.

When I approached, they immediately recognized me as an American. I asked to see the *gabbai*, the head of the *shul*, and they sent me inside. This was my first time in a big city Ukrainian *shul*. There was a gallery above for the women, solid oak seats below, an ornate chandelier, and a hand-carved holy shrine where the Torah was kept. Everything was old and worn and faded. But that *shul* carried the signs of its early beauty like a person reflects youth in old age.

I did not see the *gabbai*, so I went outside. The people pointed out his assistant walking away, and then somebody said, "Don't trust him." He was a younger man, and they thought he was a Communist Party watchdog in the *shul*.

I caught up to him and explained that I wanted to talk about Jewish life in Kiev. He invited me to walk along as he returned home for the *seder*. First I asked if there were *matzos* available for Passover. At that time stories circulated in the United States that the Soviet government would not allow *matzos* to be baked for Passover. I already had a Passover dinner with my brother-in-law and there was plenty of *matzos* on the table. The assistant *gabbai* confirmed there was no shortage.

I learned from him that there was no persecution of the Jewish religion, but it was slowly being strangled out. The practice of religion was permitted, but they could not print new prayer books or get new religious articles like *taleysim*, prayer shawls, and *yarmlkes*, skullcaps. A few young men were allowed to attend rabbinical school in Romania, but not in the Soviet Union. Nor could the Jewish people send their children to Hebrew school in the Soviet Union. It was just the older people who prayed in *shul* and maintained the religious traditions.

Finally, I asked if he, a leader of the Kiev Jewish community, would attend the twenty-year commemoration of the Warsaw Ghetto uprising to be held in Warsaw. He was never informed of such a gathering, he said, and that meant the government did not want Soviet representatives to attend. Nor did the Soviet government want any commemorations in the Soviet Union. All he could do was a *kaddish* in *shul*.

The last thing I did in Kiev was to visit Babi Yar, the site of the great Nazi massacre of the Kiev population. At that huge ravine the Nazis murdered tens of thousands of Russians, Ukrainians, and Jews. It was mostly Jews, a complete round-up of every Kiev Jew they could find, even those who weren't friends of the Soviet system. The Nazis shot them and dumped the bodies in the ravine at Babi Yar.

My friend Sophie already warned me about Babi Yar. "Don't go," she said. "You'll just have a heartache." But I wanted to see that ravine and what the Soviet government was doing there.

On the ride to Babi Yar, the cab driver also warned that there was nothing to see. He was right. The approaching roads were torn up by heavy construction equipment. There were rows and rows of new apartment buildings being built in that area. Tractors were working all over, pushing rubble into the ravine. In fact, all the rubble from Kiev was brought to fill the ravine. Babi Yar was the city dump!

I could not locate the area of the mass grave without the help of the cab driver. There was nothing preserved, like the ruins of the Warsaw Ghetto, where you could reach out and touch, where there was a monument dedicated to the victims, where you could sit down and bow your head and say a prayer. At Babi Yar there was not so much as a sign. And this, after I saw in a park near my hotel a magnificent statue of Bogdan Chemielnitskii, the seventeenth-century hero of the Ukrainian people, the bestial murderer of the Jewish people.

I was deeply disturbed by what I saw at Babi Yar. But I had heard from the assistant *gabbai* that a monument was supposed to be erected there. I was determined to learn the truth. I remembered seeing on the Kreshchatik, the main boulevard of Kiev, a huge building that was the center of Ukrainian government. Instead of returning to the hotel, I went to that government building to find out what, if anything, was planned for Babi Yar.

There were two armed sentries in front of that massive government building. I walked right by them as if I was a Soviet citizen on important business. Me! Yosele Boydick from Stanislavchik! Inside I was referred from one office to another, until finally I was directed to yet another building which housed the Kiev Department of Parks and Monuments. I knew that you only get something when you reach top leadership . . . I learned that in America. So again I went from office to office until I reached the secretary of that Department of Parks and Monuments.

I explained my confusion over the dumping ground I saw at Babi Yar and the plans I heard for a monument. The secretary replied that both were true: they were filling up the ravine to make a park, and they were drawing up plans for a monument.

"What kind of monument?" I offered to show my reprint of the monument at the Warsaw Ghetto.

She said, "We have seen it. We are having a competition between the outstanding sculptors in the Ukraine to draw up plans for a monument."

I asked, "Will there be special mention of the Jewish people who were massacred, like at the Warsaw Ghetto monument?"

"That has not been decided," she said. And then she added, "I sense you feel we are discriminating against the Jewish people. Babi Yar is a mass grave of Soviet citizens—Jews, Russians, Ukrainians, all kinds of people. Is it necessary to say so many were Jews? We don't even know how many were murdered there.

"If you want to be convinced we are not discriminating against the Jewish people, you take a walk to the Monument of the Unknown Soldier in Kiev. There you will find gravestones of a few dozen outstanding heroes of the Ukraine among the millions who perished in the war against Hitler. Among them you will find

Jewish names. That is the highest expression of appreciation we can offer."

We parted very friendly. I did visit that monument, and it was as she said. It gave credence to my belief that you cannot draw conclusions from one horror story or from one heroism report. You must listen, you must observe, you must seek the source of accurate information and form a balanced opinion.[5]

I left Kiev earlier than I originally planned. After Sorke's visit, after I decided not to travel to Stanislavchik, I felt an emptiness ... a purposelessness in staying longer, I wanted to see the family at the Zhmerinka station, and then continue my journey to Israel. But something very disturbing happened on that train trip out of Russia.

My train to Czechoslovakia pulled into the Zhmerinka station in the middle of the night. I walked out on the platform, which was virtually empty, and there was Sorke with my cousin Khayke and her family. Of course, there were embraces and tears after so many years of separation. Khayke brought Passover presents for me — some *matzos*, potato *latkes*, chicken, apples, and a bottle of wine for my train ride. We had just a few minutes to exchange greetings and express hopes to meet again. Then I returned to the train, gave the goodies to the attendant in my car, and continued on to Czechoslovakia.

When the train approached Czechoslovakia, there was an inspection by Russian border authorities. Since I was not traveling in a tourist group with arrangements for easy border passage, I accepted as normal the very thorough inspection of my luggage. But then something happened that disturbed me ... it disturbed me very deeply. The inspector asked, "Did you meet anyone at the Zhmerinka station?"

I explained what took place. Then they questioned other people in my compartment about what I got at the station and whether I destroyed any documents. Then they questioned me again very closely.

I was not concerned about my own discomfort. I was worried about my family at the Zhmerinka station. From the way I was questioned, I sensed that my family was detained for questioning too. I realized that they must have been held for hours, until I would be checked at the border.

It almost drove me crazy! My relatives carried the scars of Tsarist persecution and Ukrainian pogroms and the horrors of the Holocaust. Now they were brutally harassed just because they met me for a few minutes at the railroad station in the middle of the night. I was shaken to the depth of my soul.

After I crossed the border one of the co-travelers in my compartment, a Soviet functionary, tried to reassure me. She knew from our earlier conversation that I was a friend of the Soviet Union, that I appreciated the many positive accomplishments I found on my trip. She said it was natural for the nation to be on guard against enemies and I should feel proud that I was given an *attestat*, a clean bill of health, after thorough inspection. However, I was not troubled by their alertness, but by their brutal rudeness. It gave me concern for my family, and it gave me more of an understanding of why so many innocent people lived in fear in the Soviet Union.

When I reached Prague, I immediately went to the Soviet Consulate to obtain information about what happened to my family. The consulate officials refused to do anything. They had the attitude of people afraid to step on other toes. They just let me write a report of the entire incident, which I am certain ended up in the wastepaper basket. To this day I don't know what happened after my train left Zhmerinka. I could learn nothing from Soviet officials, and it was never mentioned in later letters from my family.

I spent a few days in Prague with Abe Chapman, whom I knew from the radical movement in New York. He had been an editor of *Jewish Life*, one of our radical Jewish publications, and he was forced to leave the United States for citizenship reasons during the McCarthy period. Now he worked for the international trade union movement in Prague. He was well informed and willing to speak freely.

Abe praised the development of socialism in Czechoslovakia. The country already was industrialized when it became a socialist society after World War II. City life, the machine, and the factory were more familiar to the Czechs than to most other East European peoples. Collectivization and mechanization, in industry and agriculture, made more sense to them. As a consequence, there was greater productivity and prosperity in Czechoslovakia than elsewhere in Eastern Europe.

Abe was proud of the democratic development of Czech socialism at that time. He attributed it to the prewar Czech experience with bourgeois democracy, which never existed in Poland or Russia. There was not the creation of a total socialist dictatorship in Czechoslovakia, like what replaced the Tsarist power in Russia and the reactionary regime in Poland. I found an atmosphere of freedom of expression and freedom of criticism that I did not see in any other socialist country.

A few years later, when the Red Army invaded Czechoslovakia, I could not accept the Soviet explanation that antisocialist elements had been taking over. I believe the Soviet leadership feared that Czech democracy might spread to other countries under Soviet control and even to the Soviet Union. That invasion, that over-throw of the Czech government, was a great tragedy for the socialist movement in the world. From my brief observation in 1963, I concluded that Czechoslovakia was developing a high level of socialism that combined collectivization of property with political freedom.[6]

My impression of Czechoslovakia pointed up my conclusions about the socialist countries I visited in 1963. As in my 1934 trip to the Soviet Union, I was impressed by the economic development and the social services. Again it was a period of digging out and rebuilding after a war. But I found a great improvement in clothing, in housing, in the general standard of living since 1934. There was excellent public education, excellent public health, and a general feeling of economic security. I appreciated the scientific production and the economic democracy in those socialist societies.

I also found things I did not like, including the attitude toward the Jewish people in the Soviet Union. A lot of the accusations in the United States were exaggerated. A lot of the fears of Soviet Jews, of my own family, were exaggerated. But there were a lot of restrictions—against the practice of religion, against a Jewish education for Jewish children, against Jewish emigration from the Soviet Union. It was unsocialist and it was unnecessary.

On my third trip in the Soviet Union in 1977, I was more sensitive to the problem of outright anti-Semitism. On this visit I was more critical on the question of simple human rights. When you dealt with government officials, you still felt the iron heel and

the whip from Stalin's time. Beyond that was the more basic
problem of total government control over the people. By 1963 the
Soviet Union, instead of becoming a classless society, had become
the dictatorship of the Communist Party over the people. There
were not real rights to freedom of expression, public disagreement, the running of opposition candidates in free elections. In
contrast to Czechoslovakia, there was no democratic spirit. There
was hardly any talking of politics at all.

I took a train to Vienna, and from there I caught a plane for Israel. I
had a joyful feeling on that El-Al flight. It was emotional memories
of my grandfather keeping his little sack of Palestine earth all the
years I was growing up ... of my mother singing songs of Israel
while plucking goosefeathers by the *hrube* ... of the stories about
ancient Israel that I read as a boy in *kheyder*. As the plane set down
at Lod airport in Tel Aviv, I had a feeling of return to my own
history.

I stayed my first week in Israel with Sheba's cousin Shayka,
whom I knew as a boy when he lived in Zhmerinka. In the early
1920's he worked with groups of *chalutzim*, pioneers, who were
organizing Jewish people to leave the Soviet Union and build a new
Jewish life in Palestine. Shayke, however, remained in the Ukraine
until he was arrested for Zionist activities. He was ordered to leave
and he went to Palestine.

Shayka settled on a *kibbutz* with other young Jews who drained
swamps, cleared fields, grew crops, and built homes. They were
the pioneers who began to develop the country. They did not have
the advantages of pioneers in the early American West, who found
rich lands, virgin forests, and abundant wildlife to rob from the
Native Americans. Palestine was a barren land, undeveloped by the
Arabs, and the Jewish settlers bought the cheapest, least fertile
lands. On top of that, they were young people from the lower
middle-class life of the *shtetl* with no experience at heavy labor,
with no callouses on their hands. In Russia it was called *belo-
ruchki*, white hands, or "white collar," as we call it in the United
States.

They were determined to do what was necessary to build a new
life for themselves ... for the Jewish people. They believed the
Jewish people would not be allowed to live peacefully in other

nations. There were periods when the Jewish people were accepted where they lived in the Diaspora, where they could assimilate to a degree. But always there was a separation and anti-Semitism. Modern Zionism grew in reaction to anti-Semitic attacks in the late nineteenth and early twentieth centuries. During World War I and the Russian Revolution, the Zionists were convinced that the Jewish people would have security only in a Jewish national homeland.

Those who came to Palestine from the time of the First World War were a new breed of Jewish immigrant. Before that it was religious people like my grandfather who came to the Holy Land to pray, to cry, and to die near the ruins of the Great Temple. The Arab people looked upon those older Jewish settlers as a strange people who came to die in their land. But the new young idealistic settlers came with the idea of making good on the Balfour Declaration, of creating a new Jewish society.

This was not a desirable development to the Arab people. There was Arab opposition—Arab anti-Semitism—all the way through the twentieth century. But these young Jewish settlers came with experience of war and with the will to defend themselves. Like other pioneers, they worked the plow with one hand and kept the gun in the other hand.

My cousin Shayka was among those young pioneers. He was a builder of Israel, an elder, a part of the generation that was honored. He met his wife on that first *kibbutz* and they raised a fine family. In 1963 Shayke was working as an administrator at the Technion, a famous technical institute in Haifa.[7]

Shayke had two beautiful daughters, Rena and Shule, who represented the new kind of Jewish people growing in Israel. They were educated, trained young people who grew up building a Jewish nation. They grew up with the struggle for the existence of Israel. It was a different kind of struggle than the Jewish resistance to anti-Semitism and pogroms in the Diaspora. They had military training in the Israeli Army. They were ready to drop the shovel and pick up the gun at the first alarm. They were minutemen, always on the watch, always prepared to defend their people and their country. They were a proud new generation.

They even looked different from the Jewish young people of the Diaspora. They had no timid expression in their faces, like the

young people I grew up with in the Ukraine, even those who
defended the life and honor of the Jewish people through self-
defense groups. These young Israelis had no fear in their faces.
They had straight backbones and strong shoulders. They was a self-
assuredness in their appearance and in their manner.

My first day in Israel I told Shayke that I wanted to visit the
kibbutz of some Israelis I met at my hotel in Kiev. They were a
group of twenty people who, like me, came to see their families in
the Soviet Union. I was amazed that one *kibbutz* could afford to
send so many people on a vacation to the Soviet Union. They said it
was possible because their *kibbutz* had developed a large profitable plywood factory.

In Kiev I asked the leader of the group if I could visit their
kibbutz Affikim when I reached Israel. That man, who was
secretary of the *kibbutz*, was very receptive. In fact, he asked me to
go there the first thing when I arrived in Israel. He gave me a small
cut-glass vase and said, "Bring this to my wife as soon as possible."

After all the time I spent in Prague and Vienna, and then a few
more days becoming reacquainted with Shayke in Haifa, that
secretary reached Kibbutz Affikim before I got there. When I
arrived, he was very aggravated that I had not delivered the cut-
glass vase earlier. He said, "You would have saved a lot of worry for
my family. Didn't you read the world newspaper reports of what
happened to me?"

I didn't know what he was talking about. He explained. When he
visited with his family in the Ukraine, he talked about his life on the
kibbutz. He described the sharing of income, the rotation of jobs,
the equality of all members regardless of status in leadership, the
collective raising of children, the eating together, the spirit of
service rather than grabbing for oneself.

This was a higher level of socialism, with a higher standard of
living, than what was practiced on a *kolkhoz* or anywhere else in
the Soviet Union. When one of the secretary's brothers, who was a
high ranking Red Army officer, heard this, he reported that
secretary, his own brother, to the authorities as a Zionist agitator
who was spreading propaganda and lies.

The secretary was arrested soon after he gave me that glass vase.
I did notice that he was uneasy in Kiev. It turned out that he had
wanted to reassure his family that he would be all right, and that's

why he wanted me to deliver the vase immediately. By the time I reached *kibbutz* Affikim he already had been arrested and deported from the Soviet Union. He said, "I simply described the reality of *kibbutz* life. They just could not visualize real socialism."

However, there was something else about *kibbutz* Affikim which explained its riches and which raised questions about its socialism. They got the bulk of their income from a large plywood factory. They imported the lumber from Africa, processed it, and sold the plywood on international markets. Since the basic life of the *kibbutz* was agriculture, and they didn't have enough labor for the factory, they hired workers from nearby communities.

I asked, "Are the factory workers considered part of the *kibbutz?*"

"No. They come from all over this area to work for us because we pay good wages, but they are not *kibbutz* members. The *kibbutz* members work the land and manage the factory."

"What about exploitation and surplus value? Do the workers share in the profits at the end of the year?" The answer was no.

It seems that *kibbutz* Affikim, while being a socialist organization, also was an industrial exploiter, squeezing profits out of the labor of others. That's how the *kibbutz* could send twenty members on a vacation to the Soviet Union and maintain a high style of living. It was a two class system, with one group of workers as the collective exploiter of another group.

I found the same thing at other *kibbutzim* I visited in Israel. It was a policy of the central organization of *kibbutzim* that each *kibbutz* should spread out from agriculture. I found one *kibbutz* with a factory producing needles, another with a sugar mill, others with facilities for the scientific production and processing of fish. Most *kibbutzim*, large and small, had some kind of industrial production with hired labor.

It seems the *kibbutzim* were following the path of capitalist industrialization with all the disease of exploitation and profiteering. There was opposition from the older generation, the pioneers, but they could not resist the pressure from the center. It was the top leadership of the central organization of *kibbutzim*, the economists who dealt with markets and economic growth, who pushed the *kibbutzim* in a capitalist direction. It also was pressure from the younger people, who wanted additional income and a better life for their families. It was the eternal struggle between the desire for something pure and just, and the desire for profit and prosperity. Time worked like a grinding stone on the original socialists ideals of the *kibbutzim*.

I found greater agricultural productivity on the *moshav*, which was a cooperative in which people owned their own homes and their own chunks of land. Even though it was individual owner-ship, they operated the land collectively, with greater specializa-tion and mechanization than the *kibbutz*. The *moshav* not only had greater agricultural production, but it was a more flexible form of organization. Each family received its share of the profits. They had their own homes and ate separately with their own families. They had more privacy and individual expression within the collective framework.

Nevertheless, I basically liked what I saw in the *kibbutz*. I was told that the *kibbutzim*, which held a small percentage of the population, produced a high proportion of army officers. It was a reflection of the discipline and the cooperative spirit of the *kibbutzim*. There was no individual competition for anything better than what the *kibbutz* could provide for everybody. Each did according to his ability, whether it was washing dishes or milking cows. All got the same with room for individual taste and needs. I would say that in the future, when the Israeli people decide to change from capitalism, they will have the *kibbutz* and the *moshav* as a yardstick for a collective society.[8]

I was as interested in the past as the future during my visit to Israel. On that trip to *kibbutz* Affikim, near the ancient city of Tiberias, the road was filled with busses and cars packed with people. I asked Shayke where they were going. He explained that once a year a great number of Jews from Arabic countries, especially Yemenite Jews, gathered at the shrine of Rabbi Mayer Baalnes, whom they believed to be a miracle man with a power to heal the sick and to bring good fortune.

I was curious to see that shrine. Shayke was reluctant. He was an Ashkenazic Jew, an East European Jew. Like me, he was influenced by modern ideas from back in Russia. He was part of the historic movement for relaxation of "the law of Moshe" in Israel. He was not interested in these pious Sephardic Jews who continued the ancient beliefs and rituals. But I insisted, and we did stop.

I was startled by what I saw at that shrine. There were hundreds of crippled people who came to be cured. Others simply came to say a prayer for a newborn child or a newly married couple. The people who came by car would open their trunks and take out a lamb or a kid goat or a chicken. Live animals! For sacrifice! Everyone brought candles. On the shrine there was a thick layer of wax from years of burning candles. There were large rooms for group prayer inside, and outside were sulphur baths, which had a healing effect.

I do not know if Mayer Baalnes was simply cashing in on those sulphur baths for his reputation as a miracle man. But that whole scene with hundreds of people coming to pray and to sacrifice took me centuries back into the past. That piety with the sacrifice of animals and the belief in the Messiah and the faith in miracles was right out of the Old Testament. Here I was traveling in Israel, with all its modern life, and suddenly I walked into the ancient world.

As I traveled in Israel, I found a sharp division between the Sephardic Jews, who came from the backwardness of Arab countries like Syria and Iraq and Morocco and Yemen, and those who came from Eastern Europe. There was a difference of a thousand years of cultural development between these two peoples. The Sephardim brought the ancient scholarship of the Torah and craft skills for the making of carpets and jewelry, but they were unfamiliar with modern ideas and modern industrial development. They were dark skinned and indistinguishable from Arabs. There was a deep cultural division—almost a racial division—in the Jewish population of Israel.

Those different peoples were united by Israel as the God given home of the Jews ... by ancient history and ancient religion as expressed in the Torah ... by the circumstances of world politics after the Holocaust and the war. I had heard there was a racist attitude toward the Sephardim, but I found something else. I found a deliberate attempt to assimilate the two peoples.

I had a long discussion about this on an overnight bus tour of the Red Sea area. When I tried to strike up a conversation with a Sephardic young woman sitting next to me, I was surprised to hear her speak a beautiful Yiddish. It seems that she was born in Syria, where she learned Hebrew and Arabic, but she grew up in Tel Aviv on the same block with Polish refugees who only spoke Yiddish. She learned Yiddish from the Polish children and helped them learn Hebrew.

She said there was government encouragement of integration, but there was resistance on both sides. "My father will never adapt to modern society," she said. "He is sweeping the streets in Tel Aviv to make a living, and he never will learn anything else. Nor does he want to mix. He does not believe the white Jew's religion is good enough for him. Their traveling and working on the Sabbath is unacceptable. He lives by the will of God: *borukh ha shem yom-yom*, praise the Lord from day to day."

"My father is too old to change," she said. "But my generation of Sephardim is encouraged in school, in the military, in every phase of Israeli life. I had an opportunity for education and now I am a teacher with the same wages as others. There is an opening of doors for equality."

She thought the process of assimilation of the two peoples was just a matter of time. I agreed. I saw mixing of Sephardic and Ashkenazic Jews in all kinds of situations during my travels in Israel. Such a process takes decades and generations, but in 1963 I already saw mixed marriages and beautiful children. I saw continuous efforts toward assimilation by the government and by the people, that will bring results much faster than the centuries of racial division in America. That problem will not persist in Israel.[9]

I found the contrast between the very ancient and the very modern throughout Israel. On my trip to the Dead Sea, again I had that feeling of return to history. The terrain of the country—the hills, the desert, the Dead Sea—evoked the feeling of ancient history. Here is where the Prophets walked, here is where the Kings ruled, here is where the Judges sat; here is where Samson fought, where King David fought, where the Maccabees fought. I felt like I was traveling through the ancient history of my people. I was elated.

That trip ended at Elath, at the top of the Gulf of Aqaba, where Israel met up with Egypt, Jordan, and Saudi Arabia. That little community at the edge of the Negev Desert was growing fast. I saw all kinds of flimsy structures that were thrown up to house new Romanian settlers. But they also were building on a permanent basis with large blocks of native stone ... building that was solid, durable, and modernistic. When I revisited Israel ten years later, I was not surprised to find that little community had become a city of twenty thousand people with paved roads, luxury hotels, cultural institutions, night life, and a prosperous economy.

Everywhere I saw the genius of the Jewish people at work to make that barren land a functioning, prospering place. There was a tremendous modern economic development in industry and agriculture. There were modern buildings, modern roads, big stores, advanced educational institutions. Everywhere there was the application of science for the improvement of life. Even in Jerusalem, where the old part of the city was under Jordanian rule in 1963, there were modern government buildings, a hospital and a university spreading out on the Israeli side. They built up that country from scratch.

Of course, there were the negative features of a developing capitalist society. There were the haves—the manufacturers, the exploiters—trying to squeeze labor and profits from the workers. It was a class society like every other modern industrial capitalist society. There was exploitation, there was a working-class movement, there was class conflict, but it was a democratic capitalist society at work.

I also found areas of poverty in the Israeli big cities that reminded me of the East Side of New York in the 1920's. I knew Americans who returned from Israel with petty criticism of all the little hole-in-the-wall stores and the pushcart peddlers on the streets. I disagreed. I learned that many people who came to Israel after the Holocaust were broken in body and spirit. They were not able to swing the pick and shovel. Did they live on charity? No, they opened little candy stores, they sold oranges in the streets, they applied their little knowledge of exchange, and they tried not to be a burden on the government. Knowing their history, I sympathized with those people. I appreciated that there was room for them in Israel when no other country would take them after the war.

At the time of my visit, despite all the economic development, life was very uneasy in Israel. It was after the 1947-1948 War for Independence, after the 1956 Suez invasion. But there was a state of undeclared war with the Palestinian Arabs. Small groups of guerrillas would cross into Israel under cloak of darkness. They would attack a *kibbutz* or sneak into homes and slit the throats of people. No one was safe. There was forever a danger of attack . . . forever an alertness by the Israeli people.

That constant threat of Palestinian attack, that sharp antagonism between Israel and the Arab world, was a cementing element for the Jewish people. Israel was a country of many borders and many enemies. Despite all their differences, the Israelis had to unite to defend themselves.

At that time, there was a cry from the opponents of Israel and even from some Jewish radicals in Israel and in the United States that the Jewish people were responsible for the suffering of the Palestinians. It was charged that during the War for Independence the Jewish people took Palestinian homes and lands. It was said that the Palestinians were a grieved people who were fighting a just struggle through guerrilla warfare to reclaim what was theirs.

I heard another view from the manager of *kibbutz* Alonim, a border *kibbutz* that was under constant threat of Palestinian attack. The father of that *kibbutz* manager, Nachman Meisel, was an outstanding writer in the American Jewish radical movement. I expected that young Meisel, whom I came to see at his father's suggestion, would give me a balanced report on the Palestinian question.

He said, "We did not chase the Palestinians from their homes. It was their own greed that did them in. They would not accept the 1947 United Nations resolution, which created an independent Jewish state and an independent Palestinian state. When the Arab nations declared war on Israel in 1948, they expected to destroy us with no trouble. They urged the Palestinians to leave their homes, join the Arab armies, and return after the Jewish population was destroyed. The Palestinians left with the promise of getting back their own homes and the Jewish homes to boot."

He continued, "We won the war. The Palestinians who remained in Israel were not disturbed. But those who went to the other side lost their homes and their chance to build a Palestinian state. Then the Arab nations that made the big promises placed the Palestinian refugees into terrible concentration camps instead of absorbing them into Arab societies. An entire generation of Palestinians grew up under those conditions with hatred toward

Israel. It is the Arab responsibility to solve the problem they created for the Palestinian people. Instead they are raising murderers in those camps."

"We cannot open the doors of Israel to people who hate Jews!" He pointed to his children and said, "Nor will I let them sneak in and kill my family. I will defend my home if I am attacked. I will not compensate those who want to slit our throats! It is the Arabs who rejected the United Nations compromise. Let the Arabs be responsible for the consequences!"[10]

The radical movement in Israel was very torn on this Palestinian question. During my 1963 trip, I visited with all kinds of left-wing institutions and marched in a May Day parade with thousands of Israeli workers. I met with left-wing leaders from the Social Democratic Party, Mapam, and from the Communist Party, Maki. Those left-wing parties wholeheartedly supported the existence of Israel and fought for a socialist society. They also believed that the establishment of friendly relations with the Arab world, particularly the Palestinians inside and outside Israel, did not brook delay.

I had followed their publications for years and thus my discussions with those left-wing leaders were like continuing an old conversation. I knew their problems. In the late 1940's, those left-wing parties received strong popular support on the basis of their demands for social justice and their friendship with the Soviet Union. Israel came into existence with Soviet support in the United Nations and Israel won the War for Independence against the Arabs with military support from Communist countries. Mapam was the second largest party in the Israeli Knesset during those years.

But then came the Cold War with all its divisions. The United States, the lifeline for Israeli existence, demanded that Israel develop closer economic ties and shift away from friendly relations with the Soviet Union. This became the policy of Mapai, the right-wing socialist party that held power in Israel. From that time the Soviet Union moved toward support for the Arab nations and the Arab nationalist movements that wanted to destroy Israel.

What could the left wing do? As Arab attacks continued, as war repeated itself, as the Soviet gun fed the Arab cause, the Israeli people responded to any mention of communism with "Russian murderers." They turned away from the left-wing parties, and the parties splintered over the correct policies toward the Soviet Union and the United States, toward the Palestinian people and the Arab nations. That early left-wing Israeli movement was a casualty of the Cold War and a great loss to the possibility of peace in the Middle East.

The left-wing Jewish movement in the United States also was very torn on this question. We supported the existence of Israel, but we also called for settlement of the Palestinian question. We believed that each people had to recognize the other's right to exist as an independent nation. In many cases, we went overboard in our criticism of Israeli refusal to help the Palestinian refugees. But it was a difficult question with just claims on both sides and no easy solutions.[11]

While in Israel, I met up with a person I knew from my youth in the Ukraine. I got in contact with her through my old friend Khayim Berger, who I knew from the year I was a printer's apprentice in Bar. For forty years after the revolution, when I was living in America and he was living in Brazil, we corresponded. When I wrote him about my travel plans, he urged me to see his cousin Masha in Tel Aviv.

I also knew Masha from Bar, because I spent a lot of time with Khayim's family that year. In fact, my boss at the printing shop also had an interest in that family . . . in Masha. Anytime he learned I was going for a visit, he would send some flowers with me for Khayim's beautiful cousin.

I called Masha in Tel Aviv and told her that I wanted to visit. I refused to tell her who I was; I just said I was an old friend of her cousin Khayim, who asked me to send personal regards. Then I bought a bouquet of the flowers I love best—the gladiola . . . red gladiolas.

When I arrived at the door, Masha said, "Who are you?"

I gave her the gladiolas and said, "I am the boy who used to bring you the flowers from Riven Wilner in 1913. This is the last bouquet I forgot to deliver."

Masha, the old lady at the door, was just a shadow of the beautiful graceful girl I remembered, but I was not exactly the boy who brought her the flowers either. We spent a wonderful afternoon engrossed in memories from the Ukraine.

I left Israel soon after that reunion. In the letter I received from my old friend Khayim, telling me to look up Masha, he also suggested that since I would be on the go, why not "hop across" the Atlantic and visit him in Brazil on my way home from Israel. I had hoped he would make that proposition, and in Israel I sent him a telegram that I would visit him in Rio de Janeiro.

The trip to Brazil was uneventful. From Israel I flew to Rome, where I caught an airplane for Rio. I was met at the airport by my old pal Khayim, whose name means "life" in Yiddish. In Brazil he took the Russian name Boris, and so I will refer to him. Boris met me at the airport with his entire family. His son Gerson, who was a member of the Rio city council, speeded me through customs, and thus began four exciting weeks in Brazil.

We had a lot of catching up to do after forty-five years. I was fascinated to hear the story of how Boris went from the Ukraine to Brazil. Before I left for America I knew he was in love with a beautiful girl from Bar, Rose, whose father already had immigrated to Brazil. Not long after I left the Ukraine, a delegate arrived to take the rest of Rose's family to her father in Brazil. Rose refused to go without her loving Khayim. He decided to go along with her to Brazil.[12]

It seems that Boris was a persona non grata when he arrived in Rio. Rose's father already had a big furniture store, and he had plans for Rose to marry a prosperous young Brazilian Jew. But Rose wanted to marry Boris. He was a handsome dark complexioned young man—intelligent and lively, the center of attention in any group, the *soul* of a party. They married and Boris went his independent way to make a living.

He started peddling on the streets of Rio without even knowing Portuguese, the language of the land. He worked his way up. He developed a furniture business, he invested in real estate, and then he became a building contractor. By the time I arrived he was a very rich man. His son Gerson, who was in business with him, was a political leader in Rio and the head of the Zionist movement in Brazil. Boris's grandchildren were securing high education. The entire family was well established in Brazilian life.

Boris not only was very rich, but he was very conservative. At that time there was a liberal government in Brazil under the leadership of João Goulart. He advanced a series of reforms, not only to redistribute land to landless peasants, but also to regulate apartment rents in favor of poor people in the cities. Boris, as a real estate speculator and builder, was very unhappy with the government reform trends.

Boris took me on a tour of Rio. It is a magnificent city, a world metropolis that has a European appearance with its wide tree-lined boulevards and old buildings. We not only walked the streets, but Boris took me up to Sugar Loaf Mountain, which overlooks the city and the magnificent shoreline. From there I saw the *favellas*, the communities of impoverished people who lived in tiny shacks made from scrap wood, tin, and cardboard. Those *favellas* reminded me of the Hoovervilles in the United States during the Great Depression.

The only good thing about the *favellas*, in Rio, was their location. They were clinging like fungus to the hills surrounding the city. Boris *kibbitzed* about it. "Our world is twisted," he said. "The poorest people are up on the hills with the fresh air and the fabulous views, and we, the poor rich, live below and look up to them." Boris explained that arrangement came about decades back, in the days of horse and carriage, when the rich did not want to climb mountains to go back and forth from the city.

I had many impressions from my weeks in Rio, my week in the supermodern capital of Brasilia, and my week in São Paulo, "the Chicago of Brazil." But I was most interested in the Jewish community of Rio.

On one side was Boris, his family, and his friends. They were rich and conservative and Zionist oriented. I had a sharp encounter with these people. Boris arranged for me to speak on my travels in the Soviet Union and Israel to a gathering of friends and relatives. That meeting took place at Rose's sister's house, which was like a palace. The entry foyer was larger than my entire house in Cotati. The living room was so large I suggested that the host provide us with walkie-talkies to communicate across the room. Everything was expensive—imported marble from Italy, fine rugs and furniture, goodies of all kinds. They were so damn rich!

They gave me a criss-cross examintion on my trip and my position on the Jewish problem. If Boris was the black sheep in his family, I certainly was the red sheep in that gathering. They argued there was no religious freedom for Soviet Jews; I insisted the Soviet

Union had a right to demand freedom from oppression of religion. They complained that Jews could not leave the Soviet Union; I agreed, but I reminded them that Soviet Jews had excellent education, improved standard of living, and full citizenship rights under the Soviet system. They opposed the Soviet Union and the Arab nations as enemies of Israel; I insisted that Israel had to recognize what was just in the historic Palestinian claims for their own nation. I described the situation as I saw it, as a friend of the Soviet Union and of Israel, but I would not hide the negative features in either country.

I also had an encounter with the left-wing Jewish movement in Rio. I had there a left-wing acquaintance, Serota, whom I met in Romania in 1919 on my way to America, and whom I met up with again in the 1940's when he visited New York from Rio. Serota was the son of a famous photographer in Zhmerinka and he became an outstanding photographer in Rio. He too was a wealthy man—my impression was that every Jewish person in Rio was wealthy—but he was part of the left-wing movement.

That movement was bubbling with activity. They had an excellent Yiddish school, a Yiddish library and a fine Yiddish newspaper, and all kinds of organizations and activities. I attended one of their cultural evenings, a gathering in honor of H. Leivick, one of the oustanding Yiddish poets in America. The reading of his poetry and the singing of his songs showed a high level of Yiddish culture. I found myself visiting another branch of my own denomination.

That cultural evening was part of a larger conference they held while I was in Rio. I was asked to give a detailed report on my travels in Europe and in Israel. In the discussion that followed, I came under attack from one of the leaders of the group, an outstanding Brazilian Jewish Communist educator. He actually lived in exile in Argentina, because he faced arrest in Brazil, but he could shuttle in and out of the country without much danger.

He had just been in Poland for the twentieth anniversary commemoration of the Warsaw Ghetto uprising. He had been on a parallel course with me, traveling through the Soviet Union and Israel before returning to South America. When I described the backwardness of Polish agriculture, he reported that he actually traveled in the Polish countryside with government officials and saw nothing but prosperity. When I reported the restrictions on Jewish life in the Soviet Union, especially the absence of Soviet Jewish representation at the Warsaw Ghetto memorial, he reported Soviet Yiddish culture was flourishing. When I reported the prosperity in Israel and the need for understanding the poverty as a legacy of the Sephardic Jews and the Holocaust, he insisted the Israeli economy was going backwards with peddlers and small business, that Israel was a corrupt society with pornography and prostitution and all the evils of capitalism.

I received just as rough treatment from the left wing as I did from Boris's right-wing Zionist friends. It is no surprise, then, that there was a sharp antagonism between the Jewish radicals and the Jewish conservatives in Rio. It was just like Petaluma.

I returned to the United States after three months of travel. It was an excellent trip, a journey of supreme interest. I visited all kinds of places I never saw before, even in the Soviet Union, but especially my visit to Israel, a place that generations in my own family yearned to see. I had a chance to see for myself how socialism was developing in the Soviet Union, how life was developing for the Jewish people in other parts of the world.

Upon return to the United States in New York and then in Petaluma, I reported upon my travels. Like in Brazil, I found that if I did not go the full hog one way or another, if I criticized some aspects of Israel before Zionists or if I called attention to some defects in the Soviet Union before leftists, I met strong opposition. I found myself battling criticism from the Right and the Left. Nevertheless, I refused to be pinned down to one simple line. Up to the present day, I believe that fair-minded people must be friends of the Soviet Union and of Israel, and as friends we must stress the positive and still call attention to the negative.

11. The Struggle Continues

*T*hrough all my years in the United States, I heard that Americans have free choice of how to work and how to live. It is ironic that I was forced out of the chicken business in California much the same as I was forced out of the knitting industry in New York. I lost my job as a hand knitter because of the introduction of power knitting machinery. That's how I became a chicken farmer. Then I was forced out of chicken farming because of new scientific production and greater capital investment in the poultry industry. My choices, my life as a hand knitter and as a chicken farmer, were changed against my will.

Over the decades, American agriculture generally has developed so that the family farmer could not receive a substantial return on his product. The family farmer has been steadily pushed out by larger operators, by huge corporations that actually built "factories in the fields." This was part of the continuous concentration of ownership in American agriculture.

When I came to Petaluma after the war, you could make a living by working a hen ranch with four thousand chickens. If you had ten thousand hens, you were one of the *kulaks*, the rich, who could afford modern homes, new cars, and children in college. However, the big feed companies were beginning to produce livestock too. They purchased grain in the carloads, they built fully automated chicken houses that held over one hundred thousand birds, they marketed the product themselves with the most modern methods. They integrated the operation, produced in volume, and cut costs at every corner. These corporations did everything possible to eliminate the nuisance of competition from the small operators. Even the most capable family farmer was driven out of business in just a matter of time.

The farmers organizations were not much help. The most powerful farm organization, the Farm Bureau, was controlled by conservative large farmers who would not act in the interests of the family farmer. I joined the Grange in the hope that it would defend the small farmer. Through our Grange chapter, I participated in attempts to enact state and federal legislation that would protect the small farmer. But there was too much talk about the value of the family farmer and too little action in the Grange.

Through the Grange, I came to appreciate the value of cooperation for small farmers, but cooperatives were difficult to organize and sustain. There was a built-in conservatism with the family farmer. He had a feeling of independence, of doing things his own way, of being his own boss. The small operator did not see the larger developments and the need for unity. He did not see that his independence was an illusion and that organization was for the good of all. This was true even with left-wing Jewish farmers who came from a trade union background and should have known better.

We did form some cooperatives in our area, but they were too small to stand up against the big poultry corporations; and when a cooperative was established on a sound basis, it inevitably pursued policies which favored the larger operators within it. We built a cooperative hatchery, for example, that eventually switched from quality production to quantity production at the demand of the larger hen ranchers with breeding flocks. That cooperative hatchery ended up selling large numbers of the best chicks at the lowest prices to our large out-of-town corporate competitors. Finally, of course, this little cooperative was swallowed up. It was not large enough to compete.

The small farmer was always being pushed around by his own organizations. The Poultry Producers Cooperative, a huge northern California institution, was the worst example in our area. In the decades before the war, that co-op was a terrific help to the small chicken farmer. It bought feed in bulk and sold it in small quantities at low prices. It paid good prices for eggs, whatever the quantity, and it paid out good dividends to the membership every year. Those who left their dividends in the co-op got higher interest rates than a bank would give.

After the war, the Poultry Producers Cooperative moved toward larger operations with the most modern methods of production and distribution. In the process of expanding, it encouraged the growth of larger co-op members by giving lower prices for the purchase of feed in bulk and higher prices for the sale of eggs in bulk. It gave out huge loans to the larger operators to further expand and modernize their egg production. The irony was that the small farmer, the majority of the co-op membership, paid for it all through the discriminatory rates, the money they had invested, and the lowered dividends.

Some of us recognized this abnormal, unfair expansion. It was legal—we couldn't take the management to court. All we could do was protest at the annual general membership meeting, but even that was not easy.

How could a handful of small farmers stand up against the management of a multi-million dollar operation? They had directors and managers and agricultural scientists and banking specialists. They had long reports with big statistics. At such a meeting your small ranch shrunk to insignificance. If you tried to speak, you couldn't explain your feelings about what was happening. You couldn't convince the other family farmers, let alone influence the management.

In the end, those of us who saw the handwriting on the wall had no choice but to withdraw our savings from the organization. It was clear that the small farmer would pay the penalties for the growth of this cooperative. When the squeeze came in the 1960's, the members who still had their savings in the Poultry Producers Cooperative got back four cents on the dollar. Many people lost their life savings.

This was only the most dramatic event in the corporation take-over of poultry and egg production in our area. Hundreds of family farmers were forced out in the 1950's and 1960's. One could say this was progress, but when a way of life for families and communities is plowed under in the name of progress, it is brutal and obscene. It is criminal.[1]

Many of the older ranchers, like myself, continued to raise chickens as long as we could get some return. I worked my ranch until 1973. In the end we avoided bankruptcy only because our land grew in value as Petaluma became a bedroom suburb of San Francisco in the 1960's. Without that, if we had sold our land as chicken ranches, we would have ended up penniless.

During these years, I participated in other popular struggles, along with the fight to save the family farmer. Most important to me was the movement by black people and other minorities to win equality and justice. There also was the great struggle to stop the Vietnam War, which gave birth to a new radical movement. I was in all of this, right here in Sonoma County. In my own small way, I was looking to build a broad based movement of justice-minded people.

In the late 1950's, I broadened out my community activities. At that time, I joined the local branch of the NAACP along with other white progressive people in the area. Those of us from the Jewish Cultural Club who joined the NAACP considered it part of the history of the Jewish radical movement to work with other minorities in the fight for improvement. Since the NAACP maintained open membership to people outside the black community, it was natural for us to join.

Within a short time, there came an incident in which a black family had some trouble moving onto a small ranch in our area. There was a neighbor, a southern bigot, who aroused the people in that community with warnings that their land would lose value if a black family moved in. The NAACP, under the leadership of Plat Williams and Gilbert Gray, organized a broad-based defense committee to visit the people in the area and counteract the racist propaganda.

When that white racist threatened to resist with a shotgun, the black family was ready to give up. But the defense committee insisted: "When will you stop running?" The family agreed to move in, and we came in numbers to help. Then we kept a watch on that ranch until the family was fully established, just as they had planned.

This first joint struggle broke down a lot of separation between progressive blacks and whites in our area. I have found that between blacks and whites, no matter what their political beliefs, there is an invisible wall of separation which traces back to the days when blacks were sold on the auction block by whites. Even though you become acquainted and share political views, it takes a long time to break down the feeling of difference. This first struggle helped us to be accepted more readily as friends.

After that some of us from the Jewish Cultural Club participated with the black community in many local struggles against racial discrimination in the courts, in hiring policies of businesses, in the schools. They became involved in our campaigns against a local Nazi hate group and a Nazi speaker in our area. We raised money for each other's causes, we attended each other's affairs, and we established close personal friendships over the years.

Of course, there were historic clashes between Jews and blacks, but there also was the common historical experience of slavery. We Jews are reminded of it every year at Passover with the words "*evodim hoyinu be-mitsrayim,* we were slaves in the land of Egypt." We have a history as antislavery fighters in the Exodus from Egypt to the Promised Land. The echoes of that historic Jewish struggle can be found in the black spiritual from slavery times: "When Israel was in Egypt land, let my people go."

Here we see the contradictions of two historical streams meeting and mixing, each with good and bad. We in the Jewish radical movement believed that Jewish people must take a deeper look into our own history to understand the black people's struggle for freedom and equality today. We thought that the history of anti-Semitism in the twentieth century made it natural for Jewish people to object to the oppression of black people, of all minorities. This was an important part of our movement in the 1930's, when we joined with black workers to fight evictions and to build trade unions. It was an important part of our movement after World War II, when we supported the black movement for equal rights. And it was no surprise to us that so many Jewish young people—our own grandchildren—participated in that historic struggle for black equality in the 1950's and 1960's.[2]

The Jewish Cultural Clubs, nationally and in Sonoma County, also supported the struggles of Latinos. There were not so many in our area, but we threw our support behind Cesar Chavez and the United Farm Workers (UFW). We contributed financially, we picketed local food stores in support of UFW boycotts, we worked to influence public opinion, we helped organize caravans of food and clothes for striking farm workers in the central valley of California.

In this we acted on the general principle of supporting minority workers in their fight for economic rights—for a living wage, for a right to the job, for protective legislation and union recognition.

That struggle was special for some of our cultural club members, because back in the 1930's one of our people was tarred and feathered in Sonoma County for helping striking apple pickers.

I had my own personal double interest in the farm workers' movement. I supported them as a former trade unionist who went through the hardships of organizing the unorganized. I appreciated the special problems, the special exploitation of rural workers, from my youth in the Ukraine when I had contact with the peasants near my father's sheep farm. I participated in that UFW struggle for years, and for that participation I was proud to receive special recognition at my seventy-fifth birthday party, when my friend Jacques Levy, the biographer of Cesar Chavez, showed up with a personal message of congratulations from Cesar. It was a recognition of all our contributions from this area.

Out of all the minority groups I have worked with, I found the Native Americans the hardest to be accepted by. Their sectarianism is not a theoretical thing. They carry in their hearts and minds the wrongs committed upon them by the white man. They carry the history of "open season" on the "Indians," when they could be shot on sight without punishment. It was a history of genocide.

Liberals and progressives in our area reached out to local Native Americans for many years. We could not do much by bringing contributions to local reservations, but we did make contact by supporting the fight to establish a Native American cultural center on the former prison island of Alcatraz. Then we participated in a local fight for government land on which to build a Native American cultural center in Sonoma County. I came to appreciate the eternal struggle of the Native Americans to strengthen their existence by regaining every possible inch of land. I appreciated their fight for dignity through preserving tradition and teaching history to the young. Here we won that patch of land, which they named *Ya-Ka-Ama,* my land, and they built a cultural center.

I was invited to the victory celebration for that cultural center, but never was I invited to any Native American council meetings. I encountered greater obstacles forming alliances with the Native Americans than with any other minority group. They were justified in the resentment they carried against white people for the mass attacks and the round-ups they suffered in American history. But I wanted them to recognize that the Jewish people had a similar history. From the days of the Tsarist system and the Russian Civil War, we knew what it was like to live under "open season" on Jews. Later our people, our own families, not only were placed in ghettos, but were subject to systematic destruction by the Nazis. There was a historical basis for unity between Jews and Native Americans.

I once discussed the Holocaust with a younger Native American leader. I wanted her to come to our Warsaw Ghetto Memorial meeting. She said, "My grandfather told me about it. He said the Jewish people walked to their massacre. He said we should never walk to a massacre." I tried to explain that it wasn't so simple, but I didn't make any impression, and she didn't come to the memorial.

The artificial walls between ethnic groups are not easily broken down, even in the left-wing movement. There is forever competition among minorities for positions in an institution, for political representation, for the dollar. Each group pulls its own way, and in some cases, there is even a contempt for another group.

These divisions are a curse to the struggle of oppressed peoples. It is an old tactic of oppressors to divide and rule. We do a great service to the establishment when we maintain divisions and weaken the base of struggle. In the 1970's there has been a slow growth of unity between minority groups and unity with non-minority groups in the struggle for equal rights. It is through this class unity and the building of a socialism with humanism that we will solve the problems of racism and nationality, and that socialism will come only through patient, persistent work to build a broad-based movement for justice.

It was precisely these requirements, understanding the need for a broad base and patience to do in-depth organizational work, that were missing in the New Left of the 1960's. That is when I came in contact with a new generation of radicals. Until then, in our area there was only a small left-wing group with a high proportion of older Jewish activists. Everything changed in the 1960's, beginning with protest against the Vietnam War.

Soon after the establishment of Sonoma State College in the mid-1960's, I saw a newspaper notice about a campus meeting on Vietnam. I went and I found others who felt a need to bring a message against the war to the local population. We formed a small committee which started antiwar agitation in the county. We issued information, we held public meetings, we organized demonstrations. As cochairman of that committee, I became deeply involved in organizational work against the war.

We argued that the war was unjust and destructive. It not only plowed under Vietnamese life, but it betrayed the promise of America in the eyes of the world and in the eyes of the younger generation in America.

When I emigrated from the Ukraine to America in 1919, the real attraction was not gold in the streets, but it was the freedom represented by the outstretched hand of the Statue of Liberty. By the time of the Vietnam War, the U.S. government supported every reactionary government around the world. Those of us who opposed the war wanted to reestablish the United States as a country that stood for freedom and justice, at home and abroad.

The struggle against the war became a broad movement here in Sonoma County and across the country. It united all kinds of people with many differences. It was a movement of a magnitude which I had not seen since the fight by the unemployed in the early years of the depression. It touched the soul of the people. I saw it as the beginning of a movement which, if properly encouraged, would develop roots in depth among a broad segment of the American population.

Here in Sonoma County our coalition became broad enough to run a peace candidate in the Democratic congressional primary. Our candidate, Phil Dratt, was different from the run-of-the-mill ambitious politician. We worked our heads off and our feet off, pushing door bells and distributing buttons. And we reached a wide segment of the population. Even though we lost, we drew ten thousand votes in the county and 40 percent of the vote in the Democratic congressional district. Similar results were achieved in other parts of the state.

Then came the question of what to do next. We held a conference of peace activists in our area, and there the young radicals denounced the Democratic Party. They were disappointed that our peace candidate did not win. They called for a new independent left-wing political party.

Some of us spoke against that position as strongly and as sharply as we could. In my view, we had used the legitimacy of the

Democratic Party to bring forth radical ideas to the people. We had established an organizational base for continuity and growth. It may not have been dramatic, but it was effective and promised success with more hard work.

I remembered the 1948 presidential campaign of Henry Wallace, the former vice president of the United States. At the time, we thought it was a great achievement for such a person to head the ticket of the Progressive Party, an independent left-wing party. But he would have been more effective if he had remained a voice inside the Democratic Party, pushing it closer to the needs of the people. In my judgment that Progressive Party campaign was a failure.[3]

In the 1960's some of us argued that a separate left-wing party would be a mistake, a reptition of the 1948 Wallace experience. I called it a betrayal of the thousands of people who voted for our peace candidate. A new left-wing party would pull the energetic, idealistic new activists away from the base, away from the people. It reflected a pessimism that they could not win the support of the people.

Ours were voices in the wilderness. Our position did not prevail at our local conference, nor did it prevail at the subsequent state conference for new politics. At that state conference, I witnessed the new militant left-wing youth pull out as leaders of a broad based antiwar movement. Thus began the California Peace and Freedom Party.

I regarded that development in my area as a reflection of the new left wing in the United States. In the next congressional primary in an adjoining district, Phil Dratt won the Democratic Party nomination. But in the general election he not only was opposed by the Republicans, but also by the new Peace and Freedom Party. That left-wing opposition from the Peace and Freedom Party helped to defeat Phil and indirectly encouraged a Republican victory in that election. It revealed the New Left as a collection of counterproductive groups which functioned for their own interest rather than for the building of a broad movement.

That New Left movement came mostly from young people on the campuses. They declared themselves as avant-garde, which is easy to do, but avant-garde of what? Advanced ideas do no good if you march off alone. Whom were they leading?

There was a romanticism in their feeling of fighting the world: "I am somebody! I am challenging a powerful system!"

I do not want to minimize the deep convictions of the young people who had the courage to stand up against the government in time of war. I do not want to criticize the romanticism itself. But that romanticism remained with them alone. Socialism cannot be created in a college laboratory. It must have deep roots among the people.

I was more disturbed by the extremism that developed in the New Left. I heard and I read that some young radicals trained with guns and bombs. That was self destructive. The Left will never have as many guns as the establishment. Such methods turned people away from our movement and invited disruption by government provocateurs. Later it was recognized as an approach of desperation and futility.

It might have been useful if the older left-wing movement provided more continuity and exerted more influence upon the young radicals. Unfortunately, that left-wing movement was greatly weakened, partly because of government persecution in the 1950's and partly because it never had a healthy base in the population. There was no established organization to criticize extremism on the Left. There was no established organization to help the young people to broaden out to the unions and the communities and the liberal organizations, to organize in depth and struggle for the daily needs of the people.

The New Left did not develop with much theory or a class point of view. It was more of a rebellion . . . a rebellion against the parents, the society, the war, and also against the older Left. They couldn't care less about our struggles for working-class rights and dignity. They actually pulled away from the working class in the 1960's. Some even brought forth the false theory that the trade union movement was part of the enemy . . . that skilled white workers had become bourgeois. They called for revolutionary change based on American minorities and peoples of the Third World.

This was completely out of touch with reality. No basic change, no revolution, could take place in the United States without participation of the broad spectrum of working people. And with the high standard of living since World War II, and with the social welfare system, the needy people did not look for avenues of total change. There were important working class battles for improvement, but it was not a revolutionary period.

Under such circumstances, it was useless for the New Left to appeal for revolutionary action by American workers. When the workers did not respond, it was even more counterproductive to call them petty bourgeois and to dismiss them as the enemy.

This is not to say there should be no criticism of the labor movement. Quite the contrary! My entire participation in the labor movement was directed against the kind of trade union bureaucracy represented by Louis Nelson and the ILGWU leadership. Nelson himself recognized what he had built. Before he died in the 1960's, he told one of our left-wing activists, "I'm leaving behind a wooden orchestra." He was right. The present leaders of the Knitgoods Union sit in an office like a Wall Street corporation. They do not want to remember the militant history of their union, and there is practically no opposition to remind them.[4]

Here in Sonoma County the central labor council also moved to the right under Teamsters Union leadership in the 1950's. I ran up against the new conservative leadership later, when we organized local support for the United Farm Workers. The Teamsters Union was trying to take over farm labor at that time and the local teamsters leaders publicly denounced the local UFW supporters.

Such leadership is the disease of the contemporary labor movement. They come into office making promises like a politician during an election campaign. These leaders will do anything to avoid a strike, including negotiating mediocre agreements and sweetheart contracts. They collaborate with the bosses, and they keep the unions in a conservative groove.

All that must be said. But the young radicals of the 1960's did not recognize the historic struggle by workers for dignity, for higher living standards, for improvement of life. For decades we in the left-wing movement gave our time, our energy, and our lives so that workers could live in better homes, buy new cars and color televisions, send children for higher education, and have some protection for unemployment and disability and old age. We believed that by winning concessions the workers would be strengthened for continuation of the struggle.

Most of the young radicals did not recognize this fight for

improvement over generations and generations. It is not surprising that they could not reach the workers, because they came as enemies. Instead of calling workers petty bourgeois, they should have said, "What you have is good. Let us work together for further improvement." You cannot reach the moon without an elevator. You cannot build socialism without a broad movement.[5]

I participated in the organizations and movements of our area as a community activist who came from the Jewish Cultural Club. There were others from our radical Jewish movement who occasionally participated—Ruby Wenger, Joe Greenspan, Louis Sisselman, Ben and Lena Fields, Yakov Levinson, and more. They too came to Petaluma with the experience of working with all kinds of people in the labor movement. After lengthy discussion they too believed that the interests of the Jewish people—the fight against anti-Semitism, the right to a home and a job, support for the state of Israel—required alliance with other Jews and with non-Jewish peoples. We considered it part and parcel of the Jewish radical movement to participate in the struggles of poor people for economic rights, to support minority groups fighting for social equality, to take part in the movement for democracy and justice and peace in the United States.

The national organization of Jewish Cultural Clubs participated in many of these activities. Our Sonoma County club also participated in the greater civic life of Petaluma, especially through the concerts of the Jewish People's Folk Chorus. Despite the relatively small size of our group, we were recognized for our contributions. In fact, our small radical Jewish community became known to the Jewish radical movement throughout the country. They read our reports about reaching out, about involvement in the entire community, about accomplishments in work with other people.

Nevertheless, I continued to believe that our Jewish Cultural Club and the radical Jewish movement nationally, was too much wrapped up with Yiddish culture as an end in itself. Our meetings, our affairs, our publications continued in Yiddish. I appreciated the creativity of our Yiddish culture, but we had to make a greater effort to reach the English-speaking population on Jewish issues in the Soviet Union, Israel, America, and elsewhere ... to explain it from a radical Jewish point of view. We had to make our

organizational know-how more useful to other people and movements. We had to spread out, to draw young participation, to
perpetuate our movement. It was not enough to say, as a Yiddish
activist once remarked, "If you can't understand us then learn
Yiddish."

I expressed these views in 1963 at a national conference of
Yiddish cultural leaders, and I still believe it today. Although
Yiddish is now taught in some schools, it is restricted to a small
part of the Jewish population. We must reach out in English, in the
language of the land. I support the efforts in this direction by the
Jewish radical movement, like the publication of *Jewish Currents*
and the publication of weekly English pages in the *Morning
Freiheit*, but it is still inadequate.

There was some bending when it came to reaching other Jewish
life around us. In our Petaluma Jewish People's Folk Chorus, there
were singers who tried to broaden the audience, to modernize the
program with some American songs and some English explanations of the Yiddish songs. They wanted to respond to invitations
to sing at out-of-town old-age homes and synagogues and Jewish
community centers. In the end the chorus did come to those
places with our songs of struggle and hope . . . songs of the Jewish
people . . . and a few American songs too.

We also tried to broaden contacts with the general Jewish
community in Petaluma, the ones who kicked us out of the Jewish
Community Center during the McCarthy era. We succeeded when
it came to fighting anti-Semitism. One time we joined them in a
successful campaign to expose a little Nazi factory that printed
hate literature and produced swastika armbands. Another time we
cooperated in a protest against a Nazi speaker at Sonoma State
College. The college president would not agree to ban that
speaker, but the Jewish community—Left and Right—showed up
and stood in silent protest during that meeting.

Slowly we began to weaken their boycott against us. It was a
hard shell to pierce, even after we had a majority of the Jewish
Cultural Club willing to enter coalitions with them. But still we
approached them year after year for cooperation, especially for a
joint Warsaw Ghetto Memorial meeting. Finally, they agreed to our
proposal. In 1967 we held our first joint Warsaw Ghetto Memorial
meeting.

The old conflict ended, and then we were drawn even closer together during the Six Day War of 1967. Our Jewish Cultural Club like the rest of the Petaluma Jewish community came to the support of Israel in her hour of danger. We of the Jewish radical movement in Petaluma and nationally did not agree with charges from the Arabs, the Soviet Union, and the general American Left that Israel fought a war of imperialist aggression. We believed Israel started that war in self-defense, after the Arab world threatened to destroy Israel and drive the Jews into the sea. It was not just threatening words, but it was actions like closing the

Sheba and Joe in a demonstration against the Vietnam War, 1968.

Aqaba Straits to Israeli shipping, sinking an Israeli ship, and moving the Egyptian Army into the Gaza Strip. There was a danger Israel would not have survived if it had not attacked in self-defense. That is why the Jewish Cultural Club came to the Jewish Community Center and joined with the rest of the Jewish community to raise money for Israel's defense.

In the years following the Six Day War, there developed some new differences of opinion over the Middle East between the Jewish Cultural Club and the general Petaluma Jewish community. These differences reflected larger national and international divisions over the refusal of Israel to give up some of the Arab lands she conquered during the Six Day War. We of the Jewish radical movement disagreed with the Jewish majority in Israel and in the United States who defended Israel's right to keep that territory as the spoils of war. That military occupation gave ammunition to the charges that Israel was bent upon imperial conquest. There could be no peace in the area without return of conquered land. Jewish peace forces in Israel and in America supported United Nations Security Council Resolution 242 as a basis for return of conquered land, settlement of the Palestinian problem, and guarantees of security for all sides. We wanted a political solution to the problems between Jews and Arabs.

I agree with those who criticize American Jewry for not taking an independent position from the Israeli government. It has not influenced Israel to pursue more moderate policies in the Middle East, especially toward the Palestinian people. American Jewry, which gave so much help to Israel, could have been a constructive force in the life of Israel and the Middle East. It could have supported the peace forces in Israel. Instead, most of American Jewry defended everything the Israeli government did right or wrong. It did Israel a great disservice by encouraging occupation and reaction. Israel and the American Jewish community missed a golden opportunity for peace after the 1967 war.[6]

I had an opportunity to examine developments in the Middle East more closely during my second visit to Israel in 1973. On this trip too, I had the feeling of traveling through ancient history, especially when I walked through the Old City of Jerusalem, which Israel conquered from Jordan in the Six Day War. Again I was impressed by the modern scientific and industrial development, which was far advanced over what I saw in 1963. On this second visit, I could not help thinking about what Israel and the entire Middle East could have become, or can become, with a change toward peace and the full use of resources for improvement of life.

In 1973, however, Israel was determined to keep the lands it occupied and the people it conquered during the Six Day War. That was a source of eternal conflict with Arab nations and Arab peoples. I saw that Israel would be exhausted under the weight of hostility from neighbors, of terrorist attacks from Palestinian guerrillas, of ruling over a million new Palestinian Arabs in Israel. It required that small young nation to maintain extraordinary military strength. It required a population that was ready to run for the gun at any moment. That kind of military readiness saps juice out of the economy and out of the people.

During that visit I had some contact with Palestinian Arabs inside Israel. One day Sheba and I rented a cab and traveled through the occupied territory of the Jordan Valley. We were joined by our old friend Rabbi Bick with whom we had worked on Ukrainian war relief and who now lived in Israel. Our cab driver was a Palestinian who was born in Jericho and now lived in Jerusalem. During the day, between one stop and another, we conversed with this man.

Rabbi Bick asked him, "How do you like living and working in Jerusalem under Israeli control? Here, my friend will pay you fifty dollars for a day's work. You make a better living than you would do under an Arab government."

"Yes," he said, "our standard of living is higher. It is not as high as the Jews, but we appreciate that it has been raised."

"And you live in a democracy in Israel."

"Yes, it is a democracy, but we have little political influence. We live under Jewish rule. Israel is our occupier. Even if our economic life has been improved, we are not a free people. We are not happy."

"What about King Hussein? Would you rather live under Jordanian rule?"

"No, Hussein is not our friend."

"What is the way of freedom for you?"

"We want an independent state with our own industry, our own commerce, our own culture. We want a Palestinian state, just as the Jewish people have their own state of Israel."

"Then do you support the Palestinian Liberation Organization?"

"No, the PLO does not solve anything by guerrilla warfare and terror. It feeds reaction by the extremists in Israel, and that feeds reaction among the Arabs. The PLO is aggravating the situation. But I do not see any other way now."

We had other conversations with Palestinians who desired a peaceful political solution to the conflict with Israel. On our trip back to the United States in London's Hyde Park, we had a chance meeting with a young Palestinian couple. It was neutral ground with no ties or obligations, with no reason not to be frank. We asked the same questions and received the same answers. They did not like PLO terror, but they saw no other way for Palestinian independence.[7]

That Palestinian attitude was partly the result of an uncompromising position by Israel. During my 1973 visit, I found the Israelis were still dizzy with their success in the Six Day War of 1967. They thought nothing could prevent them from keeping the occupied Arab lands and the conquered Palestinians from the last war. They believed they were invincible, that the Arabs would not dare fight another war. It was not a racist attitude, but they were contemptuous of the fighting ability of the Arabs. They gloated over two and a half million Jews defeating a hundred million Arabs, over little David slaying the modern Goliath. It was an arrogant, super-nationalistic glorification of their military achievements.

I did meet people on the Left who saw the need for peace. There was a peace movement that called for a plan to settle disputes with Arab neighbors and to establish an independent Palestinian state, with secured borders for both sides. But at that time it took almost as much courage to stand up against the Israeli war machine and the right-wing socialist government and the out-and-out reactionaries, as it did to fight on the battlefields.[8]

Just a few weeks after our visit, the Israelis like the Arabs learned a big lesson about the need for a political solution to the problems in the Middle East. In the Yom Kippur War of 1973, due to lack of alertness Israel suffered terrific losses in the first two days. They were staggered at the beginning, and yet they got up from their knees and turned the war around. Once again they won a resounding military victory over the Arab nations.

That war revealed Israel could not be defeated by the Arabs, even after a sneak attack. It was a lesson that the Arabs must pay a high price for any attack upon Israel.

But Israel also learned a lesson. The Yom Kippur War showed that the Arabs could inflict great damage, perhaps irreparable damage. It was a lesson that the Arab people were mastering modern military hardware.

The Yom Kippur War showed both sides there was a lot to lose from further military conflict. It opened the door for direct Arab-Israeli negotiations on the basis of give-and-take by both sides. The recent Camp David Agreement with compromises by Israel and Egypt marks a start toward a political solution of the differences between Jews and Arabs.

Developments in the Middle East had an impact on the handling of the Jewish problem in the Soviet Union. While we were in Israel in 1973, we met some recent Russian Jewish émigrés. One young couple told us they left the Soviet Union because of anti-Semitic discrimination against advancement on the job. Another young couple left for fear that Soviet Jews would be made the scapegoat for the Soviet Union's disappointments in the Middle East and for any other Soviet problem at home or abroad. We met a distinguished mathematician, a member of the dissident movement, who came from a Russified Jewish family. He left after the 1969 Soviet invasion of Czechoslovakia, when he concluded there was no hope for democracy in the Soviet Union. They all wanted a better, more secure life for their children.

In the United States I heard many such stories about Jewish people who left the Soviet Union after the Six Day War of 1967. I believed many of these stories were exaggerated, but I did not dismiss the émigrés' criticisms of the Soviet Union. I continued my attempts to get to the truth, to appreciate the positive and denounce the negative, to maintain a balanced position. But those firsthand discussions in Israel got me closer to the problem than anything I could read in the United States . . . closer than the excellent reporting of *Jewish Currents* and of the *Morning Freiheit*, the Yiddish newspaper put out by the radical Jewish movement in New York. In 1977, when I took a third trip back to the

Soviet Union, I learned for myself about the Jewish problem there. This time Sheba joined me.

On this visit, like my trips in 1934 and 1963, I was deeply impressed by the economic improvement and the spirit of pride. We came at the time of the sixtieth anniversary of the revolution. Everywhere we found scrubbing, repairing, and rennovating in preparation for a celebration. It was like the day before Passover in Stanislavchik, when everything in the house was taken outside to be cleaned. There was a mood of jubilation across the Soviet Union.

In Leningrad, in Moscow, in Kiev we saw no remnants of devastation from World War II. These cities were rebuilt far beyond what existed before the Nazi invasion. In Moscow and Kiev, which I visited in 1963, there were new boulevards, new hotels, miles and miles of new housing. The clothing, the store goods, the food were much better than anything I saw in 1963. The cities and the people had a polished look.

During this trip to the Soviet Union, Sheba and I took a two-week tour into the Siberian area around Lake Baikal and into the South Central Asian republic of Uzbekistan, near the border with Afganistan and Iran. On that trip we got a greater appreciation for the vastness of the Soviet Union, the multi-national composition of the population, and especially the modern economic development.

We traveled in airplanes that matched anything in the capitalist world. In Siberia and in Uzbekistan we saw traditional life mixing with modern hotels, solid new housing, factories, paved streets, advanced educational institutions, and department stores filled with goods and customers. We saw the great dam at Lake Baikal, which provides electricity to tap the vast resources of that permafrost area. We saw great green patches in the Kizyl Kum Desert, the product of modern scientific agriculture, and we heard about a great engineering project to divert a Siberian river for irrigation. Everywhere we saw young families, young life, and building for the future.

My 1977 travels in the Soviet Union deepened my appreciation for the historic Soviet economic development, for raising the standard of living, for spreading modern education. However, what

we saw and what we heard about the treatment of Soviet Jewry
was disturbing.

The first report came from a Jewish engineer we met by chance
in Leningrad; he complained that he was limited in advancement
on the job because he was Jewish. Then, in Moscow, Sheba's
cousins told us about insults on the streets: "Hey, *Zhid!* Go back to
Israel!" On our trip to Uzbekistan in Tashkent, we were visited at
our hotel by the brother of a Jewish Cultural Club member in
Petaluma. He came up to our room, but his family remained
outside the hotel because authorities demanded to see passports
of those who came in. "I am an old man," he explained, "and I can
take my chances. But my children will not enter the hotel."

We learned that others in our Siberian tour group heard the
same things from friends and relatives, but still we could hardly
believe it. Sheba and I tried to hold judgment, to keep an open
mind, until we really could confirm what was happening when we
reached family and friends in the Ukraine.

We concluded our trip to the Soviet Union with a week in Kiev
and Vinnitsa. We had applied to stay there three times as long, but,
for whatever reasons, we were limited to a few days. With so little
time, we did nothing but see a continuous flow of relatives and
friends in both cities. Each wanted us to visit his home, stay for
dinner, have a party. We had to schedule the hours—who and
where and when—and we had to combine visits. There were so
many people to see . . . so much to talk about. We were so busy
with people that we saw nothing of Kiev and Vinnitsa, except from
the window of a taxi cab.

The economic position of the people again confirmed what I
saw on earlier visits. The Jewish people had opportunity for
education, good jobs, and comfortable living. At each home we
visited we found banquets prepared—from caviar to champagne
with gefilte fish and stuffed cabbage between . . . meals that could
not even be dreamed about in 1963. The people were not rich, but
there was an air of affluence about them. America, with the
insecurity of work and the lack of health insurance and the
expense of education, was not an economic attraction to them.
They insisted their economic position was much better in the
Soviet Union.

It took more than one visit, however, to learn what did bother them about life in the Soviet Union. You had to watch carefully, listen carefully, and establish confidence. I never was certain whether our radical record, which our family and friends knew about, encouraged them to speak openly or discouraged them. Only after we met up with people a second and third time would they discuss controversial matters. That is when we heard bitter complaints, and even then I do not think they were fully frank.

Again and again we heard the same reports of anti-Semitic statements in Soviet publications, of anti-Semitic insults on the job and in the neighborhood, and especially of discrimination against Jewish advancement to higher positions. We heard it from mechanics, from service workers, from teachers and engineers. They made good wages, and they lived comfortably; they were not threatened with loss of job; but they could not advance on the job. A few people—Communist Party members—denied it. But everyone else we spoke with told some story of discrimination.

I raised the question: "After Jewish life blossomed out in the early years of the revolution, after so many decades of economic development and improvement of life in the Soviet Union, why is there an outburst of anti-Semitism now? Why are so many Jewish people trying to leave?"

They answered as I had read the explanation in the *Morning Freiheit*. Anti-Semitism ran deep in Russian history. After the revolution it was combatted under the Soviet system. However, the Nazis revived it in a more bestial manner than ever before when they occupied large parts of the Soviet Union. Remnants of that anti-Semitism persisted after the war.

Then came developments in the Middle East. During the Cold War, Israel shifted from neutrality to alliance with the United States and became an opponent of the Soviet Union. In the Six Day War of 1967, Israel soundly defeated the Soviet Union's Arab allies. The Soviet Union, which spent billions of dollars building those Arab armies, was sorely disappointed with the results of that war. It denounced Israel from the public platforms of the world, from the United Nations, as an aggressive Nazi-like state.

The non-Jewish Russian people, it seems, were not able to distinguish between political Zionism—which is what the Soviet government officially attacked—and the general Jewish population. Therefore, anti-Semitism began to show itself among workers in the shops and neighbors on the block. The Soviet government, rather than discourage that anti-Semitism, allowed the printing of all kinds of anti-Semitic publications. Hence the growing discrimination against the Jewish people.

In Vinnitsa I got a more intimate understanding of these Soviet attitudes, when I was approached for an interview by a Ukrainian journalist who overheard me speaking in Russian and English at the hotel. After some hesitation I spent an hour telling him my impressions of the improvements in the Soviet Union from when I left in 1919 and from my visits in 1934, 1963, and now in 1977. Just as were parting, he asked my opinion about the establishment of Israel. I understood immediately that he knew I was Jewish. I told him that I considered the establishment of Israel a positive development in the history of the Jewish people.

He accused me of taking a one-sided position against the Arabs. I told him, "That is not so. I agree with the position taken by Andrei Gromyko, the foreign minister of the Soviet Union, at the United Nations in 1947. The Soviet Union supported the creation of a Jewish state and a Palestinian state at that time. When the Arabs rejected the United Nations decision and declared war on Israel in 1948, the Soviet Union helped Israel by sending guns through Czechoslovakia."

He replied, "That is your story. I never heard about Soviet support for Israel, and I do not accept your statement. *Eto ne pravda*, it is not true."

I told him to check the old issues of *Pravda* and see for himself. After we parted, I wondered what kind of history is being circulated in the Soviet Union. This was a man of learning who was supposed to educate the people through the newspapers. It was another disturbing example of how the Jewish problem was being handled in the Soviet Union.

At first, the Soviet Jewish people did not believe the Soviet government was tolerating discrimination and anti-Semitism. But the young people heard from the *babushka* and the *dedushka*, the grandparents, the old warning that whenever there was a disturbance in Russia in the past, the Jewish people were singled out as scapegoats. The older folks remembered the pogroms and urged the young people to save themselves. This new anti-Semitism did not carry the pogrom character of the Tsarist system, but the younger Jewish people felt no guarantee that their children would even be able to reach their level in Soviet society. *That* was the deepest, most damning criticism.

During my 1977 visit, many people asked me about life in the United States for Soviet Jewish émigrés. We answered that some were doing well, but others had a hard time starting a new life. Sometimes their questions were very detailed. When we asked if they had any desire to come, they said they would like to visit but they had no desire to live in America. In the year following our trip, several of those people did immigrate to the United States. It seems that they were carefully soliciting information from us in preparation for leaving the Soviet Union.

I understood their uneasiness. From my own youth in the Ukraine, I understood the warnings of the older folks that the Jewish people became a scapegoat in times of restlessness. I understood why they wanted to leave, and I thought the Soviet Union should let them go with no obstacles. Those who left and became disappointed with life in the capitalist world . . . those who would return to a life they found superior in the Soviet Union . . . would become the ones to brake the outflow of Jewish people from the Soviet Union.

Instead, Soviet Jews found themselves in a position where it was difficult to leave and difficult to find a secure place where they were. They could not develop as Jews, because the Soviet Union systematically discouraged the Jewish people from maintaining their traditions, their culture, their religion. They could not fight for rights, because such resistance would be crushed in the Soviet Union. They could assimilate, but it was a forced assimilation, and under such circumstances of anti-Semitism they became even more self-conscious as Jews. Besides, even if they did try to assimilate, Hitler showed that assimilation was no guarantee of protection against anti-Semitic attack.

There is an old Russian expression which explains the predicament of Soviet Jewry: "*Biut, u plaket' ne daiut,* you are whipped and you are not permitted to weep."[9]

While in Vinnitsa I got permission to visit my home town Stanislavchik. The trip was under official supervision with arrangements for an automobile, a driver, and a guide.

The ride took us from Vinnitsa to Zhmerinka and then to Stanislavchik. The roads were completely new ... the towns and countryside did not look familiar. Finally we reached the outskirts of Stanislavchik, where our peasant uprising took place during the Russian Civil War. I recognized the area, but after fifty-eight years the thicket of trees was gone.

Further along we passed over a little stone bridge that was made by my grandfather Alter Khaskel, who had been a stonemason. Then we passed the Jewish cemetery where my grandfather and parents were buried. The *geder*, the stone fence around the cemetery, also was the work of my grandfather. It was crumbling apart, but it still stood upright.

Before reaching the *shtetl*, I saw a roadside sign: *Selo* Stanislavchik. It used to be called *mestechko*, which was the Russian word for *shtetl*. *Selo* referred to a peasant village. That new designation for Stanislavchik reflected the destruction of Jewish life during the Nazi occupation.

Soon I was riding along the road where the landlord's estate house used to be on one side and the stone houses of the richer Jewish merchants on the other. That is where we used to walk on a Saturday afternoon ... out to that well with the sweet water. Now those fine stone houses looked tired, belabored, very much run-down from the time of the last war.

As we entered Stanislavchik the old synagogue and the two towering churches, which had been confiscated by the Soviet government after the revolution, no longer were there. The old stores, also confiscated by the Soviet government, were gone. Most of the old Jewish homes were gone. There were a lot of new homes with tin roofs ... homes that were occupied by Ukrainian peasants.

Before I started out for Stanislavchik in Vinnitsa, I met briefly with a distant cousin. She said her sister still lived in Stanislavchik and told me how to reach her. I visited with that sister, who told me about another Jewish family living there. It was the youngest sister of my old friends Nokhem and Rose.

I rushed over to their house. It took a little while to introduce myself. She was only seven when I left Stanislavchik. But she remembered my father, Yisroel Boydik, and then came embraces.

It was a warm meeting with exchange of information about our lives. Again I heard the story of destruction during the Holocaust. She was one of the people who fled and survived. She and her husband, a tailor, were one of three Jewish families still living in Stanislavchik. She didn't say too much about how they got along with the Ukrainian peasants. But I learned that her brother, my old pal Nokhem whom I had failed to find in Kiev in 1963, had died while I was in Kiev on this trip. Their sister Rose, who married the third pal, Mayer, was alive and staying with her daughter near Dniepropetrovsk. I also learned that Mayer, who had been murdered in the Stalin terror of the late 1930's, had been exonerated after the death of Stalin.

It was a meeting of high excitement and great nostalgia with someone from a family I was so close with in the past. I wanted to talk longer, but I had so little time and there was so much I wanted to see. And then, too, I was followed everywhere by my guide—right into the house of Nokhem's sister—which caused much uneasiness.

On my first visit back to Stanislavchik in 1934 I found it like a ghost town from what was there when I left in 1919. It was old buildings, old people . . . just a shadow of the older Jewish life.

This time there was almost no Jewish life at all. Stanislavchik—*selo* Stanislavchik—was the village base of a *kolkhoz*, a collective farm. The peasants were living much better, but Jewish life was almost completely wiped out. The people, the stores, the synagogues, the homes were gone. My own home was gone . . . completely gone.

As the time for my visit ended, on the way out of Stanislavchik, we stopped at the Jewish cemetery. I wanted to see the graves of my parents, my grandparents, and the generation before. I thought I remembered where they were buried, but I didn't. The gravestones were made of sandstone, not granite, and time made it impossible to read the inscriptions. I walked from stone to stone in that cemetery, but I couldn't remember where they were buried and I couldn't find a name I could read. Only my memories were alive.

This is how I left Stanislavchik. My coming was not with joy. My parting was with sorrow.

As time passed the radical Jewish movement was dwindling down in the United States. Here in Sonoma County, as the family farmer was forced out of business over the years, our people left the chicken ranches and moved to the cities. But even in the cities our movement suffered losses for biological reasons, and we had no young blood for new growth. Our left-wing organizations got smaller and smaller. In Sonoma County the Jewish People's Folk Chorus, the Yiddish theater group, and the Jewish Women's Reading Circle all disbanded. The Jewish Cultural Club, which used to draw over a hundred members for a meeting, is now dwindled down to a handful.

Our Jewish radical movement wanted continuity through the next generation. In this we were like the religious Jew who wanted his son to go to *shul*, make a *bar mitzvah* at thirteen, and marry under the *khupa*, the wedding canopy, according to the Law of Moses. The Jewish radical had his own Torah, his own ideas about heaven on earth, that he wanted his children to accept. In this we were disappointed.

It was not because of our devotion to Yiddish language and culture. It was rare that any Jewish immigrants or any immigrant group could maintain a cultural stranglehold on their children in America. Those of us who were born in the Old World, who did not dissociate from our heritage, were a strange thread in the cloth of American society. And as Jewish people we were not just immigrants, but we were immigrants without roots, immigrants without a country, and immigrants without a Christmas tree. We were, we are, a different people with special problems.

It is no surprise that there was a pull-away in mass, the second generation from the first. The children did it through the parents' encouragement to get an education, make a better living, lead an easier life. Many of the children from a left-wing background became good liberals and joined a Jewish congregation. The stream flowed in the direction of the society in which they lived.

It was their children, the third generation, who searched for some continuity. They were less fearful than their parents. They were raised with an American lullaby, with the language and ideas of the land. They inherited the promise of the Constitution and the Bill of Rights. When something went against that inheritance, many of these young people, grandchildren of the immigrants, went on the picket lines to protest.

I observed a high participation of Jewish young people in the protest movements of the 1960's. I saw a bridge from the grandparents to the grandchildren. It was not just the idea of improvement of life through education. Something echoed from the radical struggles of the grandparents. When those Jewish young people took up the fight for freedom and justice and peace, the threads were not completely broken from the grandparents. The radical Jewish young people whom I knew, when they began to demonstrate, found a warm corner in the hearts of their grandparents, and sometimes they found themselves marching shoulder to shoulder with their grandparents in the same demonstrations.[10]

Many of the young Jewish radicals, however, did not and do not understand the Jewish problem. I continue to meet young Jewish left wingers who denounce Israel as a racist, imperialist state and who throw all their sympathies to the Arabs. They point to reactionary Israeli leaders who call for national expansion and a tooth for a tooth policy.

They do not think about the centuries long oppression of the Jewish people. They do not know the pain and insult of a pogrom . . . the insult of someone taking a shot at you in the street just because you are Jewish . . . a resentment that stays with me to this day. They cannot grasp the destruction of the Holocaust and the condition of the Jewish people after that. They do not understand the historic Jewish struggle for survival.

They do not appreciate the lessons we have learned in the Jewish radical movement—that Israel must be recognized as historically justified, that Israel's existence must be supported, and that Israeli governments must be criticized when they do not act in a just manner. We must demand justice for the Palestinian people, but not at the expense and welfare of our own people.

Some of these young people do not recognize the Jewish problem right before their eyes, here in the United States. Most of them come from the lower middle class, and they see only their own background. They believe the American Jewish people have "made it"—that American Jewry is an economically comfortable, respected bourgeoisie. It is true that there has been economic improvement, that these young people participate more fully in American life today, that there is more intermarriage. But still there is a segment of poverty-stricken Jewish people.[11] And still there is anti-Semitism, open and covert, in America. I encounter it.

As long as that anti-Semitism exists, regardless of the economic and cultural success of American Jewry, there will be a separation of the Jewish people. Ilya Ehrenburg, an outstanding Soviet Jewish writer who was almost completely Russified, put it this way: "As long as there is anti-Semitism, I am a Jew." Shouldn't that be the attitude of the American Jewish radical?

Ilya Ehrenburg made that remark to protest the Nazi persecution of the Jewish people, but today it can stand as a protest against anti-Semitism anywhere in the world, including the Soviet Union. The recent resurgence of anti-Semitism in the Soviet Union has been a terrible disappointment for me ... for the entire Jewish radical movement. From when I was a little boy in Stanislavchik ... when I heard stories about socialists like Mitka Dobrovolskii and Sasha the bagelmaker in the 1905 Revolution . . . I believed in the promise of socialism for the Jewish people. I started to appreciate it for myself during the civil war, when the Red Guard protected my *shtetl* from pogroms. I joined the radical movement in America with the belief that socialism would bring salvation for the Jewish people and for all humanity. And I saw evidence for it when I returned to Stanislavchik in 1934. That is why my 1963 visit to the Soviet Union was disturbing; that is why my last visit in 1977 was shocking. I have seen anti-Semitism growing in the Soviet Union.

Despite that disappointment, I continue to believe that socialism can be the answer for the Jewish people and for mankind in general. I believe that a society organized to end economic exploitation and religious prejudice will solve the basic problems of all oppressed peoples, including the Jewish people. Socialism, more than any system of society, promises to end the social divisions and to unlock the creative genius of the people to serve the people.

Today, however, I am less concerned with the "ism" or the party or the leader. I speak for myself, and in my own small way I am looking for a broad movement that stands for basic social change. The accumulation of wealth and power in the hands of a few—in the hands of gigantic international corporations and capitalist governments—does not serve the interests of the people. I believe that radicals . . . that all justice minded people . . . must unite to build a different kind of world system.

Today, eighty years old, I have seen a lot of change, a lot of improvement, in all kinds of forms. I have witnessed the Russian people overthrow Tsarist reaction and embark upon the road to socialism. Years ago, at a celebration honoring Paul Robeson on his fiftieth birthday, I heard W. E. B. DuBois say that colonial oppression was ending once and for all. I have seen that, and I have seen the challenge to neo-colonialist rule. Today we see the people of the Third World continuing the struggle for freedom and human rights.

The American government and the American economic rulers have not yet learned the lesson, but in America too they have been forced to make concessions. There have been some improvements of living standards, some improvements of social welfare protection, some improvements for ethnic minorities. I have participated in these struggles, and I have seen life improve as a result.

Still, we have a long way to go. There is a gigantic struggle taking place—a struggle away from corporation dominated capitalism in the United States and in the world. The change will not be as easy as the shift from feudalism to capitalism. The great corporations seek to tighten their stranglehold on the people wherever they can. But time and power are on the side of the people.

I have unwavering confidence that basic change will come, but I also know it will be a struggle all the way. And in that struggle the radical movement must be ready to take a fresh look at where we are going and how. A lot has changed since Karl Marx first wrote about the struggle between labor and capital. Marxism . . . socialism . . . was and still is the only scientific proposal for a thorough change of society. But can we say that humanity will reach a point of finality even with the establishment of socialism?

We in the radical movement must see socialism as the beginning of a process of change, not the end. The human mind has brought mankind to the point where we can destroy in minutes what took billions of years to create. So too can the human mind improve society in ways as yet undreamed. We in the radical movement must keep an open mind. We must avoid sectarianism. We must learn from history. Otherwise we will stay petrified in the past. We will become guilty of *khvostism*, tailism, of being in the tail of events.

In the coming struggle the radical movement must win support from the majority of the people. Basic change cannot take place at the point of a bayonet, especially when an *atomic bomb* dangles from that point. It must be in accordance with the economic, cultural, and historic traditions of each country.

Basic change cannot take place through a small sect and left-wing extremism. It cannot take place even through the working class alone. It must be based on the broadest part of the population.

We must bring a radical message to a broad spectrum of the people through existing institutions. It should be a constitutional approach ... a democratic approach. It should be a practical gradual approach. We must continue to be impatient with oppression, but we must have the patience to reach out, to educate, to organize on a solid basis. I still accept Georgii Dimitrov's historic 1935 speech, when he made a ringing call for a broad coalition of the people to fight reaction and to build a movement for social change.

The struggles of the 1960's have left us with a legacy to build this movement in the 1980's. We can see it today in the struggles of workers, of minorities, of young people and older people. We see it in the fight to save the earth from those who would destroy it with nuclear weapons and nuclear pollution.

The task before us is greater than ever before. People who despair against the darkness we face in the world must do more than complain. The demand of our time is to join the movement to build a better world. I accept the view of the philosopher who said, "Don't curse the darkness. Light a candle."

Notes

1. Stanislavchik

1. From the eighteenth-century dismemberment of Poland up to World War I, the Jews of Tsarist Russia were restricted to habitation within the Pale of Settlement. This great ghetto, stretching from the Baltic Sea to the Black Sea, included Congress Poland, Lithuania, Byelorussia, and the Ukraine. By 1897 almost four million Jews lived there. This constituted 94 percent of the total Jewish population of Russia and 12 percent of the population of the area. Half were in cities and towns; half were in villages and hamlets.

    For a brief introduction to traditional East European Jewish *shtetl* life see Irving Howe, *World of Our Fathers: The Journey of the East European Jews to America and the Life They Found and Made* (Harcourt, Brace, Jovanovich, 1976), ch. 1. For more substantial accounts see Maurice Samuel, *The World of Sholom Aleichem* (Alfred A. Knopf, 1943); Mark Zborowski and Elizabeth Herzog, *Life Is with People: The Culture of the Shtetl* (Schocken Books, 1962).

2. The majority of the Russian Jewish population eked out a marginal living at petty commerce, artisanry, and service occupations. Russian Jews were steadily driven toward pauperization from the 1880's up through World War I. With the enactment of the May Laws of 1882, Jews were prohibited from owning or renting land outside cities, discouraged from living in rural areas, subject to quotas in higher education, and dislodged from liberal professions and more skilled trades. Through these legal restrictions and the forces of industrialization, Russian Jews increasingly came to live in urban ghettos rather than the rural *shtetl*.

    For an excellent survey of Eastern European Jewish history see Lucy S. Dawidowicz, *The Golden Tradition: Jewish Life and Thought in Eastern Europe* (Holt, Rinehart and Winston, 1967), pp. 5-90. Also see the more extensive treatment in Howard Morley Sachar, *The Course of Modern Jewish History* (Delta Books, 1958); Salo W. Baron, *The Russian Jew under Tsars and Soviets* (The Macmillan Company, 1964).

3. From the mid-nineteenth century, traditional East European Jewish life came under increasing assault from the *Haskala* (the Jewish Enlightenment), as well as from industrialization and from Tsarist

persecution. One important consequence was a rebellion against religious orthodoxy, a growing skepticism and secularism. Joe's youthful rebellion against his family's religious strictures suggests that the decay of traditional Jewish life was reaching the *shtetl*, too, by the early twentieth century.

4. These beliefs, all absorbed from Slavic folk tradition, are an interesting example of the unconscious cultural exchange that occurred between the Jewish and Ukrainian communities. Note the mixture of symbols: the Russian house spirit (*domovoi*) is exorcised by Hebraic incantations.

5. The Kishinev massacre in April of 1903 was triggered by charges of a Jewish ritual murder of a peasant boy. Over a period of twenty-four hours crowds killed forty-five Jews, wounded and crippled another eighty-six, and destroyed fifteen hundred stores and homes. Eye witnesses described the murder of babies, stomachs cut open, tongues cut off, women's breasts cut off, men castrated, blindings, and hangings. The massacre, instigated by the Tsarist government, triggered outraged protests throughout Europe and the United States.

6. From the accession of Alexander III to power in 1881 through World War I, the Tsarist government regularly whipped up hatred of Jews as a means of maintaining popular support. Before World War I, the most savage wave of attacks took place between 1903 and 1907, the period of the Russo-Japanese War and the 1905 Revolution.

    The Black Hundreds, an arm of the Union of the Russian People, was established by high government officials in 1904. It was the first modern instrument of Russian anti-Semitism, attacking the Jews as an emergent middle class and as revolutionaries, as well as an "unassimilable" people. By 1906 there was a network of three thousand cells across Russia, a virtual second government that carried out regular attacks upon Jewish communities.

7. Most sources on East European Jewish life call attention to the development of class conflict among urban Jews from the late nineteenth century. They note the existence of social divisions within the *shtetl*, based upon learning and wealth and family status, but they do not emphasize the significance of divisions between rich and poor. See Zborowski and Herzog, *Life Is With People*, pp. 239-65; Sachar, *Modern Jewish History*, p. 289; Howe, *World of Our Fathers*, p. 10.

    Joe does consider these divisions between Jewish rich and Jewish poor to be significant, particularly during the Russian Revolution. His view is borne out by the most recent scholarship. See Ezra Mendelson, *Class Struggle in the Pale* (Cambridge University Press, 1970); Henry J. Tobias, *The Jewish Bund in Russia from Its Origin to 1905* (Stanford University Press, 1972).

2. War and Revolution

1. Despite the massive participation of Jewish young men in the Russian Army, the Tsarist government issued charges of Jewish shirking, promoted intensified anti-Semitism, and treated the Jewish population of the Pale as an unpatriotic people during the war. Perhaps the most devastating government policy in the early war period was the forced expulsion of six hundred thousand Polish and Lithuanian Jews into the Russian interior.

    For further information on Russian Jews during World War I and the Russian Revolution see Howard Morley Sachar, *The Course of Modern Jewish History* (Delta Books, 1958), 296–304; Solomon M. Schwartz, *The Jews in the Soviet Union* (Syracuse University Press, 1951), ch. 7; Salo W. Baron, *The Russian Jew Under Tsars and Soviets* (The Macmillan Company, 1976), chs. 10, 11.

2. Tsar Alexander II (1855–81) inaugurated his rule with a collection of liberal reforms, including the abolition of serfdom. These reforms touched the Jewish people, especially with the discontinuation of the drafting of Jewish children into the army to foster Jewish assimilation. His early reform policy, never completed, was replaced by increasing reaction from the 1863 revolt in Congress Poland. After his assassination, Alexander III (1881–94) sought to re-establish uncompromising autocracy with the repression of all tendencies toward revolution and reform. This reaction included a renewal of government attacks on the Jews with a pogrom wave in 1881 and the May Laws of 1882.

3. The Provisional Government that emerged from the chaos of the February Revolution was composed primarily of members of the Kadet Party, which sought to replace Tsarist autocracy with liberal democracy on the Western model. It also promised autonomy for the non-Russian nationalities. Alexander Kerenskii, a lawyer with confused socialist leanings, first was minister of justice in the Provisional Government and then became prime minister in July 1917.

4. The politicization of segments of the Jewish population was well underway by World War I. The Jewish Bund, a Marxist oriented movement that advocated a separate organization for the Jewish proletariat within a broader socialist movement, competed with the Social Democrats for the allegiance of Jews, mainly in the cities and the towns. The penetration of political ideas and movements into the *shtetl* was considerably weaker, but all Jewish political tendencies were sharpened during the revolution.

5. The soviet had first emerged as a parallel form of government in the 1905 Revolution. Based on the 1905 model, the 1917 Soviet of Workers and Soldiers Deputies became a parallel governing force along with the Provisional Government. The relationship between the two bodies from February to October 1917 was referred to as a

system of dual power. From the beginning the Soviet placed great pressure on the Provisional Government for democratization of the army.

6. Jewish hopes were raised by the early Ukrainian nationalist movement. During the months following the overthrow of the Tsar, the newly established Ukrainian People's Republic promised national rights and equality to all peoples, including the Jews, in the Ukraine. However, by 1918, the various tendencies within the Ukrainian nationalist government were mobilizing popular support and maintaining military cohesiveness by diverting all discontent against the Jewish people. They associated the Jewish people with capitalist exploitation and with Bolshevik expropriations.

7. Bogdan Chmielnitskii (1593–1657), hetman of the Zaporozhan Cossacks, led a Cossack uprising to liberate the Ukraine from Polish rule. Urban Jewish merchants, who played a powerful economic role as mediators between the Polish nobility and the Ukrainian peasantry, exacerbated old religious and cultural tensions between Jews and Ukrainians. However, there hardly was any opportunity for the Jewish people to join the Chmielnitskii revolt, as Joe suggests, because anti-Semitism was one of the animating forces of revolt. During a decade of upheaval, tens of thousands of Jews were murdered.

8. Despite charges that the Red Army also instigated pogroms, the Bolsheviks alone among the contending forces in the Ukraine instituted an explicit policy of opposition to anti-Semitism. The Bolsheviks not only recognized anti-Semitism as contrary to socialist principles, but they regarded it as a dangerous threat to the revolutionary struggle. However, there probably were individual acts of anti-Semitism from within the Red Army, since anti-Semitism was a deeply rooted attitude among Great Russians as well as Ukrainians.

9. The flowering of Yiddish culture in Stanislavchik during the revolution very likely represented the final penetration of nineteenth-century currents of Jewish cultural modernism into all corners of Russian Jewish life. It also probably reflected the intensification of Jewish nationalist aspirations during the revolution. It is noteworthy that Joe sees—in contrast to most historians—signs of vitality even amid the unprecedented Jewish destruction during the Russian Civil War.

10. Joe's characterization of a "genocidal" logic in this period is not at all exaggerated. The dislocations of World War I and the Russian Civil War, particularly the attacks by the Ukrainian peasantry and the Ukrainian Nationalist Armies, completed the pauperization of East European Jewry which began with the policies of Alexander III in 1881. Between 1918 and 1919 an estimated fifty thousand Jews were slain in Ukrainian pogroms and perhaps another hundred thousand died as an indirect result of attacks. This constituted 10 percent of

the Ukrainian Jewish population, a significant prelude to the final assault from German fascism.

11. The attitudes and actions of Joe's self-defense group are at complete variance with the commonly held image of Jewish passivity and submission in Eastern Europe. That stereotype of Jewish passivity, derived from the Holocaust, has persisted despite the record of growing Eastern European Jewish self-defense and politicization from the 1880's through the Russian Revolution.

12. Most sources emphasize Jewish support for the liberal democracy established with the February Revolution and Jewish opposition to the Bolshevik program for proletarian dictatorship, expropriation of private property, and attack upon religion. Throughout his recollection, Joe calls attention to various divisions within his own *shtetl*— old and young, religious and secular, rich and poor—and among Jews generally. There not only was significant participation of Jews as individuals in the Bolshevik leadership, but the civil war and the Ukrainian pogroms undoubtedly induced a shift to the Left among younger, secular Jews from poor families like Joe.

3. Emigration

1. Historians of U.S. immigration have debated the causes for European emigration in the nineteenth and twentieth centuries. Some, like Oscar Handlin, have emphasized the European forces of displacement: the development of commercial agriculture and industrialization. More recent scholars, like Philip Taylor, have stressed the activism of the emigrants—their seeking out prosperity and democracy in America. See Oscar Handlin, *The Uprooted: The Epic Story of the Great Migrations That Made the American People* (Grosset & Dunlap, 1951), ch. 1; Maldwyn Jones, *American Immigration* (University of Chicago Press, 1960), ch. 7; Philip Taylor, *The Distant Magnet: European Emigration to the U.S.A.* (Harper & Row, 1971), ch. 3.

    All historians agree that Tsarist persecution and Slavic anti-Semitism, beginning with the pogroms of 1881 and the May Laws of 1882, was a major factor encouraging mass migration of Eastern European Jews. From the reign of Alexander III up to World War I, about one-third of the Jewish population emigrated from the Russian Empire. By 1920 approximately three million of them had arrived in the United States. See Oscar Handlin, *Adventure in Freedom: Three Hundred Years of Jewish Life in America* (McGraw-Hill Publishing Company, 1954), pp. 80-85; Howard Morley Sachar, *The Course of Modern Jewish History* (Delta Books, 1958), pp. 305-16; Salo W. Baron, *The Russian Jew Under Tsars and Soviets* (The Macmillan Company, 1976), pp. 69-74.

Joe is a good example of someone who was seeking a better life even while he left because of persecution and dislocation. See Irving Howe, *World of Our Fathers: The Journey of the East European Jews to America and the Life They Found and Made* (Harcourt, Brace, Jovanovich, 1976), pp. 26-29, 34-35.

2. Over a period of several decades there developed an international network of Western European and American organizations to help East European Jewish emigrants. The Joint Distribution Committee, established in the United States during World War I, was one of the newer such organizations.

3. Between 1881 and 1930, approximately one million East European Jews settled in Western Europe, Britain, Canada, South America, and Palestine. By 1925 there were seventy six thousand Jewish settlers in Palestine. With the enunciation of the Balfour Declaration in November 1917, the British government promised the establishment of a Jewish national homeland in Palestine. Despite the vagueness of the declaration, it stimulated a new movement of idealistic young Jews to settle in Palestine.

4. Romania was one of the less preferred routes of emigration due to the extreme anti-Semitism of Romanian authorities. From the mid-nineteenth century Romanian governments, like the Tsars of Russia, invoked anti-Semitic outbursts and enacted restrictive legislation against Jews as a tactic to deflect popular discontent and revolutionary activity. By 1920, however, after the depredations of the civil war in Russia, even Romania looked good to Jewish immigrants such as Joe Rapoport.

5. In 1921 the United States legislated quotas restricting further immigration to three percent of the numbers of foreign born nationality groups in the United States as of 1910. The Johnson-Reed Act of 1924 reduced the quotas to two percent and changed the base year to 1890, before any significant numbers of Italians, Slavs, or Russian Jews had arrived in the United States. England, Canada, Argentina, and Brazil quickly followed with similar legislation.

4. America

1. The Jewish Bund, formed in 1897, was the first Jewish socialist organization with a mass following in the Pale of Settlement. After the collapse of the 1905 Revolution, many Bundists immigrated to America, where they quickly became influential in the emergent Jewish socialist and trade union movements. The Bund advocated trade union organization, socialism, and the development of a modern secular Jewish culture. In America the Bund helped establish the Jewish Socialist Federation as an autonomous branch of the Socialist Party in 1912. For more on the influence of the Bund in

America see Irving Home, *World of Our Fathers: The Journey of East European Jews to America and the Life They Found and Made* (Harcourt, Brace, Javanovich, 1976), pp. 292-95; Arthur Liebman, *Jews and the Left* (John Wiley & Sons, 1979), pp. 178-82.

2. There was skimpy coverage of the knitgoods strike in the *New York Times*, February 15, 1923, 31:1; February 16, 1923, 24:2; February 28, 1923, 20:1; March 12, 1923, 16:7.

3. During the revolution the Soviet government declared the Jewish people a national minority group with Yiddish as their official language. In the first decade after the revolution, there was lavish state support for Yiddish schools, for the publication of Yiddish literature, and for the development of the Yiddish theater. Even the Hebrew language, which was considered an expression of religion and bourgeois nationalism, was not officially attacked until the late 1920's. During that decade there was a renaissance of Russian Yiddish culture, with a vitality that equaled Yiddish developments in the United States. It was fueled by the breakdown of traditional Jewish life and by the new problems and opportunities presented to the Jewish people by the building of Soviet socialism.

   For further information on Soviet Jewish life during the first decade after the revolution, see Howard Horley Sachar, *The Course of Modern Jewish History* (Delta Books, 1958), pp. 248-54; Solomon M. Schwartz, *The Jews in the Soviet Union* (Syracuse University Press, 1951), ch. 10; Salo W. Baron, *The Russian Jew Under Tsars and Soviets* (The Macmillan Publishing Company, 1976), chs. 12-14.

4. For further information on this remarkable network of Jewish left-wing social and cultural institutions, including the workers' cultural clubs, see Melech Epstein, *The Jew and Communism: The Story of Early Communist Victories and Ultimate Defeats in the Jewish Community U.S.A., 1919-1941* (Trade Union Sponsoring Committee, 1959), chs. 26, 27; Howe, *World of Our Fathers*, pp. 341-45; Liebman, *Jews and the Left*, pp. 305-25.

   Throughout the 1920's the U.S. Communist Party, with a largely immigrant membership, attempted to Americanize the orientation of the Party. Nathan Glazer treats this subject in *The Social Basis of American Communism* (Harcourt, Brace & World, 1961), ch. 2. However, Glazer simply ignores the persistent vitality of left-wing immigrant cultural activity.

5. See Irving Howe's incisive comments on the hunger for learning among immigrant Jewish workers, as well as their difficulties with night classes at the public schools, in *World of Our Fathers*, ch. 7.

6. The radical New York Yiddish newspaper *Freiheit*, known today as *Die Morgn Freiheit* or the *Morning Freiheit*, has had a shaping influence on the politics of Jewish radicals from its inception in 1922 up through the present. During that time it had been involved in a

ferocious rivalry with the *Forward*, known in Yiddish as *Der Forverts*, the most influential of the Yiddish newspapers. For the most recent polemics (in English) on the history and character of the two newspapers, see Howe, *World of Our Fathers*, pp. 241-47, ch. 16; Paul Novick, *The Distorted "World of Our Fathers": A Critique of Irving Howe's Book* (Pamphlet published from a book review in the *Morning Freiheit*, 1977), pp. 3-7, 22-28.

7. There is no underestimating the impact of the Russian Revolution, Soviet socialism, and the early development of Soviet Jewish life on immigrant Jewish radicals in the United States. This topic has been virtually ignored in current studies of the American Jewish radical movement.

8. Nathan Glazer, in *The Social Basis of American Communism*, pp. 84-89, treats the Communist Party of the 1920's as "a peculiarly effective Americanizing device." This kind of analysis from hindsight omits the immigrants' own reasons for joining the Left and thus distorts their historical experience. Joe's explanation, calling attention to issues of class and nationality, as well as to immigrant social and cultural organizations, is consistent with the most recent scholarship on immigrant working-class cultures in the United States. See Herbert Gutman, *Work, Culture and Societ in Industrializing America: Essays in American Working Class and Social History* (Alfred A. Knopf, 1976), pp. 40-46. Also see Irving Howe's strictures against treating Jewish radicalism as "an episode in the adjustment of immigrants to American society" (*World of Our Fathers*, pp. 322-24).

9. The Trade Union Education League (TUEL) was the organizational center for American left-wing trade unionists in the 1920's. William Z. Foster, who founded the TUEL in 1920, had been a member of the Socialist Party, a member of the IWW, and an AFL leader in the great steel strike of 1919. In 1921 Foster's TUEL was adopted as the American section of the Red International of Labor Unions—the Profintern. That marked the beginning of Foster's leadership in the American Communist movement.

The TUEL stood for the establishment of industrial trade unionism —the organization of all workers, skilled and unskilled, into comprehensive unions for each industry. It opposed the "dual unionism" tactics of the IWW—establishing separate radical unions—and advocated working within the mainstream unions of the AFL. The TUEL was strongest among the Jewish workers of the New York garment trades.

For more information on the TUEL and the early years of American Communism, see William Z. Foster, *History of the Communist Party of the United States* (Greenwood Press, 1968), pp. 203-208; Theodore Draper, *The Roots of American Communism* (Viking

Press, 1957), pp. 315-22; Bert Cochran, *Labor and Communism: The Conflict that Shaped American Unions* (Princeton University Press, 1977), p. 21.

10. The mid-1920's witnessed a complex, bitter conflict for control of the trade unions in the garment industry. Rank-and-file discontent with the trade union leadership, dating back to world War I, was given aggressive new leadership by TUEL groups from the early 1920's. The left-wing fur workers, led by Ben Gold, did win control of the Fur Workers Union. The left wing made little headway in the Amalgamated Clothing Workers or the Millinery Workers Union. There was a virtual civil war in the International Ladies Garment Workers Union, which the radicals lost, and which left the union in ruins until the coming of the New Deal.

The most balanced accounts of the conflict can be found in Joel Seidman, *The Needle Trades* (Farrar & Rinehart, 1942), ch. 9; Liebman, *Jews and the Left*, pp. 236-40. Also see the more partisan accounts, from a left perspective in Philip S. Foner, *The Fur and Leather Workers Union: A Story of Dramatic Struggles and Achievements* (Nordan Press, 1950), chs. 10-27; and from various anti-Left perspectives in Benjamin Stolberg, *Tailor's Progress: The Story of a Famous Union and the Men Who Made It* (Doubleday, Doran & Company, 1944), ch. 7; David Dubinsky and A. H. Raskin, *David Dubinsky: A Life with Labor* (Simon and Schuster, 1977), ch. 4; Irving Bernstein, *The Lean Years: A History of the American Worker, 1920-1933* (Penguin Books, 1966), pp. 136-38.

Irving Howe's recent analysis of this conflict in *World of Our Fathers* is a polemic directed against the Jewish Communists. Howe acknowledges that the radicals had majority support in the Fur Workers Union and in the ILGWU; yet he blames the radicals for the failings and connivances of the established union leaderships they opposed. Communism and radicalism are areas of American Jewish life to which Howe cannot bring a sympathetic understanding, and his chapter "Breakup of the Left" suffers greatly for it. For replies to Howe's polemic see Paul Novick, *The Distorted "World of Our Fathers"*, pp. 15-21; Morris U. Schappes, *Irving Howe's "The World of Our Fathers": A Critical Analysis (Jewish Currents* reprint, 1978), pp. 25-29.

11. For further information on the 1920's factional struggles within the American Communist Party see Foster, *History of the Communist Party*, pp. 269-75; Theodore Draper, *American Communism and Soviet Russia: The Formative Period* (Octagon Books, 1977); Irving Howe and Lewis Coser, *The American Communist Party: A Critical History* (Praeger, 1962), chs. 2-4.

12. For a first hand account of growing up in the Los Angeles radical Jewish community, including the Foster-Lovestone factional struggle,

see Peggy Dennis, *The Autobiography of an American Communist: A Personal View of a Political Life, 1925–1975* (Lawrence Hill & Company, 1977), pp. 19-26, 31-33.

5. Organizing the Unorganized, 1929-34

1. The late 1920's witnessed a new Soviet assessment of world conditions and the inauguration of the "Third Period" of international communism. It was based upon expectation of world capitalist crisis and an impending era of working class revolution. Through the Comintern (Communist International) and the Profintern (Red International of Labor Unions), the Soviets called upon foreign radicals to break with all liberal and socialist movements and to establish their own revolutionary organizations.

    Academic historians have argued that this led to left-wing dual unionism and the establishment of the Trade Union Unity League in the United States in 1929. See Theodore Draper, *American Communism and Soviet Russia: The Formative Period* (Octagon Books, 1977), ch. 18; Irving Howe and Lewis Coser, *The American Communist Party: A Critical History* (Praeger, 1962), pp. 164-74, 253-57; Bert Cochran, *Labor and Communism: The Conflict that Shaped American Unions* (Princeton University Press, 1977), pp. 43-45.

    Joe, in contrast, emphasizes American working-class militancy and AFL conservatism as factors contributing to left-wing dual unionism and the establishment of the TUUL. Joe's union, the National Textile Workers Union, was established in September 1928, in the wake of the New Bedford textile strike, when the AFL United Textile Workers Union expelled its left wing. This was more than half a year before the establishment of the TUUL.

    For various left-wing views of the birth of the TUUL, see Al Richmond, *A Long View From the Left: Memoirs of an American Revolutionary* (Delta Books, 1975), pp. 144-48; James Weinstein, *Ambiguous Legacy: The Left in American Politics* (New Viewpoints, 1975), pp. 38-56; William Z. Foster, *History of the Communist Party of the United States* (Greenwood Press, 1968), pp. 270-75.

2. For further information on the textile strikes of the 1920's, especially the Gastonia strike, see Irving Bernstein, *The Lean Years: A History of the American Worker, 1920–1933* (Penguin Books, 1966), pp. 1-43; Vera Bush Weisbord, *A Radical Life* (Indiana University Press, 1977), chs. 5-12. Vera Bush Weisbord also describes her brief stint as a knitgoods worker in 1928 (pp. 170-71).

3. There has been little scholarship on the Unemployed Councils movement of 1930-32. It was the beginning of radical protest during the depression and an important prelude to the trade union organiz-

ing drives later in the 1930's. See Bernstein, *The Lean Years*, pp. 426-35; D. J. Leab, "United We Eat': The Creation and Organization of the Unemployed Councils in 1930," *Labor History* 8:3 (Fall, 1967): 300-15; Roy Rosenzweig, "Organizing the Unemployed: The Early Years of the Great Depression, 1929-1933," *Radical America* 10:4 (July-August, 1976): 37-60.

4. It is noteworthy that the first thing these rank and filers wanted was help from an established trade union organization. Several New Left historians, writing from an anarcho-syndicalist position, have argued that established trade union organizations inhibit the natural militancy of rank-and-file workers. See Jeremy Brecher, *Strike!* (Fawcett Premier Books, 1974), pp. 306-14; Stanley Aronowitz, *False Promises: The Shaping of American Working Class Consciousness* (McGraw-Hill Publishing Company, 1974), ch. 4.

5. The return of the American left-wing trade unionists back into the AFL usually is attributed to the 1935 shift in Soviet policy toward the creation of Popular Front alliances. However, several years prior to this shift in Comintern-Profintern policy, there were indications that American rank-and-file radicals were moving back toward the AFL and the mainstream of the American labor movement. Many rank-and-file radicals never were happy with the dual union strategy, and they were not simply puppets following international Communist policies. This effort by Joe's knitgoods group to align with the ILGWU rather than with their "own" NTWIU is one example. Others occurred among miners, auto workers, steel workers, maritime workers, and longshoremen. See Weinstein, *Ambiguous Legacy*, pp. 61-68.

6. The NRA, the National Recovery Administration, was enacted in June 1933 as a first attempt by the Roosevelt administration toward economic recovery in industry. It called for the establishment of industrial codes of fair practice, which would include provisions regulating employment. Section 7A of the legislation offered federal guarantees of the right for workers to organize and to bargain collectively.

Employers, large and small, resisted independent unionization by workers. Instead, they used the fair practice codes to limit competition among themselves and to organize company unions. The tactics of employers with the help of government interpretations of the NRA prompted angry attacks from the entire labor movement. Not until the Wagner Act in July 1935 did the federal government throw its full weight behind independent trade union organization and collective bargaining.

Nonetheless, contemporary observers and subsequent historians have emphasized Roosevelt's NRA as the effective take-off point for labor organization in the 1930's. Joe, while sharing this view, stresses the formative work done by radical trade union activists in the years preceding Roosevelt's election. His view is confirmed by the experience of other rank-and-file activists. See Wyndham Mortimer, *Organize! My Life as a Union Man* (Beacon Press, 1971), pp. 54-68; James J. Matles and James Higgins, *Them and Us: Struggles of a Rank-and-File Union* (Beacon Press, 1975), p. 32.

7. For another example of this emphasis on rank and file activism and shop group democracy see the story of the United Electrical Workers in Matles and Higgins, *Them and Us*, ch. 1. Also see Alice and Staughton Lynd, *Rank and File: Personal Histories by Working Class Organizers* (Beacon Press, 1973).

8. Ben Gold, the most charismatic leader of the left-wing Jewish trade union movement, is discussed at length in Philip S. Foner, *The Fur and Leather Workers: A Story of Dramatic Struggles and Achievements* (Nordan Press, 1950). Foner also provides a sympathetic account of the Needle Trades Workers Industrial Union (ch. 28).

9. With the approach of the NRA hearings, the ILGWU undertook a major organizing drive in mid-1933. The union effectively organized the New York needle trades with a series of general strikes in each trade, beginning with a huge dressmakers strike on August 16, and continuing with other needle trades strikes into October. See Irving Bernstein, *The Turbulent Years: A History of the American Worker 1933-1941* (Houghton Mifflin Company, 1971), pp. 84-89.

   It is difficult to determine the comparative strength of the NTWIU at that point. Among the sixty thousand dressmakers who struck, the NTWIU claimed fifteen thousand, while the *New York Times* reported NTWIU strikers at five thousand. See *New York Times*, August 16, 1933, 3:1 and August 18, 1933, 3:1.

10. Jay Lovestone was expelled from leadership of the U.S. Communist Party in June 1929 for his theory of American "exceptionalism" to the Third Period analysis of world capitalist development. After the break, Lovestone and his followers embarked upon a long political and trade union struggle against communism. In 1931 David Dubinsky allowed a group of them back into the ILGWU, where they spearheaded the battle against communism in the needle trades. Charles "Sasha" Zimmerman, a Communist leader in the needle trades struggles of the 1920's, became manager of ILGWU Local 22 and the most prominent Lovestonite in the needle trades. See Zimmerman's own account in David Dubinsky and A. H. Raskin, *David Dubinsky: A Life With Labor* (Simon and Schuster, 1977), ch. 4.

11. Most sources, past and present, have noted the jurisdictional dispute between the ILGWU and the United Textile Workers during the knitgoods strike, but have not acknowledged the participation of Joe's knitgoods local of the NTWIU. These distortions—in the press, in the memoirs of labor leaders, and in academic history—underscore the need for historical accounts of this period from left-wing

participants. See *New York Times*, September 28, 1933, 10:4 and September 29, 1933, 28:2; Melech Epstein, *Jewish Labor in the USA: An Industrial, Political and Cultural History of the Jewish Labor Movement* (2 vols. Ktav Publishing House, 1969), pp. 200-201; Max D. Danish, *The World of David Dubinsky* (World Publishing Company, 1957), p. 79; Bernstein, *The Turbulent Years*, p. 88.

12. There has been little investigation of the Left and problems of trade union democracy in the 1930's. See the brief discussion in Weinstein, *Ambiguous Legacy*, pp. 70-71.

13. See the strike reports in the *New York Times*, August 1-23, 1934, particularly August 1, 7:5; August 9, 2:7; August 18, 4:2; August 22, 2:4. The *New York Times* reports include a few disparaging allusions to the "the Communists" in the period leading up to the strike, but the reports completely ignore the NTWIU during the strike.

6. The Soviet Union, 1934

1. For more on the trial and flight of Gastonia strike leaders see Irving Bernstein, *The Lean Years: A History of the American Worker, 1920-1933* (Penguin Books, 1966), pp. 25-28; Vera Bush Weisbord, *A Radical Life* (Indiana University Press, 1977), chs. 11, 12; Fred Beal, *Proletarian Journey* (Human-Curl, Inc., 1937).

2. Acts of sabotage, a phenomenon difficult to document, undoubtedly were commonly perpetrated by opponents of the Soviet system. Such acts also may have been committed by less politically conscious workers who resented the hard work and small rewards required by the First Five Year Plan. Often, too, industrial inefficiency was labeled sabotage.

3. Sergei Mironovich Kirov, the Leningrad Party Secretary, was assassinated on December 1, 1934. The official explanation was that a conspiratorial Trotskyite organization committed the murder. Subsequent evidence, including hints in Khrushchev's secret speech of 1956, indicates that Stalin himself may have ordered the assassination, fearing Kirov's popularity and opposing Kirov's more moderate policies toward industrialization and government terror against internal enemies. See Robert Conquest, *The Great Terror: Stalin's Purge of the Thirties* (The Macmillan Company, 1968), ch. 2; Roy Medvedev, *Let History Judge: The Origins and Consequences of Stanlinism* (Alfred A. Knopf, 1971), ch. 5.

4. From August 1936 through 1938, the Soviet government conducted a bloodbath against great numbers of Soviet citizens. It began with the public trial of sixteen Old Bolsheviks and grew to include all former Bolshevik opposition leaders, Red Army leaders, most of the trade union leadership, intellectuals, former members of other socialist parties, and a multitude of ordinary citizens. It has been

estimated that eight million people were arrested. See Conquest, *The Great Terror*; Medvedev, *Let History Judge*.

5. Peasant resistance to collectivization, combined with the absence of mechanized implements for large scale cultivation, resulted in agricultural disaster under the First Five Year Plan. Between 1929 and 1933 peasants resisted collectivization by slaughtering massive amounts of livestock. The derogatory term *kulak* was applied indiscriminantly to such peasants. An estimated eight to ten million peasants died from a combination of deportation and the famine of 1932-33. See M. Lewin, *Russian Peasants and Soviet Power: A Study of Collectivization* (W. W. Norton & Company, 1975), chs. 16, 17.

6. Soviet policy toward Jews and all nationalities vacillated enormously in the first two decades after the revolution. The conflicts centered on how to develop national cultures within the framework of Soviet society. The Jews were a special problem among Soviet minorities insofar as they had an international identity as part of a diaspora, they practiced the Jewish religion as an expression of their national identity, they were largely petty bourgeois, and they never had been even a quasi-political entity with their own geographic boundaries.

Although anti-Semitism was vigorously combatted in the new Soviet system, Jews were subject to all the general economic and religious restrictions in the building of Soviet socialism. Western scholars of Soviet Jewry, usually writing from an anti-Soviet perspective, have characterized the creation of the Soviet system as a "trauma" and a "catastrophe" for the Jewish people.

Joe's emphasis on the opening of new opportunities for Jews under the Soviet system is consistent with the evidence—but not the interpretations—of these scholars. His generational distinctions, positing his own generation as transitional in Jewish adaptation to the Soviet system, does not appear in the historical literature. Most scholars simply distinguish between those Jews who suffered through dislocations in the creation of the Soviet system and those Jews who were born into the Soviet system.

The bibliography on Jews in the Soviet Union is not very good. See Solomon Schwartz, *The Jews in the Soviet Union* (Syracuse University Press, 1951), chs. 7-13; Salo W. Baron, *The Russian Jew Under Tsars and Soviets* (The Macmillan Company, 1976), chs. 12-14; Howard Morley Sachar, *The Course of Modern Jewish History* (Delta Books, 1958), ch. 17. Also see B. Z. Goldberg's account of his 1934 visit to the Soviet Union and investigation of Soviet Jewry in *The Jewish Problem in the Soviet Union: Analysis and Solution* (Crown Publishers, Inc., 1961), pp. 23-43.

7. Jewish sympathy for Trotsky is not documented, but there is no reason to doubt this unique piece of evidence.

Western scholars have called attention to the purge trials of 1936-38, which virtually eliminated Jewish Communist leadership, as the first public manifestation of anti-Semitism under the Soviet system. Whether or not there was popular Jewish support for those Jewish leaders, their elimination must have been deeply disturbing.

8. For a fascinating account of Americans living in Moscow and working for the Comintern during this period see Peggy Dennis, *The Autobiography of an American Communist: A Personal View of a Political Life, 1925–1975* (Lawrence Hill & Company, 1977), ch. 3.

9. Georgii Dimitrov, a Bulgarian Communist, had a well-known history of militant antifascism. By 1933, as the Soviet Union became more aware of the Nazi threat, it abandoned the Comintern Third Period policies in favor of cooperation with any group opposed to German fascism and Japanese militarism. This new policy, called the Popular Front, was introduced in a 1935 speech by Georgii Dimitrov at the Seventh Congress of the Comintern. See Franz Borkenau, *World Communism: A History of the Communist International* (University of Michigan Press, 1962), chs. 22, 23.

7. United Front, 1935–41

1. The term United Front applied to working-class unity, especially Socialist and Communist workers. The term Popular Front applied to antifascist political coalitions of workers, small farmers, and sectors of the middle classes.

2. There has been little substantive study of the Trade Union Unity League or the general labor movement between 1929 and 1933. Most historians agree that the dual unions of the TUUL remained small and isolated, without a mass following. They disagree with Joe's assessment of the value of the TUUL and dismiss it as detrimental to the labor movement, but they tend to ignore the AFL expulsions that fostered dual unionism, the AFL inertia during this period, and the achievements of some of those TUUL unions. They do agree with Joe that the TUUL developed a corps of experienced radical organizers who became leaders in the AFL and CIO organizing drives of the 1930's. See Irving Howe and Lewis Coser, *The American Communist Party: A Critical History* (Praeger, 1962), pp. 256–57, 269–70, 371–72; Irving Bernstein, *The Lean Years: A History of the American Worker, 1920–1933* (Penguin Books, 1966), p. 141; James Weinstein, *Ambiguous Legacy: The Left in American Politics* (New Viewponts, 1975), pp. 42–43.

3. The TUUL officially dissolved in March 1935. Joe again argues that the change in left-wing policy, now toward United Front alliances, must be understood with respect to the American political situation and the impulses of American workers as well as the consequence of international developments and shifting Soviet policy.

 For a similar view from another 1930's left-wing activist, see Al

Richmond, *A Long View from the Left: Memoirs of an American Revolutionary* (Delta Books, 1975), pp. 225-27. Irving Howe and Lewis Coser, Socialist critics of American Communism, argue that the policy change was dictated by the Soviet Union but happened to accord with the needs of American workers (*The American Communist Party*, pp. 321-24). James Weinstein, writing from the perspective of the New Left, seems to agree with Howe and Coser, but does emphasize the independent movement of American radical activists toward working within the AFL before the United Front became official Communist Party policy (*Ambiguous Legacy*, pp. 57-68).

4. For more information on the merger of the NTWIU members into the ILGWU, see Joel Seidman, *The Needle Trades* (Farrar & Rinehart, 1942), pp. 206-208; Benjamin Stolberg, *Tailor's Progress: The Story of a Famous Union and the Men Who Made It* (Doubleday, Doran & Company, 1944), pp. 247-49; Philip S. Foner, *The Fur and Leather Workers Union: A Story of Dramatic Struggles and Achievements* (Nordan Press, 1950), chs. 40, 41.

   Stolberg, writing from the perspective of the ILGWU leadership, notes the sympathy of the ILGWU rank and file toward the United Front and the consequent leadership fears that the Communists would take over ILGWU locals.

5. Stolberg, who provides a flattering portrait of Louis Nelson, notes that "Manager Louis Nelson of Local 155 of the knitgoods workers was the only progressive [referring here to the Lovestonite dominated Progressive Group] who refused all dealings with the reds" (*Tailor's Progress*, pp. 248, 259-60).

6. See the strike reports in the *New York Times*, July 14-August 30, 1936, particularly July 15, 3:8; August 12, 19:2; August 18, 35:1; August 25, 12:6. For the subsequent grand jury probe into the strike "riots" and "kidnapping," see the *New York Times*, October 15, 1936, 1:3. Four union officers, including Joe, were indicted for conspiracy and coercion through acts of violence. The charges were not dismissed until 1939.

7. The CIO, the Committee for Industrial Organization, later known as the Congress of Industrial Organizations, was formed at the end of 1935 as an industrial union group within the craft-oriented AFL. After expulsion from the AFL in August 1936, the CIO mobilized a huge campaign to organize industrial unions in mass production industries. For the role of the ILGWU in the development of the CIO, see David Dubinsky and A. H. Raskin, *David Dubinsky: A Life with Labor* (Simon and Schuster, 1977), ch. 9.

   Howe and Coser argue that the Communist Party leadership, reacting from the experience of dual unionism in the Trade Union Unity League, opposed any splits in the AFL and did not support the CIO until the spring of 1936 (*The American Communist Party*, pp.

368-71). Weinstein argues that the Communist Party leadership did support the establishment of the CIO from the beginning, but cautiously so (*Ambiguous Legacy*, p. 60). No one disputes the sympathy of rank-and-file left wingers for the industrial union movement from the very beginning.

8. New Left historians have argued that the Communist Party of the 1930's, instead of advocating socialism, was preoccupied with defending democracy against fascism, instituting social welfare programs, and fighting for trade union organization and immediate material gains. As a consequence, these historians argue, the Communist Party mobilized working people on behalf of corporate liberal reform. See Weinstein, *Ambiguous Legacy*, ch. 3; Stanley Aronowitz, *False Promises: The Shaping of American Working Class Consciousness* (McGraw-Hill Publishing Company, 1974), ch. 4; Jeremy Brecher, *Strike:* (Fawcett Premier Books, 1974), ch. 5.

9. Several Old Left activists—former Communist Party leaders rather than trade union organizers—have responded to the New Left historians' criticisms of the Communist Party in the 1930's. Like Joe they criticize the subordination of the American left wing to the Soviet Union, they defend Popular Front coalitions as a socialist strategy, and they defend the struggle for trade unions and immediate gains. See Richmond, *Long View from the Left*, ch. 8; Max Gordon, "The Communist Party of the 1930's and the New Left," *Socialist Revolution* 29 (January-March 1976): 11-66; Peggy Dennis, "On Learning from History," *Socialist Revolution* 29 (July-August 1976): 125-43.

Where these former Communist Party leaders concede that the Communist Party sacrificed too much of its independence to the Popular Front coalitions in politics and trade unions, Joe argues that the Left should have made greater efforts to preserve coalition struggle to build trade unions and to win immediate improvements in workers' standard of living. This syndicalist orientation is even more pronounced in the memoirs of other left-wing trade union organizers, who relate the building of trade unionism with virtually no reference to the Communist Party, the New Deal, and the problems of reform and revolution in the 1930's. See Wyndham Mortimer, *Organize: My Life As a Union Man* (Beacon Press, 1971); Alice and Staughton Lynd., ed., *Rank and File: Personal Histories of Working Class Organizers* (Beacon Press, 1974); James J. Matles and James Higgins, *Them and Us: Struggles of a Rank-and-File Union* (Beacon Press, 1975). Len DeCaux, a radical who was not a trade union organizer but who was in the CIO leadership, does discuss problems of politics and trade unionism in *Labor Radical, from the Wobblies to CIO: A Personal History* (Beacon Press, 1971), pp. 239-47, 315-22.

8. "*Evreiskii Vopros*," The Jewish Question

1. See the fascinating account of personal life and left-wing politics in Peggy Dennis, *The Autobiography of an American Communist: A Personal View of a Political Life, 1925–1975* (Lawrence Hill & Company, 1977). For an account of personal life in the left-wing movement, without reference to politics, see Vivian Gornick, *The Romance of American Communism* (Basic Books, 1977).

2. There was a small impoverished settlement of fifty-five thousand Jews in Palestine by World War I. Many were pious mendicants who came in the first *Aliyah*, the first wave of Jewish emigration to Palestine, dating from Tsarist repression of Russian Jewry in the early 1880's. The second *Aliyah* (1900-14) and especially the third (1919-24) included young immigrants who were more oriented toward colonization and establishment of a Jewish national homeland. By 1925 there were some eighty thousand Jewish settlers in Palestine. During the 1920's and 1930's, they were augmented by several waves of Jewish refugees fleeing anti-Semitism in central Europe, bringing the Jewish population to approximately four hundred thousand by World War II. See Howard Morley Sachar, *The Course of Modern Jewish History* (Delta Books, 1958), chs. 13, 18.

3. The most extensive and most balanced treatment of the relationship between Jewish radicals and the general American Jewish community in the 1930's can be found in Arthur Liebman, *Jews and the Left* (John Wiley & Sons, 1979), chs. 6-8. For anti-Communist polemics on the subject see Melech Epstein, *The Jew and Communism: The Story of Early Communist Victories and Ultimate Defeats in the Jewish Community, U.S.A. 1919–1941* (Trade Union Sponsoring Committee, 1959), chs. 32-39; Irving Howe, *World of Our Fathers: The Journey of the East European Jews to America and the Life They Found and Made* (Harcourt, Brace, Jovanovich, 1976), pp. 344-47.

4. For a balanced treatment of this incident see Liebman, *Jews and the Left*, pp. 348-49, 503-504. For an example of more recent anti-Communist polemics on this incident see Nathan Glazer, *The Social Basis of American Communism* (Harcourt, Brace & World, 1961), pp. 151-54. For further information on the 1929 Arab attacks on the Palestinian Jewish community, see Sachar, *The Course of Modern Jewish History*, pp. 384-92.

5. See the thoughtful reflections of Al Richmond on American left-wing confusion during "the tortuous twenty-two months between the Nazi-Soviet nonaggression treaty in August 1939 and the Nazi invasion of the Soviet Union in June 1941." Like Joe, Richmond argues that "our troubles essentially stemmed from a compulsion to turn Soviet diplomatic necessity into an American political virtue." Al Richmond,

A Long View from the Left: Memoirs of an American Revolutionary (Delta Books, 1972), pp. 283–85.

William Z. Foster, in contrast, defends the U.S. Communist Party position as opposed to British imperialism, as advocating a peaceful Soviet-American solution to the conflict, and as consistent with the views of the majority of Americans who opposed U.S. involvement in the war. William Z. Foster, *History of the Communist Party of the United States* (Greenwood Press, 1968), chs. 26, 27.

For more extensive treatment of the special ramifications of these developments for American Jewish radicals see Liebman, *Jews and the Left*, pp. 507-10.

6. For more on the case of Victor Alter and Henryk Ehrlich, see Yehoshua Gilboa, *The Black Years of Soviet Jewry* (Little, Brown, & Company, 1971), pp. 42-45.

7. Most left-wing writers criticize the U.S. Communist Party for its subordination to Soviet and American war goals. Especially interesting is Len DeCaux's explanation of how "Lefty never had it so good" as during the war, when Communists became allies rather than enemies. See Len DeCaux, *Labor Radical: From the Wobblies to CIO, A Personal History* (Beacon Press, 1970), ch. 16.

8. For a historical study of the Russian war effort from the perspective Joe expresses here, see Alexander Werth, *Russia at War, 1941-1945* (Avon Books, 1965).

9. Irving Howe has characterized the *landsmanshaft* as the Jewish immigrant institution "closest in voice and spirit to the masses." See *World of Our Fathers*, pp. 183-90.

10. For an interesting analysis of the controversy triggered by the publication of Hannah Arendt's book, see Norm Fruchter, "Arendt's Eichmann and Jewish Identity," *Studies on the Left* 5:1 (Winter, 1965): 22-42. Also see Hannah Arendt's own reflections on the controversy in Hannah Arendt, "Postscript," *Eichmann in Jerusalem* (Viking Press, 1965), pp. 280-98.

11. From the mid-1930's to 1949 the American Jewish left wing gradually moved toward "a positive attitude to the rights and interests of the Jewish people, to the special needs and problems of our own Jewish national group, and to the interests and rights of the Jewish community in Palestine" (Communist Party U.S.A. resolution, *Political Affairs*, November 1946). However, the Communist Party and the Jewish left wing opposed unlimited Jewish immigration into Palestine and insisted upon Arab agreement to a Jewish national state, until the Soviet Union voted for the creation of Israel in November 1947.

See the cursory treatment of this revealing dilemma in Glazer, *The Social Basis of American Communism*, pp. 155-56; Foster, *History of the Communist Party of the United States*, pp. 479-81; Liebman,

Jews and the Left, 511-12. For further information see primary sources like Alexander Bittleman, *Program for Survival: The Communist Position on the Jewish Question* (Pamphlet, New Century, 1947); A. B. Magil, *Israel in Crisis* (International Publishers, 1950); and the periodic statements of left-wing positions on the Middle East in *Political Affairs* between 1945 and 1950.

12. For more on this infamous Nazi massacre of Ukrainian Jews and the controversy surrounding Soviet commemoration of the massacre, see Chapter 10 for Joe's pilgrimage to Babi Yar during his 1963 visit to the Soviet Union.

9. Jewish Chicken Ranchers and the Cold War

1. For a recent analysis of the impact of the Cold War and the Red Scare on the labor movement, see David Caute, *The Great Fear: The Anti-Communist Purge under Truman and Eisenhower* (Touchstone Books, 1979), part 5.

2. For the ILGWU leadership position on the Cold War and American communism see David Dubinsky and A. H. Raskin, *David Dubinsky: A Life with Labor* (Simon and Schuster, 1977), pp. 271-82.

3. There has been a small but rich tradition of Jewish agricultural settlements in the United States. The best single source of information is the Jewish Agricultural Society's publication *The Jewish Farmer*. The finest full-length study of American Jewish agricultural life is Joseph Brandes, *Immigrants to Freedom: Jewish Agricultural Communities in Rural New Jersey since 1882* (University of Pennsylvania Press, 1971). Also see my forthcoming study of the Petaluma Jewish community.

4. The U.S. government practice of officially listing radical organizations as subversive, first instituted by Attorney General A. Mitchell Palmer at the end of World War I, was revived during World War II and then expanded with the Truman administration's federal loyalty program. The first Truman administration list of subversive organizations was published in 1948. For further information, including federal persecution of the International Workers Order, see Caute, *The Great Fear*, pp. 169-74.

5. For amplification of Joe's argument that the Rosenberg case was a U.S. government attempt to mobilize popular support for Cold War policies, see Walter and Miriam Schneir, *Invitation to an Inquest: Reopening the Rosenberg "Atom Spy" Case* (Penguin Books, 1973); Robert and Michael Meerepol, *We Are Your Sons: The Legacy of Ethel and Julius Rosenberg* (Ballantine Books, 1976).

There has been little analysis of the special Jewish dimensions of the case, even though the Rosenberg defense committee did charge anti-Semitism was involved in the prosecution. See Julius Rosen-

berg's own view in Meerepol, *We Are Your Sons*, pp. 183-85. Also
see the suggestions of the Schneirs, *Invitation to an Inquest*, pp.
176, 179. Both accounts note that the social democratic *Forward* did
protest the death sentence applied to the Rosenbergs.

6.   With the waning of British and French colonial power in the 1940's
and 1950's, there was an enormous growth of American economic
and political power in the Middle East along with a determined
American effort to check revolutionary movements and Soviet
penetration of the area. There has been considerable debate over
whether the United States, the Soviet Union, or Israel bore fundamental responsibility for the end to Israeli neutrality and its align-
ment with the United States between 1949 and 1953. See the recent
exploration of this problem in Nadav Safran, *Israel, the Embattled
Ally* (Harvard University Press, 1978), pp. 334-47.

7.   There has been extensive exploration of the role of the American
Jewish community in the shaping of American policy in the Middle
East and of American Jewish fears that the United States would align
with the Arabs rather than with Israel. There has been no treatment
of how these fears might have fostered American Jewish anti-
Communism. See, for example, Melvyn I. Urofsky, *We Are One!
American Jewry and Israel* (Anchor Books, 1978).

8.   The resurgence of Soviet government anti-Semitism between 1948
and 1954 is not entirely explicable to this day. It seems to have been
the most extreme manifestation of more general Stalinist policies of
internal terror. The sharpness of the attacks on Jews undoubtedly
was connected to persistent Slavic anti-Semitism, resurgent Soviet
Jewish nationalism, and Soviet-Israeli antagonism with the development of the Cold War. For further information, including the Jewish
Doctor's Plot, see Yehoshua Gilboa, *The Black Years of Soviet Jewry,
1939-1953* (Little Brown and Company, 1971). Also see Joe's
exploration of the problems of Soviet Jewry since World War II in
chapters 10 and 11.

9.   Joe's analysis of how and why the mainstream American Jewish
community—social democrats and liberals—reacted to the postwar
Red Scare is a unique contribution to the understanding of recent
Jewish American history. Most analysts of American Judaism have
celebrated Jewish pragmatic liberalism and defense of civil rights,
Jewish opposition to Joe McCarthy, growing Jewish participation in
the mainstream of American life, and the American pluralism which
has encouraged Jewish integration into American life. They have
been silent about American Jewish attitudes toward the Rosenberg
case and toward attacks on the civil liberties of Jewish radicals. Nor
have they explored how liberal anticommunism in the American
Jewish community was shaped by a complex of international as well
as national political developments. See, for example, Lawrence H.
Fuchs, *The Political Behavior of American Jews* (The Free Press,

1956), chs. 5-7; Nathan Glazer, *American Judaism* (University of Chicago Press, 1957), ch. 7; Oscar Handlin, *Adventure in Freedom: Three Hundred Years of Jewish Life in America* (McGraw-Hill Publishing Book Company, 1954); Irving Howe, *World of Our Fathers: The Journey of the East European Jews to America and the World They Found and Made* (Harcourt, Brace, Jovanovich, 1976), pp. 621-26. A recent exception can be found in Arthur Liebman, *Jews and the Left* (John Wiley & Sons, 1979), pp. 514-17.

Joe's analysis of Jewish liberal anticommunism, which shows the interplay of government Red Scare policies and popular political and social anxieties, offers an important perspective for the emerging radical analysis of McCarthyism. Left-wing scholars, attempting to locate the origins of the Red Scare in official government policy under the Truman and Eisenhower administrations, have ignored why the Red Scare was tolerated and even embraced by the American populace. There is an implicit assumption that popular political attitudes can be completely shaped from above. See, for example, Lawrence S. Wittner, *Cold War America from Hiroshima to Watergate* (Holt, Rinehart and Winston, 1978), ch 4.

10. See my forthcoming study of the Petaluma Jewish community for other community members' explanations of what happened there during the McCarthy period.

    For other accounts of the Left in California during the Cold War see Al Richmond, *A Long View From the Left: Memoirs of an American Revolutionary* (Delta Books, 1975), chs. 10, 11; Jessica Mitford, *A Fine Old Conflict* (Vintage Books, 1978). Note in particular Jessica Mitford's shrewd and hilarious comments on her dealings with the left-wing Jewish chicken ranchers of Petaluma (pp. 86-91).

11. The Grange is a fraternal organization of small farmers founded in 1867. At its peak in the 1870's, it included a million and a half farmers in a movement to establish cooperatives, to regulate railroad corporations and grain elevator companies, and to run candidates for state offices. It was a precursor to larger farmer protest movements in the 1880's and 1890's. The Grange continued into the twentieth century as a social, educational, and cooperative organization for small farmers and remains one of the largest farmer organizations in the United States.

12. Nikita Khrushchev's 1956 revelations of Stalinist terror had a shattering impact on American Communists and Communist sympathizers. It was the culminating blow in the virtual collapse of the U.S. Communist Party during the decade following World War II. That collapse was the consequence of U.S. government persecution, the purge of the Communist Party from the CIO, the disastrous Progressive Party campaign of 1948, and the Party's loss of a socialist vision. Khrushchev's 1956 speech and the subsequent Soviet invasion of Hungary triggered a four-year period of intense debate and factional

struggle over reform of the U.S. Communist Party. All the while there were mass defections, and the Party was reduced to virtual irrelevance in American political and social life. See David Shannon, *The Decline of American Communism: A History of the Communist Party of the United States since 1945* (Harcourt, Brace and Company, 1959), chs. 9, 10, conclusion; Irving Howe and Lewis Coser, *American Communism: A Critical History* (Praeger, 1962), ch. 10; Joseph R. Starobin, *American Communism in Crisis, 1943–1957* (Harvard University Press, 1972), chs. 7–10.

Little has been written about the special impact of Khrushchev's speech on American Jewish radicals. Their reaction was stronger due to revelations of Stalinist anti-Semitism, categorical denials of continued Soviet anti-Semitism, and refusal of the U.S. Communist Party to press the issue. Radical Jewish publications like the *Freiheit* and *Jewish Currents* did not fully break with the Communist Party until after the Six Day War of 1967, but the immigrant Jewish radical movement began to chart a course of independent, non-Communist Party radicalism from the time of the Twentieth Party Congress. The best account of this shift can be found in Liebman, *Jews and the Left*, pp. 517-26.

10. Travels in 1963

1. The postwar era, particularly between 1948 and Stalin's death in 1953, witnessed an official resurgence of Great Russian nationalism, anti-Westernism, and internal terror in the Soviet Union. Thousands of returning soldiers, allegedly contaminated by contact with the West, were incarcerated in forced labor camps. Joe's friend Harry Eisman might have been all the more suspect, because he was Jewish and because of his early years in the United States. See Arie Eliav's perceptive speculations on this subject in *Between Hammer and Sickle* (Signet Books, 1969), pp. 31-33.
2. After the complete destruction of Soviet Yiddish cultural institutions between 1948 and 1953, the Soviet government allowed the creation of a new Yiddish literary journal, *Sovetish Haimland*, in 1961. For further information on *Sovietish Haimland* and its editor Aaron Vergelis see Joseph Brumberg, *"Sovyetish Haimland,"* in Roland I. Rubin, editor, *The Unredeemed: Anti-Semitism in the Soviet Union* (Quadrangle Books, 1968), pp. 83-89.

    Official Soviet Jewish spokesmen like Aaron Vergelis have answered charges of Soviet suppression or nonencouragement of secular Yiddish culture with insistence that the older generations who were a part of that culture have been dying out and that the younger generations simply are not interested. They call attention to parallel developments in the United States. These issues continue to generate more heat than light in the scholarship on Soviet Jewry.

Issues of Jewish culture, Jewish assimilation, and government policy require comparative study of Jews in the Soviet Union, the United States, Israel, and elsewhere. See the suggestive comments of Zvi Y. Gitelman in *Jewish Nationality and Soviet Politics: The Jewish sections of the CPSU, 1917–1930* (Princeton University Press, 1972), pp. 500-507.

3. For a less sanguine view of postwar Soviet economic development see Harry Schwartz, *The Soviet Economy Since Stalin* (J. B. Lippincott Company, 1965). For a view similar to Joe's, from another sympathetic Jewish visitor to the Soviet Union, see B. Z. Goldberg, *The Jewish Problem in the Soviet Union: Analysis and Solution* (Crown Publishers, 1961), pp. 114-21.

4. Most other commentators give more emphasis to all-pervasive fear of government by Soviet Jews during this period. They also give more emphasis to official and unofficial Soviet government policies of anti-Semitism.

    For the most eloquent account of the state of Soviet Jewry by a visitor during this period see Elie Weisel, *The Jews of Silence: A Personal Report on Soviet Jewry* (Holt, Rinehart and Winston, 1965). For the most probing and perceptive account see Eliav, *Between Hammer and Sickle*. For an interesting account from another left-wing Jewish visitor see Goldberg, *The Jewish Problem in the Soviet Union*, ch. 3. Also see scholarly analyses such as Salo W. Baron, *The Russian Jew Under Tsars and Soviets* (The Macmillan Company, 1976), ch. 17; Rubin, *The Unredeemed*; Lionel Kochan, ed., *The Jews in the Soviet Union since 1917* (Oxford University Press, 1970).

5. There have been persistent controversies, inside and outside the Soviet Union, over precisely who and how many the Nazis massacred at Babi Yar, over the response of the non-Jewish Kiev population to the Nazi massacre of Kiev Jews, over the reluctance of the Soviet government to put up any monument at Babi Yar, and over the refusal of the Soviet government to specify the Babi Yar massacres as a symbol of Nazi genocidal attacks on Jews (the Soviet government instead preferring to regard it as a Nazi attack on Soviet citizens of many nationalities). The controversy began at the end of the war, reached a high point with the events surrounding Evgenii Evtushenko's poem "Babi Yar," and continues over the present Babi Yar monument, which makes no explicit mention of the Jewish victims.

6. Czechoslovakia was the most "Western" of the socialist bloc countries, with high industrialization and well-developed democratic traditions which predated World War II. It also had the largest indigenous Communist Party of all East European countries with a genuine popular base even before it assumed full power with the 1948 coup. Thereafter, the Czech Communist Party leadership emerged as one of the most Stalinist in the East European socialist

bloc and one of the slowest to institute reform after the Twentieth Party Congress. Joe's reference to the democratic spirit of Czech political life points to a strong layer of socialist dissent beneath the tightly controlled Stalinist state apparatus. That dissent very likely stemmed from the indigenous Czech socialist tradition as well as from the Czech democratic tradition.

For the reflections of other American radicals on their visits to Czechoslovakia and the implications of Czech developments for the American Left see Al Richmond, *A Long View from the Left: Memoirs of an American Revolutionary* (Delta Books, 1975), pp. 409–27; Peggy Dennis, *The Autobiography of an American Communist: A Personal View of a Political Life, 1925–1975* (Lawrence Hill & Company, 1977), pp. 272–73, 278–79.

7. Joe's capsule account of Jewish settlement in Palestine and Arab response closely follows the interpretation of Israeli writer Arie Eliav, *Land of the Hart: Israelis, Arabs, The Territories, and a Vision of the Future* (Jewish Publication Society of America, 1974), ch. 1. For further information from historians with perspectives sympathetic to Zionism see Walter Laqueur, *A History of Zionism* (Holt, Rinehart and Winston, 1972); Howard Morley Sachar, *A History of Israel: From the Rise of Zionism to Our Time* (Alfred A. Knopf, 1976). For historians with perspectives sympathetic to the Arabs, see Sami Hadawi, *Bitter Harvest: Palestine between 1914 and 1967* (New World Press, 1967); Abdelwahab M. Elmessiri, *The Land of Promise: A Critique of Political Zionism* (North American Publishers, 1972).

8. The *kibbutz* and the *moshav* were the most powerful expressions of the idealism of twentieth-century Zionist pioneers, who sought to create a new Jewish society based on agricultural labor and socialist principles. These institutions flourished after the creation of the state of Israel, so that by 1965 there were 229 *kibbutzim* with 78,000 inhabitants and 336 *moshavim* with 120,000 inhabitants. They provided the base of agricultural production in Israel, and they claimed to be among the most modern, efficient agricultural institutions in the world. The weakening of idealism on the *kibbutz* has been a subject of considerable debate and inquiry within Israel. See Sachar, *A History of Israel,* pp. 149–51, 407–408, 478, 517–18.

9. Jews from Arabic countries in the Near East and North Africa immigrated to Israel in huge numbers during the decade following the Israeli War for Independence. They were displaced from Arabic societies by varying forms of anti-Semitic persecution, ranging from outright pogrom to government economic confiscations. Known in Israel as "Orientals," they constituted 25 percent of the population in 1948, 45 percent in 1961, and 55 percent by 1967.

Israel's first decade witnessed bitter cultural conflicts between Oriental and European Jews. The gap between the two peoples was narrowing at the time of Joe's visit. By 1969, 17.4 percent of all Jewish marriages in Israel were between Orientals and Europeans.

For treatment of this topic from a perspective close to Joe's, but with more emphasis on the depth of the problem and on the culpability of European Jews, see Sachar, *A History of Israel,* pp. 395–409, 415–24, 538–42.

10. The 1947–48 Israeli War for Independence created between half a million and three-quarters of a million Palestinian Arab refugees, while approximately one hundred fifty thousand Palestinian Arabs remained in Israel. Since that time bitter controversies have raged over the causes of the Palestinian Arab exodus from areas under Jewish control during the war, over the fate of Palestinian Arabs inside and outside Israel, and over attempts by Palestinian Arabs to create their own state. See, for example, the eloquent treatment of these problems in Eliav, *Land of the Hart* and in Fawaz Turki, *The Disinherited: Journal of a Palestinian Exile* (Monthly Review Press, 1972).

11. American radicals have maintained divided allegiances towards the struggles for national survival of the Jewish people and the Palestinian people—a conflict of two just causes, the legacy of British imperialism, the Holocaust, and World War II. Unfortunately, there has been no systematic scholarly treatment of the policies of the American Left toward Israel, the Palestinians, and the Middle East. For an older study reflecting the position of the immigrant Jewish American Left, see A. B. Magil, *Israel in Crisis* (International Publishers, 1950). The most compelling spokesman on the American Left in recent years has been Noam Chomsky, who has condemned the role of the great powers in the Middle East and has advocated the creation of a binationalist socialist state in Palestine. See Noam Chomsky, *Peace in the Middle East?: Reflections on Justice and Nationhood* (Vintage Books, 1974). Also see I. F. Stone, *Underground to Palestine: and Reflections Thirty Years Later* (Pantheon Books, 1978); Paul Jacobs, *Between the Rock and the Hard Place* (Random House, 1970).

Joe expressed his position on the Arab-Israeli conflict in a "Letter to the Editor," *People's World,* August 5, 1967:

"The two articles by Peggy Dennis (PW, July 8 and 15) were supposed to deal with 'two highly explosive problems' of Israeli-Arab relations:

"(a) 'Arab refusal to accept the reality of the State of Israel,' and their unrelenting position of a continuous state of war against Israel; and

"(b) The military victories of Israel, its seizure of Arab territory, and Israel's refusal to share responsibility for solving the refugee problem.

"In developing the reasoning around these problems, point (a) was lost. The articles dealt mainly with the 'injustices' committed by Israel and its inhuman attitude toward the refugees.

"Let us keep the record straight. It was the Arabs who refused to accept the decision of the UN to establish an Israeli state in Palestine; hence the war of 1947-48. They lost the war and got stuck with hundreds of thousands of Arab refugees who fled the area, accepting the promises of Nasser and others that the Jews will be pushed into the sea, that their homes would be returned to them, that they would inherit the possessions of the Jews. The statement that the Arabs were driven out by the Jews was incorrect 19 years ago and it is misleading today about the refugees of the Western triangle of Jordan. We all agree, however, that the aggravated refugee problem has to be solved with the participation of Israel.

"To accuse the 'progressive Jews in Israel and politically radical-minded Jews in the U.S.' that they fell in line with 'the reactionary pro-Western imperialist domestic and foreign policies of the Israeli Government' is to display ignorance.

"The Communist party of Israel ('Makai'), and its many supporters were, for many years, accused by the other political parties of being more pro-Arab than Israeli. The 'Makai' always criticized the Israeli administration for not working for more amicable relations with the Arabs, for not meeting squarely the refugee problem, for not taking a neutralist position in world affairs.

"Placing the blame for the situation in the Near East, mainly on the shoulders of Israel, isolated 'Makai' from the masses of Jewish people. The party finally realized that there are two sides to the story, that the extreme nationalism of the Arabs is an equal—if not a greater—obstacle to peace in the area. This was one of the issues on which the party was split. It is the Vilner (minority) group that walked out and maintains the old position which was so completely accepted by Peggy.

"The slur against the progressive Jews is contradicted by Peggy, herself, when she quotes S. Mikunis, Communist leader and member of the Knesset (Parliament), who called upon the Israeli Government to act 'not as conquerors and oppressors' towards the Arab population in Israeli-occupied Jordan and Gaza, but rather in 'cooperation and friendship.'

"Israel does not want war; it never threatened to push the Arabs into the sea. But it will not and should not permit itself to be destroyed and allow another chapter of martyrdom of Israel.

"The progressives in Israel, in the U.S., and elsewhere, have, through the years, criticized the handling of the Arabs within Israel. Discrimination against Arabs in Israel, which smacks of racism, is weakening peace efforts in the area. But they are justified in bitterly rejecting the cruel and false accusation that the Arabs live in Israel under 'regulations strongly parallel to the Hitler restrictions imposed upon the Jewish ghettos in Europe.'

"Yes, the refugee problem is an aggravated one and should be solved by all concerned; but perhaps we should remember that while streams of Arab refugees found their way out of Israel into the Arab countries, hundreds of thousands of Jewish refugees were expelled from the Arab contries, robbed of all of their possessions and made their way to Israel.

"These problems and the problem of the military territorial occupation and the establishment of peace in the area, are not one-sided. It will have to be settled by direct negotiations between the Arab states and Israel and helped by the major world powers. While the Soviet Union and the United States have opposite interests in the Near East, as elsewhere in the world, yet, they find some areas of agreement. Narrow as those areas may be, they are important to world peace. A serious effort has to be made by them and other major powers to calm the turbulent waters in the Near East for the good of the Arabs, for Israel, and for the peace of the world."

12. For further information on Jewish settlement in Latin America, including Brazil, see Howard M. Sachar, *The Course of Modern Jewish History* (Delta Books, 1958), pp. 510-18.

11. The Struggle Continues

1. For further information on the development of a corporate chicken industry and the industrialization of chicken raising, see Page Smith and Charles Daniel, *The Chicken Book* (Little, Brown and Company, 1975).

2. For an introduction to the policies of the American Left, particularly the Communist Party, toward the problems of black Americans, see William Z. Foster, *History of the Communist Party of the United States* (Greenwood Press, 1968). For a brief critical treatment of these Communist Party policies see James Weinstein, *Ambiguous Legacy: The Left in American Politics* (New Viewpoints Books, 1975), ch. 4. Harold Cruse offers a sharper criticism of the white Left, particularly Jewish Communists, in *The Crisis of the Negro Intellectual* (William Morrow & Company, 1960), pp. 147-70. Also see Nell Irvin Painter, *The Narrative of Hosea Hudson: His Life as a Negro Communist in the South* (Harvard University Press, 1979).

3. Henry Wallace (1888-1965), former vice president under Franklin Delano Roosevelt, resigned as secretary of commerce in 1946 to protest the Cold War policies of the Truman administration. At the end of 1947, he allied with the Left, especially the Communist Party, to form the Progressive Party and oppose the developing Cold War.

The new party did not win support from the CIO, Negro organizations, or liberal New Deal groups. Wallace and the Progressive Party, with a narrow base of support and facing merciless Red-baiting, ended up with a disappointing one million votes in the 1948 presidential campaign. This campaign marked the effective end of Wallace's political career and served to further isolate the Left from the trade unions and liberal Democrats.

4. By the 1960's the ILGWU retained its old Jewish social democratic leadership with some influx of middle-aged Jewish lawyers and labor experts, but with a membership that was largely black and Puerto Rican. The new members, including knitgoods workers, have charged the older leadership with racial domination and have mobilized oppositional challenges for power. For further treatment of this topic, from a perspective sympathetic to the old Jewish leadership, see Irving Howe, *World of Our Fathers: The Journey of the East European Jews to America and the Life They Found and Made* (Harcourt, Brace, Jovanovich, 1976), pp. 635-37.

5. For contrasting analyses of the New Left from more sympathetic perspectives see Weinstein, *Ambiguous Legacy,* ch. 7, 8; Stanley Aronowitz, *False Promises: The Shaping of American Working Class Consciousness* (McGraw-Hill Company, 1974), ch. 8.

    Joe was unusual among older leftists in his ability to work with the young militants of the New Left. Other Old Leftists offer a similar critique of the New Left, but they provide few insights from actual participation. See Al Richmond, *A Long View From the Left: Memoirs of an American Revolutionary* (Delta Books, 1972), pp. 394-98; Peggy Dennis, *the Autobiography of an American Communist: A Personal View of a Political Life, 1925–1975* (Lawrence Hill & Company, 1977), pp. 275-78.

6. For other left-wing criticism of the American Jewish community similar to that of Joe, see Noam Chomsky, *Peace in the Middle East?: Reflections on Justice and Nationhood* (Vintage Books, 1974), pp. 51-54; I. F. Stone, "Confessions of a Jewish Dissident," *Underground to Palestine: And Reflections Thirty Years Later* (Panetheon Books, 1978), pp. 229-40. The growth of such American Jewish criticism in recent years can be traced in the journal *New Outlook.*

7. For further analysis of Palestinian Arab life in Israel see Sabri Jiryis, *The Arabs in Israel* (Monthly Review Press, 1976).

8. For an expanded treatment of Israeli attitudes and policies during this period, from a perspective similar to that of Joe, see Howard Morley Sachar, *A History of Israel: From the Rise of Zionism to Our Time* (Alfred A. Knopf, 1976), pp. 714-28.

9. Joe's account of the dilemma of Soviet Jewry after the Six Day War is largely consistent with the perspectives of most Western commentators. See, for example, Salo W. Baron, *The Russian Jew Under Tsars and Soviets* (The Macmillan Company, 1976), ch. 18; Ronald I.

Rubin, ed., *The Unredeemed: Anti-Semitism in the Soviet Union* (Quadrangle Books, 1968); Lionel Kochan, ed., *Jews in the Soviet Union since 1917* (Oxford University Press, 1970).

10. See Irving Howe's interesting discussion of the origin and character of these changes over generations in *World of Our Fathers*, pp. 249-55, 608-38.

11. For further information on Jewish American poverty, especially among aging immigrants in New York and Florida, see Howe, *World of Our Fathers,* pp. 611-12.

Index